Environmetrics 81:
Selected Papers

SIMS

The SIAM Institute for Mathematics and Society was established in 1973 by the Society for Industrial and Applied Mathematics. Its purpose is to develop, promote, support and maintain research in the application of mathematics in the study and solution of social problems. To this end SIMS conducts conferences relevant to its objectives, a transplant program wherein mathematicians are "transplanted" for two years into university interdisciplinary centers to work as members of a team on societal problems, and university research and education studies on statistics and environmental factors in health.

SIAM—SIMS CONFERENCE SERIES

1. ECOSYSTEM ANALYSIS AND PREDICTION. Simon A. Levin, editor. Proceedings of SIMS Conference, Alta, Utah, July 1-5, 1974.

2. EPIDEMIOLOGY. Donald Ludwig and Kenneth L. Cooke, editors. Proceedings of SIMS Conference, Alta, Utah, July 8-12, 1974.

3. ENERGY: *Mathematics and Models.* Fred S. Roberts, editor. Proceedings of SIMS Conference, Alta, Utah, July, 1975.

4. ENVIRONMENTAL HEALTH: *Quantitative Methods.* Alice Whittemore, editor. Proceedings of SIMS Conference, Alta, Utah, July, 1976.

5. TIME SERIES AND ECOLOGICAL PROCESSES. H. H. Shugart, Jr., editor. Proceedings of SIMS Conference, Alta, Utah, June-July, 1977.

6. ENERGY AND HEALTH. Norman E. Breslow and Alice S. Whittemore, editors. Proceedings of SIMS Conference, Alta, Utah, June 26-30, 1978.

7. FLUID MECHANICS IN ENERGY CONVERSION. John David Buckmaster, editor. Proceedings of SIMS Conference, Alta, Utah, June 25-29, 1979.

8. ENVIRONMETRICS 81: Selected Papers. Selections from USEPA-SIAM-SIMS Conference, Alexandria, Virginia, April 8-10, 1981.

Environmetrics 81: Selected Papers

Selections from a Conference sponsored and supported by the U.S. Environmental Protection Agency, the Society for Industrial and Applied Mathematics, and the SIAM Institute for Mathematics and Society.

 Philadelphia

1981

Library of Congress Catalog Card Number: 81-84060
ISBN: 0-89871-178-9

Contents

FOREWORD

This volume presents seventeen "Selected Papers" which were given at Environmetrics 81, a conference held in Alexandria, Virginia April 8-10, 1981. These papers describe a number of research results in areas relating to environmental quality where mathematics and statistics have played a significant role and at the same time they often point to new topics awaiting future investigations. The papers are in part expository in nature; it is hoped that they will be useful to researchers for reference and that they will serve at the same time as an introduction for those who may be entering the field.

Environmetrics 81 was sponsored by the U.S. Environmental Protection Agency (USEPA), the Society for Industrial and Applied Mathematics (SIAM), and by the SIAM Institute for Mathematics and Society (SIMS); financial support for Environmetrics 81 was provided by the USEPA Environmental Monitoring Systems Laboratory and Health Effects Research Laboratory, both of Research Triangle Park, North Carolina.

D. L. Thomsen, Jr.
President, SIMS
June 30, 1981

KEYNOTE ADDRESS

Environmetrics: Mathematics and Statistics
in the Service of the Environment

J. S. Hunter*

This meeting, Environmetrics 81, is not the first the EPA has
sponsored in an effort to bring together experts concerned with the
applications of mathematics and statistics in the environmental
sciences. An earlier meeting was held in April 1976 in Cincinnati.
The objective of this earlier conference was to review the state of
the art of modeling and simulation, and to discuss associated computer
requirements.

In his keynote address to the first conference, Dr. Andrew Breidenbach commented that an environmental conference on modeling and simulation seemed natural yet unique. Certainly the environmental
scientist recognized the value of models. However, Dr. Breidenbach
noted that the concept of the mathematical model was only the beginning to take hold in the minds of most environmental decision makers,
managers, legislators and the public. On review of the technical
papers being presented at that meeting, he chided his listeners to
create a simpler language to assist in communication between modelers
and decision makers. And he asked that we give serious attention to
the task of creating a consistent methodology for verifying models.

I'm not sure we have met Dr. Breidenbach's objectives, but we have,
at least, coined a new word to describe what it is we do: "Environmetrics." Ah, an impressive sounding word. It tumbles easily from
the tongue and has a nice iambic beat. And it combines a sense of
science: "metric," with a sense of social usefulness, "environment."
Altogether, a good catchy word. And as for its meaning? Well, the
subtitle for this talk is "mathematics and statistics in the service
of the environment."

That's an encompassing definition. To begin, I think it would
include all the statistical aspects of environmental data collection,
storage and retrieval, data laundering, exploratory data analysis,
and data exposition including the interactive use of the computer and
graphics. I would have it encompass data quality assurance, beginning

*Professor, Civil Engineering Department,
 Princeton University, Princeton, New Jersey 08544

with the establishment of good measurement methods, the comparison of alternative measurement methods, and the control of these methods across diverse users, that is, the control of the measurement system. I would have it include concern for the problems of calibration, for the establishment and use of standard reference materials, and the statistical analysis of trace results so close to zero that one may question whether the response is actually quantifiable or merely detected. I would include under environmetrics the problems of the statistical design of experiments and the spatial location of sensors. I would include the analysis of personal dosimeter data, the determination of health effects and the estimation of risk. I would certainly include the statistical problems associated with taking decisions under uncertainty and estimating the cost of uncertainty. Nor would I leave out time series analysis, multivariate methods, and even nonparametric methods. And will this audience also allow me to be Bayesian?

And as to areas of application for environmetrics: we are destined to hear papers addressing problems in monitoring, modeling and analysis in both air and water quality applications bearing on toxic substances, on regulatory risk assessment, on health effects, on hazardous substances, on regional air quality indices, on ozone pollution, acid rain, and groundwater flows. One could go on...

If you can't find your topic of interest amongst those mentioned thus far then perhaps you are attending this meeting to learn about the newer and innovative applications of statistics and mathematics to the environment. You'd like to learn more about the van-Belle-Fisher statistic, or about Kriging to estimate spatial patterns, or cluster analysis, or about information weighted splines.

From the sound of things, it would appear that the statisticians and mathematicians flaunting their new title of "environmetricians" have just about subsumed unto themselves all the quantitative problems facing the Environmental Protection Agency! Certainly, a description of what they say they do has managed to include rather large chunks of the turf already inhabited by a host of administrators, regulators, engineers and scientists already working for the EPA. The lowly statistician now claims to be lord of all! Perhaps it's time to remind, at least the statisticians, that in earlier days in the ancient town of Nuremberg, the only place they were permitted to meet was on the basement floor of the Hangman's Guild!

Thus, before we environmetricians claim too much it would be wise to gain some perspective as to what we can contribute to the resolution of environmental problems, and just where we do stand with respect to our administrative and scientific peers.

Dr. Breidenbach asked us to make our models understandable, our language simpler. Both are easier said than done. The English language can be a miserable conveyor of statistical information, so

poor a conveyor we often resort to symbols to enhance the meaning of
our words. For example, the union and intersection symbols help us
distinguish between the words "and" versus "both" and between the
inclusive and exclusive uses of the word "or." And how often we use
Greek and Roman letters to distinguish between parameters and statistics so that we can reduce the confusion generated by the words
mean (μ) and average ($\bar{x}$)! But how many engineers do <u>you</u> know who
employ the word "correlation" (carefully defined by statisticians to
be a measure of association between two random variables) to suggest
a <u>casual</u> relationship? And even we are not too careful with our own
technical words. Consider "independent". What administrator knows
what that important word connotes? In probability, it means that,
amongst random variables $P(A \cap B) = P(A) \times P(B)$. But in fitting
deterministic (regression) models, the statistician is prone to speak,
once again, of "independent variables." Here the word independent
suggests that the contribution of variable x_1 in forcing changes upon
a response η is clear of the contribution of x_2. The effect of x_1

and x_2 are additive, that is the full change in η is obtained by
superpositioning the changes separately due to x_1 and x_2, that is,
$F(x_1, x_2) = g(x_1) + h(x_2)$. Of course, we get around the failure of our
variables x_1 and x_2 to act independently by postulating "interaction terms. Ah, now all we have to do is explain what <u>that</u> <u>word</u>
<u>means</u>! And if you would like some other key words, try "confidence,"
or "significant."

   My point in providing these illustrations is to emphasize that
statistics uses many common words in a unique way. Statistics is
largely a language. In fact, it is a characteristic of a profession
to have a special language. As members of the profession, the
cognoscente, we speak this language to one another in our meetings,
and in our technical papers.

   Speaking of technical papers, we have each received a copy of the
Summaries of Conference Presentations "Proceedings of Environmetrics
'81." This very professional appearing publication raises the issue
as to whether it is time to consider establishing a technical journal
so that we may more regularly follow developments in our field. We
have been very fortunate thus far in having our meetings financed by
the EPA, with additional sponsorship from professional societies.
The establishment of a new journal will require much collaborative
effort, and provides a topic for all of us to consider during these
meetings.

   But the key question remains: "How well do we communicate with non-
statisticians?" Here the statistician runs into a very interesting
problem. Words like average, mean, correlation, independence, interaction and significant occur frequently in the vernacular, the
language of the common man, and he uses such words casually. And when

the common man hears us using these everyday words he attaches what-
ever convenient rationale suits his immediate needs. And when he
employs these words, he expects us to grasp his meaning. Since we
both use the same words, the impression is abroad in the land that
anyone can speak the language of statistics, and write it too.   Unfortunately, it is usually done very poorly. If examples are needed,
read any issue of the Federal Register.

    Well, it's difficult to do much about this problem of language.
Perhaps we could have followed the early lead of Karl Pearson and
employed more Greek derivative words such as "heteroscedastic" and
"leptokurtosis." But we have largely missed that opportunity.
Certainly if we complained every time our peers misused our language
there would be little time for us to do much else. And if we attempt
to educate them to the nuances of our meanings, they will have little
opportunity to do much else. How then, can we reduce this problem of
language and its attendant diminished communication? There are a few
things. We can make a better effort to communicate the meanings of
our statistical-environmental-analyses so that others can grasp the
essential kernels of information. And perhaps more importantly, we
should try to convey what the data do not say, and cannot support.

    And we can begin to insist, as all professionals should, that if
statistical matters are to be discussed by non-professionals, then
they should consult a statistician. No responsible person reporting
on an environmental problem would run the danger of misstating a
chemical reaction or describe the results of a cost model, or comment
on the structure of some new law without first consulting with his
chemist - his accountant, - or his lawyer! We must begin to make the
point more aggressively to our peers. If you're going to address
statistical problems, to either speak or write statistical language,
consult your statistician. Perhaps a little doggerel will help
emphasize the point.

> Before your stick your long neck out
>   spouting percentages and means
> Before you claim numerical support
>   for your pet social schemes
> And claim causation based upon a
>   correlation coefficient
> Go my friend and search him out
>   CONSULT YOUR STATISTICIAN
>
> Before your scheduled court appearance
>   as an expert witness
> Before your give your evidence
>   showing excellent curve fitness
> Be sure your data does support
>   your inference and decision
> Go my friend and search him out
>   CONSULT YOUR STATISTICIAN

Before your spend your money on
    new instruments and claim
That everyone who breathes the air
    will die in exquisite pain
Remember that the sampling points
    must be in good position
Go my friend and search him out
    CONSULT YOUR STATISTICIAN

But, once again, before we get too high and mighty, it might be
wise to return to Dr. Breidenbach's concern about models. What do we
mean by the word "model?"

One could say that a "model" was something fashionable. More
seriously, a model is commonly taken to be a replica, a physical
structure that appears or acts in a manner analogous to reality. An
electric train set, or a doll house, come to mind. Similar hands-on
models of greater consequence exist to aid in the construction of
factories, others are designed to characterize water flows in large
river basins. Models are made of hulls of ships destined for some
sailing competition, or more ominously, for great undersea battles.
Models of complex molecules are a common sight. Sometimes, models
become vast simulation exercises involving many players and instruments,
as in a war game.

But at this meeting we are speaking about mathematical-statistical
models. No hardware aspects are involved. Rather the model brings
together <u>mathematical</u> forms and structures. Such models are cerebral,
they are based upon assumptions and work by evoking the axioms of
deductive logic. The analogy to the real world is a formal one.

As a statistician, most of the models that I deal with arise in an
effort to give structure and form to a collection of data, to "stiffen"
the data analysis. Usually there are one or more response variables,
$y_1, y_2, \ldots$ and several proposed forcing variables, $x_1, x_2 \ldots$ and the
objective is to illustrate <u>how</u> the x's influence the y's. The models
produced are empirical, they are a deliberate simplification of the
real world. These models seldom depend upon prior theoretical development, i.e., a more basic or ancient model that requires enhancement in
the light of new information. Instead, they are convenient mathematical
simplifications that spring into life as Taylor or Fourier approximations to unknown functions. Such models are tuned, that is, their
parameters (and perhaps their structure) are adjusted so that their
ability to forecast the recorded history is excellent. We trust, of
course, this ability to predict the history will continue to operate
when it comes to predicting the future, although as statisticians we
often err by saying very little about this aspect.

We also consider models of a more sophisticated nature. Here the
modeller begins to evoke mathematical forms of a more mechanistic or
theoretical context, that is, he draws upon relationships long tested

in the real world. The statistical modeller now finds himself in
close collaboration with a subject matter expert. For example, if he
would construct a model useful for forecasting the fate of some
pollutant in the atmosphere, it would be good to know something about
transport mechanisms, photo-chemical pathways, and the sensing abilities
of various instruments. The resulting model thus becomes a complex
mathematical structure, likely non-linear in the parameters. The
problems of parameter estimation, and more seriously, the problems of
how best to collect meaningful data in such cases, represent work on
the frontiers of statistics. Further the problem of comparing competing models of this kind, each possessed of different empirical and
theoretical components, is a topic of great concern. The point to
remember here is that useful empiric-theoretic models are usually
the consequence of good statistics, good mathematics and good subject
matter theoretical knowledge. The models require collaboration.

    Finally, and occasionally, there springs from the study of natural
events with their associated data, and empirically based models, an
inspiration - a theoretical model. Its characteristics are usually
its simplicity... its ability to provide additional insights, and to
impart new concepts beyond those embodied in the immediate data. The
model synthesizes, and suddenly nothing is ever quite the same again.
If statistical models have a role here, it is in their ability to
uncover and exposit all the scintilla of information that lie in a
data set, hopefully in as vivid a way as possible, so as to stimulate
imaginative leaps on the part of the subject matter expert.

    As statisticians and mathematicians, we are skillful in constructing
models. And certainly, for almost every problem of monitoring,
regulation and control faced by the Agency, models have been provided
and have proved useful. But again, a little perspective will help.
The EPA is charged with the responsibility of improving the quality
of our environment. The Agency recognizes that the discharge of
pollutants into the air, or into a stream, changes the quality of
that system.   But before an overall control and improvement of the
environment can occur, it is essential to quantify the forcing
variables (the changing concentrations of the pollutants) and to
quantify the quality of the environment.   The Agency's problems are
thus forced to shift from a broad canvas containing general objectives
down to specific choices of measurements on variables and responses.
For example, the Agency measures the SO_2 in the air and the pH of the
rainful; or it measures the amounts of organics dumped into the
stream, and then uses dissolved O_2 as the surrogate for stream water
quality. The general objective: improving the quality of the environment, is thus reduced to the collection of sets of numbers purporting
to be good measurements of certain specific environmental qualities.
It is these limited data that we use in our attempt to model the
environment.

    Missing from these data are all the non-quantifiable aspects of
the problem, as well as all the quantifiable variables that might be

important, if only we knew their names. Nevertheless as modellers we
trust our efforts are helpful to those with the responsibility for
making decisions bearing on the more general problems of environmental
management, as for example on the establishment of regulatory limits
determining appropriate controls, for capital expenditures decisions,
and for extending scientific knowledge.

It is important to remember that our environmental data and models
capture only part of the larger environmental scene faced by the EPA,
or for that matter, by our government and the nation. The resolution
of controversies arising from the environment must combine scientific
knowledge with social and political realities. We take a quantitative
approach hopefully purged of our prejudices and based upon deductive
principles and empirical verification. Our models and expertise do
not take in the vast panoply of non-quantifiable elements that surround
most issues of concern. Such issues generate controversies that
engage social and political elements as well as the contribution of
environmetricians and other environmental scientists. Individuals
with the authority to make public policy decisions will do so. The
degree to which these decisions will utilize the contributions of the
environmetrician will undoubtedly vary. Fortunately our contributions
are bound to be part of the decision making process. No modern
institution that hopes to survive can afford to truncate its source
of information, particularly if quantitative, or worse still, lie to
itself. Our professional role may be a limited one, but it is
essential! The environmetrician is one of the few around the decision
maker who doesn't confuse data with information, or quantification
with science. He is about the only professional available to the
decision maker who knows the technical hazards of inductive inference
and who appreciates the errors of decisions under uncertainty. And
just as the environmetrician has seen his past efforts on the part
of data quality assurance and standardized computing procedures
become generally accepted, so too will the day come when his value to
the decision maker will become patently obvious.

Unhappily, that day is being delayed by many unfortunate endemic
factors; some of which will be a long time in passing. Too often we
are compelled to obtain a quick decision, so that some legislative or
administrative deadline may be reached. On other occasions, we must
take part in adversary proceedings to support some higher authority's
decision made against our better judgment, and on other occasions we are
pressured to reduce or eliminate good statistical analysis by economic
strictures. These conditions enhance intolerance towards information
that does not suit immediate needs, or lead to the selection of bits and
pieces of the available analyses most conducive to the immediate
argument. The desire for the quick answer persists. Particularly
desirable then are executive summaries accompanied by an executive
statistic or two: something numerically simple, impressive sounding,
and as non-informative as possible. And finally, rather than call in
a statistical expert, many non-statisticians may decide it is the
simplest to merely be his own statistician or data analyst, or worse,

to instruct his statisticians as to exactly what models and statistics are required.

Of course each time we willingly participate in such shenanigans, we are self-defeating. Somehow our non-statistical associates, the nation's managers and directors, lawyers and doctors, legislators and regulators, and members of the 4th estate, have got to be told: obtaining information from data is a serious business. How many times have we heard statements such as "Only a fool is his own lawyer," or "If pain persists see your doctor," or as a child, "If you are lost, find a policeman." It's time we began to pound out a similar message: "Consult your statistician," or in our immediate case, your environmetrician.

> Before your boss takes data from
>   your files and recorders
> And demands you fit a model of high
>   polynomial order
> You might remind him gently 'bout
>   the variance of the prediction
> And ask him to leave the modelling to
>   his local statistician.
>
> The next time your boss comes to you
>   demanding statistical analysis
> Proving, for example, that drinking water
>   leads to paralysis
> Then professionally, and in your role
>   as his personal statistician
> Wish your boss a long and painful
>   journey to perdition.

Environmetrics: mathematics and statistics in the service of the environment. Not "subservient to" but "in the service of." This means to me that we have a lot of hard, yet enjoyable, work to do. We have to learn how to adapt our available tools of mathematics and statistics to meet the problems of the environment, and the environmentalist, and we must develop new and innovative tools as the need unfolds. And, we must do a better job of communicating our results, and demonstrating their value.

There is little doubt that environmetrics has become, in the space of a few years, an identifiable, productive, intellectual force. The breadth and depth of the topics scheduled for these meetings is but one impressive example. We have, perhaps, too full a platter at this meeting, and most of us will have to miss sessions we'd dearly love to attend. But this meeting not only provides an opportunity for the arts of mathematics and statistics to mesh with the practical problems of the environment, it provides a gathering place for statisticians and mathematicians to become better environmentalists, and the environmentalist to become a better environmetrician. In most ways our work together has only just begun.

AIR POLLUTION
MODELING AND ANALYSIS

Air Pollution Modeling
as a Problem in Statistics

Robert G. Lamb*

Abstract. An heuristic, statistical basis for air pollution model-
is presented. We use it in this paper to explore answers to some of
the fundamental questions underlying regional scale diffusion modeling. Among these are: What constitutes "turbulence" on regional
scales? How is its effect on material dispersion parameterized? To
what extent can the impact of a given source on air quality at a re-
mote site be predicted?

1. Introduction. Up until the mid 1960's, air pollution modeling
dealt almost exclusively with the prediction of concentration levels
within a few kilometers of point sources. The well known Gaussian
plume formula was an early outgrowth of this work. Being an empirical relationship (based largely on diffusion data collected during
the Prairie Grass experiments), the plume formula provides quite well
defined concentration estimates (approximately 15 minute averages at
fixed points in space) in terms of well specified input parameters.
The chief weakness of the plume formula is that strictly speaking, it
is limited in its applicability to the immediate environs of ground-
level sources of nonbuoyant, chemically inert material.

Beginning in about the mid 60's, the focus of air pollution modeling
shifted to urban scale problems. Here the need was to simulate concentration levels, in particular hourly averaged values, of photochemical pollutants over regions of up to 100 km in spatial extent
arising from many sources of many different pollutants. Realizing
that the complexity of this problem precluded the development of a
viable empirical model analogous to the plume formula, model developers
turned to the classical K-theory diffusion equation as the modeling
basis. This was motivated primarily by the belief that atmospheric
turbulence is an intrinsic property of the atmosphere whose effect on
material concentration is described generally by the K-theory equation.

* U.S. Environmental Protection Agency, Environmental Science Research
Laboratory, Research Triangle Park, NC 27711. (On assignment from the
National Oceanic and Atmospheric Administration.)

In implementing K-theory in this role, several fundamental questions
had to be confronted. One was the evaluation of the eddy diffusivity
itself. Here Taylor's [1] statistical theory of turbulence was usually
invoked to support the premise that for large scale diffusion the
eddy diffusivity is proportional to the variance of the turbulence
velocity, $\overline{u'^2}$ say, times the Lagrangian integral time scale T of the
turbulence, i.e.,

$$(1) \qquad K \sim T \, \overline{v'^2}.$$

Since T is not an easily measurable quantity its value was usually
inferred from diffusion data (see, for example, Draxler [2]). However,
if one examines the theoretical implications of (1), one discovers an
interesting paradox of which apparently few modelers are aware.
Briefly, the integral time scale T of a stochastic process is nonzero
only if the energy spectrum of the process has finite amplitude in the
limit as the frequency $\omega \to 0$ (we show this later). But the zero frequency component of atmospheric motion is contained in the time averaged wind $\bar{u}$ which is substracted from the instantaneous velocity u
to define the turbulent, or stochastic component $u' = u - \bar{u}$. Consequently, the integral time scale of atmospheric turbulence u' should
always be zero! The existence of this paradox is an indicator that
basic features of existing diffusion models are not well defined. We
will consider this problem again later.

A second important question that results from the use of K-theory
is whether the equation yields ensemble, time or space averaged concentrations, or mixtures of these. The most common belief is that
they are roughly hourly averaged values at fixed points. The arguments for this are that the equation is usually solved using hourly
averaged wind data; and that the temporal scales of "atmospheric turbulence" are smaller than one hour. It is also thought that the averages are ensemble averages but that under the tenets of the ergodic
theorem and assumptions concerning the temporal scales of "atmospheric
turbulence," these averages are roughly equivalent to hourly averages.
Venkatram [3] has pointed out that this is not generally true.

In short there are two fundamental questions underlying regional
scale diffusion modeling that currently are unanswered: What is it
that models do or can predict? What input information is required to
make these predictions? An answer to the first question is essential
not only in the assessment of the ability of model predictions to meet
regulatory needs but also in the design of appropriate model validation experiments. A proper definition of the input data requirements
is essential for obvious reasons.

We believe that these unresolved questions are attributable to the
ad hoc bases on which air pollution modeling is now predicated. All of
the basic concepts now used in regional scale modeling were taken or
extrapolated from the theory developed for analyzing turbulent diffusion

very close to the source or from molecular diffusion theory. In this
transfer of concepts, tacit assumptions were made which are incorrect.
The purpose of this paper is to derive a modeling basis from first
principles that hopefully overcomes the problems and uncertainties
cited above.

Another objective is to emphasize the inherent limits of the predictability of quantities associated with turbulent flows and to build
into the modeling bases the capability of delineating these limits
quantitatively. Air pollution modeling seems to be pervaded by the
notion of determinsm, i.e., that given accurate descriptions of the
physical laws that govern material concentrations in the atmosphere,
accurate input data, and a large enough computer, one can predict any
quantity of interest. This premise is not supportable, however, because the quantitative specification of the initial state of the atmosphere and the conditions at its boundaries that are essential in
the use of physical laws in prognostic roles is far beyond our measurement capabilities. The situation is analogous to that of a set of
dice. We know what laws these dice supposedly obey once they are
thrown, but we cannot describe quantitatively the initial positions
and speed of the dice and other parameters that would be needed to
predict the outcome of a throw on a given occasion.

In the next section we summarize a statistical basis for pollution
modeling which is developed in more detail in [4].

2. Statistical Basis for Air Pollution Modeling. We regard diffusion modeling as akin to games of chance inasmuch as one can determine, based on the definition of the system, the family of possible
outcomes but not the outcome itself on a given occasion. Only mean
properties of the family of outcomes (the ensemble) can be specified.
In some instances, the corresponding values associated with each member of the ensemble cluster around this mean value so closely that in
the majority of realizations, the value observed is close to the predicted mean value.

The steps developed in [4] for modeling a given space-time domain
$(\mathcal{D}, T)$ are the following:

(i) First, we represent the actual flow field $u(x,t)$ in $\mathcal{D}$ within a
given time interval T in terms of its complex Fourier transform $U(k,\omega) = (U,V)$:

(2) $$u(x,t) = \frac{1}{(2\pi)^{n+1}} \int \int U(k,\omega) e^{i(k\cdot x + \omega t)} dk d\omega.$$

(ii) The set of possible U is the global family Γ of complex functions
that satisfy realizability conditions such as

(3a) $U*(k,\omega) = U(-k, -\omega)$

(3b) $U*(-k,-\omega) = U(k,\omega)$

where $U*$ denotes the complex conjugate; physical laws such as mass continuity, which for an incompressible 2-D fluid reads

(4) $k_x U(k_x, k_y, \omega) + k_y V(k_x, k_y, \omega) = 0;$

momentum, entropy and other laws. Figure 1 depicts the global family Γ of velocity transforms U schematically.

(iii) The probability of occurrence of a given U varies from one domain D to another and can be determined only from observations of flow in D. If continuous time averaged wind records are available at N sites x_1, $x_2 \ldots x_N$ in D over M time intervals $t_m \leq t \leq t_m + T$, i.e., we have the set of observations

(5) $\bar{u}_{nm}(t) = \frac{1}{2T} \int_{t-T}^{t+T} u(x_n, t') dt'$ $n = 1, 2, \ldots N$
                                                                           $t_m \leq t \leq t_m + T$
                                                                           $m = 1, 2, \ldots M$

we <u>approximate</u> the probabilities to be nonzero for only those U in the subset E of Γ whose subset mean values, denoted by $<>$, satisfy the integral equations

(6a) $\tilde{u}(x,t) = \int \int <U(k,\omega)> \frac{\sin\omega T}{\omega T} e^{i(k \cdot x + \omega t)} dk d\omega,$

(6b) $R(x,x';t,t') = \int \int \int \int <U(k,\omega)U*(k',\omega')> \frac{\sin\omega T}{\omega T} \frac{\sin\omega' T}{\omega' T}$

$$e^{i(k \cdot x - k' \cdot x' + \omega t - \omega' t')} dk dk' d\omega d\omega'.$$

Here $\tilde{u}(x,t)$ represents a least squares fit of the mean values

(7a) $\tilde{u}_n(t) = \frac{1}{M} \sum_{m=1}^{M} \bar{u}_{nm}(t)$, $n = 1, 2, \ldots N$

and R is a least squares fit of

(7b) $R_{jk}(t,t') = \frac{1}{M} \sum_{m=1}^{M} \bar{u}_j(t_m + t)\bar{u}_k(t_m + t')$, $j,k = 1, 2, \ldots N$

We assume that the probabilities of each U in E are equal, so E is also the ensemble of flows associated with $(D, \tilde{T})$.

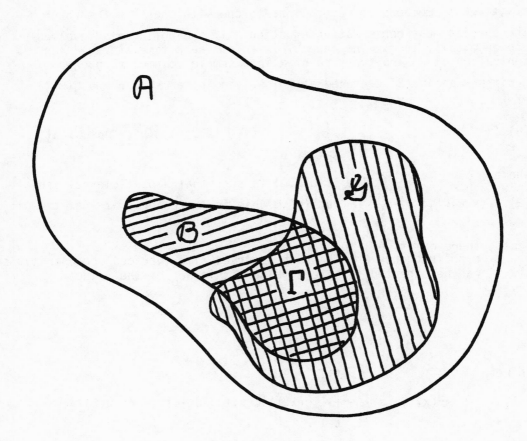

Figure 1. Illustration of the set Γ of complex functions
$\tilde{U}(k,\omega)$ that comprise the global family of fluid
flow velocity Fourier Transforms. Set $\mathcal{A}$ represents
functions that satisfy purely mathematical constraints
like Eq. (3). Set $\mathcal{B}$ represents the set that satisfy
mass continuity relationships, like Eq. (4); and set
$\mathcal{L}$ denotes functions that satisfy all other laws
like momentum and entropy. The intersection Γ of
$\mathcal{B}$ and $\mathcal{L}$ defines the global family of $\tilde{U}$.

(iv) For given pollutant species and their source emission rate distributions $Q(\underset{\sim}{x},t)$, there exists an ensemble E of concentration fields $\underset{\sim}{c}(x,t)$ whose members correspond one-to-one with the u in E through the species mass conservation equation. If the pollutants involved are chemically inert, the ensemble mean of their time averaged concentration at an arbitrary point x in a sample volume δv, over an arbitrary period $2T$ centered at t is given in terms of E and $Q(\underset{\sim}{x},t)$ by

$$(8) \qquad <\overline{c}(\underset{\sim}{x},t)> = \frac{1}{2T\delta v} \int_{t-T}^{t+T} \int \int_{0}^{t'} <\phi(x,t'|x'',t'')>Q(\underset{\sim}{x}'',t'')dt''dx''dt'$$

where

$$(9) \quad \phi(\underset{\sim}{x},t|x',t') = \begin{cases} 1 \text{ , if } u(k,\omega) \text{ is such that a particle released} \\ \qquad \text{at } (\underset{\sim}{x'},t') \text{ is in } \delta v \text{ centered at } x \text{ at time } t; \\ 0 \text{ , otherwise.} \end{cases}$$

(Note: there exists a ϕ for each u in Γ.)
The average frequency λ with which observed time averaged concentrations $\overline{c}(\underset{\sim}{x},t)$ can be expected to have a value within $\pm\varepsilon_0$ of the value $<\overline{c}(\underset{\sim}{x},t)>$, given by (8), satisfies

$$(10) \qquad \lambda \geq 1 - \frac{<\varepsilon^2>}{\varepsilon_0^2}$$

where

$$(11) \qquad <\varepsilon^2(\underset{\sim}{x},t)> = \frac{1}{4T^2} \int_{t-T}^{t+T} \int <c(\underset{\sim}{x},t')c(\underset{\sim}{x},t'')>dt'dt'' - <\overline{c}(\underset{\sim}{x},t)>^2$$

and

$$(12) \qquad <c(\underset{\sim}{x},t)c(\underset{\sim}{x},t')> = \int \int_{0}^{t} \int_{0}^{t'} <\phi_2(\underset{\sim}{x},t;\underset{\sim}{x},t'|\underset{\sim}{x}'',t'',\underset{\sim}{x}''',t''')>$$

$$Q(\underset{\sim}{x}'',t'')Q(\underset{\sim}{x}''',t''')dt''dt'''dx''dx'''$$

$$(13) \qquad \phi_2(\underset{\sim}{x},t;\underset{\sim}{x},t'|\underset{\sim}{x}'',t'';\underset{\sim}{x}''',t''') = \begin{cases} 1 \text{ , if } u(k,\omega) \text{ is such that a} \\ \qquad \text{particle released at} \\ \qquad (x'',t'') \text{ and one released} \\ \qquad \text{at } (\underset{\sim}{x}''',t''') \text{ are found at} \\ \qquad (x,t) \text{ and } (x,t'), \text{ respec-} \\ \qquad \text{tively;} \\ 0 \text{ , otherwise.} \end{cases}$$

(v) We define the <u>conditional ensemble</u> C as the subset of E whose members U satisfy the integral equations

(14) $$\bar{u}_n(t) = \frac{1}{(2\pi)^3} \int \int U(\underset{\sim}{k},\omega) \frac{\sin\omega T}{\omega T} e^{i(\underset{\sim}{k}\cdot\underset{\sim}{x}_n + \omega t)} dkd\omega \quad n=1,2,\ldots N.$$

Here $\bar{u}_n(t)$ is a given time averaged wind observation at $\underset{\sim}{x}_n$. The corresponding conditional ensemble of concentrations is denoted by C. Its mean values of $\bar{c}$ and ε^2 are obtained by the same formulas as cited in the preceding step, except the ensemble averaging <> is over C rather than E. The conditional ensemble properties are relevant to conventional type modeling studies where one attempts to predict concentrations from given wind data $\bar{u}_n(t)$. The general ensemble E applies when estimates of expected future concentrations and their frequencies are to be made for postulated source distributions Q. The flow field ensembles E and C are depicted in Figure 2.

3. <u>Remarks</u>.

   A. <u>The character of diffusion at long range</u>. Consider for the moment the case where only a single wind observation site exists within D and that a point source of material exists at $\underset{\sim}{x}_0$ near that site. Then, E and C are defined in terms of data at that site only, i.e., $N = 1$ in (14) and implicity in (6). If we were to superpose the trajectories originating at $\underset{\sim}{x}_0$ in each member of C defined for a given, observed wind vector $\bar{u}(t)$, we might find a pattern like that shown in Figure 3. The spread of these trajectories is what we regard as the manifestation of turbulent dispersion.

   Since each member of C satisfies (14), all trajectories have the same general direction, namely that of $\bar{u}(\underset{\sim}{x}_0,t)$, near the source. But farther downstream there is increasing freedom in the direction that the local flow, and hence the trajectories, can take and still satisfy (14). For example, on some occasions when the wind vector is $\bar{u}(t)$ at $\underset{\sim}{x}_0$, the flow turns cyclonically downstream while on other occasions, with an identical flow at $\underset{\sim}{x}_0$, it turns anticyclonically. Without more information than simply the wind vector at $\underset{\sim}{x}_0$, there is no way to say which direction the trajectories will take. Indeed, it appears obvious from this perspective that the spread of trajectories far from the source is in no way controlled by small scale wind fluctuations at $\underset{\sim}{x}_0$, yet this is the implication of the conventional method of estimating material spread at long range.

   Specifically, using the so-called turbulent velocity fluctuation u' defined at $\underset{\sim}{x}_0$ by

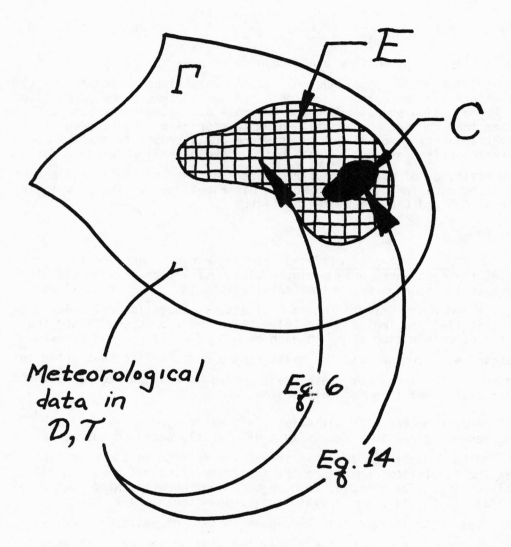

Figure 2. Schematic illustration of the ensemble E and the
conditional ensemble C of flows U associated with
a given (D, T) and their relation to the global
family Γ.

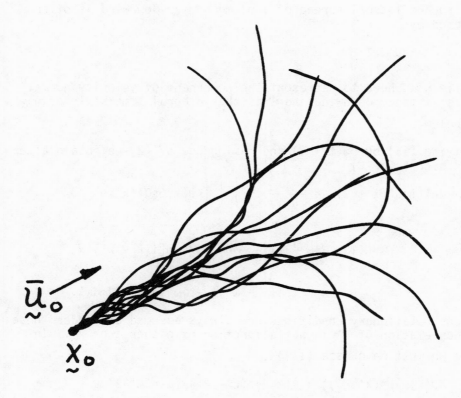

Figure 3. Trajectories of particles eminating from x_o in the
ensemble C conditioned on the observation $\bar{u}_o$.

(15) $u'(t) = u(x_o,t) - \bar{u}(x_o,t)$,

the mean square lateral spread of a plume σ^2 far downwind is often approximated by

(16) $\sigma^2 \sim <u'^2>T \dfrac{x}{u}$

where u' is used here to represent the component of velocity normal to $\bar{u}$, x is distance downwind and T is the integral time scale of u' defined below.

   Multiplying (15) by $u'(t + \tau)$ and making use of (2) we obtain after averaging over E (or C)

(17) $<u'(t)u'(t + \tau)> = \dfrac{1}{(2\pi)^6} \int \int \int \int <U(k,\omega)U*(k',\omega')>$

$$[(1 - \frac{\sin\omega T}{\omega T})(1 - \frac{\sin\omega' T}{\omega' T})]\exp[i(k - k')\cdot x_o$$

$$+ i(\omega - \omega')t - i\omega'\tau]dkdk'd\omega d\omega'.$$

Homogeneous, stationary conditions are always assumed and under these the autocorrelation of u' is not a function of either t or x_o. In this case we must have (see (17))

(18) $<U(k,\omega)U*(k',\omega')> = \Psi(k,\omega)\delta(k - k')\delta(\omega - \omega')$

and with this (17) reduces to

(19) $<u'(t)u'(t + \tau)> = \dfrac{1}{(2\pi)^6} \int \int \Psi(k,\omega)(1 - \frac{\sin\omega T}{\omega T})^2 e^{-i\omega\tau} dkd\omega.$

Setting $\tau = 0$ in this equation, we get $<u'>^2$ in terms of the mean ensemble properties of U. By definition

(20) $T = \dfrac{1}{<u'^2>} \displaystyle\int_o^\infty <u(t)u(t + \tau)>d\tau.$

As we noted in the introduction, values for T are usually inferred from empirical data. But we can calculate T from (19) and (20):

$$(21) \quad T = \frac{1}{2(2\pi)^6} \int \int \Psi(\underset{\sim}{k},\omega)(1 - \frac{\sin\omega T}{\omega T})^2 \int_{-\infty}^{\infty} e^{-i\omega\tau} d\tau d\underset{\sim}{k} d\omega$$

$$= \frac{1}{2(2\pi)^5} \int \int \Psi(\underset{\sim}{k},\omega)(1 - \frac{\sin\omega T}{\omega T})^2 \delta(\omega) d\underset{\sim}{k} d\omega$$

$$= 0.$$

The only way for T to be nonzero is for the wind averaging time T to be infinite. Stated another way, the use of nonzero values for T in estimates of plume spread implies that the "turbulence" consists of all scales of motion, which contradicts the conventional definition (15). The problem is simply that (16) is misapplied. Close to the source, the constraint of the observation $\overline{u}(t)$ permits freedom in only the small scale wind fluctuations (provided the source is near a met station) which normally are regarded as the "turbulence" u' (see (15).

However, with increasing distance from a met observation site, the constraint of the observation $\overline{u}$ on large scale flow features diminishes gradually so that far away there is freedom in the ensemble over a much broader spectrum of fluctuations than close in.

   B. Parameterization of dispersion. If we increase the number of met stations in $\mathcal{D}$ from 1, as in the example above, to N, the added constraints on U change the character of the E and C ensembles and therefore, also, the pattern of particle trajectories. Thus, dispersion is an artifact of our observations, rather than an intrinsic property of the atmosphere, and it must be treated in this manner when attempting to approximate it.

   For example, to estimate the effective value of eddy diffusivity for use in a diffusion equation model, one should proceed as follows.

   First, calculate <c> for the C ensemble, as summarized at the beginning of this section.

   Secondly, define a transport wind field by fitting some function to the mean winds <u> in C.

   Finally, using the known <c> and <u> solve the diffusion equation "in reverse", i.e., the inverse problem, for the diffusivity K. Lamb and Durran [5] illustrate this process.

   C. Predictability of concentration at long range. We want to emphasize that models predict ensemble mean concentrations and these may differ greatly from the values one might measure on a given occasion.

This discrepancy stems from our inability to specify atmospheric motion in its full detail and is not attributable to deficiencies in the model. The latter compound the problem; but even if the model equations and input data were perfect, differences would still exist between the observed and predicted values. Recognizing this inherent limitation and being able to quantify it are essential not only in the design of appropriate model validation experiments but also (and more importantly) in the proper use of model predictions in decision making processes. We introduced a predictable parameter $<\varepsilon^2>$, see (11), which provides through Eq. (10) an estimate of how frequently one can expect observed, time averaged concentrations $\bar{c}$ to differ by an arbitrary amount ε_0 from the predicted ensemble mean concentration $<\bar{c}>$. Using this parameter, we will illustrate briefly below that the scatter of observed values $\bar{c}$ and $<\bar{c}>$ increases with distance from the source.

Referring to Figure 4, let's assume that the two plumes shown represent the extreme lateral deviation from the x axis of all plumes in the C ensemble. By "plume", we mean the superposition of particle trajectories originating continually at the source over some small time interval for each $\tilde{u}$. Thus, the plume envelopes in the figure represent the locus of travel of the particles released during this small time period. Also, the plumes shown assume that C is an ensemble in which a wind observation site is located at the source but that no other observations are available.

For simplicity, let's assume that the concentration aurocorrelation has the form

$$(22) \qquad <c(t)c(t + \tau)> = \begin{cases} <c^2> , & \tau \leq T, \\ <c>^2 , & \tau > T, \end{cases}$$

where T is arbitrary and independent of t and x. Assuming that within C, plumes are equally distributed over the lateral ranges L_1 and L_2 shown in Figure 4, and their width ℓ is nearly the same within C for a fixed x, we obtain by straightforward calculations based on the definition of ensemble averaging

$$(23) \qquad \begin{aligned} <c_1^2> &= <c_1>^2 \, L_1/\ell_1 \\ <c_2^2> &= <c>^2 \, L_2/\ell_2 . \end{aligned}$$

Now from (22) and (11) we obtain assuming stationarity

$$(24) \qquad <\varepsilon^2> = \frac{T}{T} \left(2 - \frac{T}{T}\right)(<c^2> - <c>^2),$$

where, it will be recalled, ε is the difference between an observed concentration averaged over a moving interval T and the corresponding predicted ensemble mean value $<\bar{c}>$. Making use of (23) and assuming $\ell_1 \simeq \ell_2 = \ell$ we get

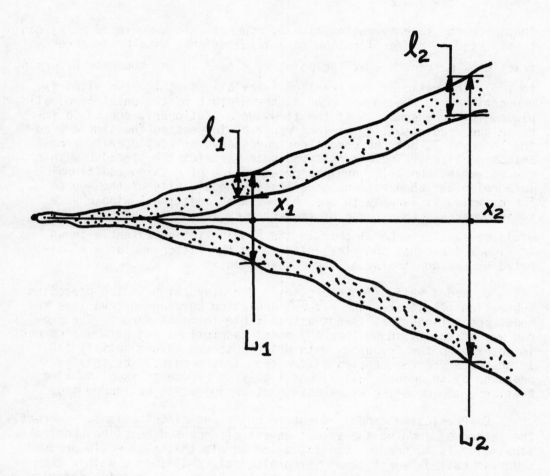

Figure 4. Plumes from the C ensemble that mark the limits
of lateral motion.

$$
(25) \qquad \frac{<\varepsilon_2^2>}{\overline{<c_2>}^2} = \frac{<\varepsilon_1^2>}{\overline{<c_1>}^2} \left(\frac{L_2 - \ell}{L_1 - \ell} \right).
$$

Thus, for the same averaging time T, concentrations measured at x_2 can be expected to differ from the mean value at that site by a larger fractional margin than at the point x_1 closer to the source. According to (25), the ratio of the fractional deviations at the two sites is proportional to the square root of the width L of the envelope of all plumes in the ensemble. If the flows were stationary, one could improve the predictability at long range by increasing the time averaging interval T, but the conditions necessary for stationarity are seldom realized. The alternative is to restrict the spread L within the ensemble, and this requires redefinition of C using additional meteorological observations at sites in the vicinity of the source. For example, it is easy to see that with an additional wind observation near x_2, the spread of trajectories in the new ensemble C would be less in general than in the single station ensemble shown in Figure 4 because some trajectories in the latter would be eliminated by the constraint of the observation at x_2.

D. Model validation exercises. Our discussion in the preceding subsection illustrates the natural deviation between observations and model predictions that is not attributable to model error. The proper way to establish whether the model assumptions and data are correct is to examine the frequency with which observed values satisfy (10). If the observed frequencies differ from that predicted by this expression by an amount that is not likely to be due to sampling fluctuations, the modeling hypotheses must be judged to be inadequate.

E. Predicting impact of future emissions distributions. Currently the method of judging the effectiveness of proposed emissions control strategies is to predict concentration levels that they would produce under so called "worst case" meteorological conditions. Within the context of the approach we have developed here, this entails defining the conditional ensemble C for the set of "worst case" meteorological conditions N and then computing $<c>_C$ and $<\varepsilon^2>_C$ for the proposed source distribution $Q(x,t)$, where $<>_C$ denotes averaging over the subset C.

However, since meteorology and the source distribution jointly effect concentrations, the concept of "worst case" meteorology is not well defined in the abstract. A more meaningful approach, therefore, is to compute $<\overline{c}>_E$ and $<\varepsilon^2>_E$. These quantities give the expected concentration and its variance for a given region and emission distributions, taking into account the full range of flows likely for that region as revealed in the climatological data on which the corresponding flow ensemble E is based.

REFERENCES

[1] G. I. Taylor, <u>Diffusion by continuous movement</u>, Proc. of London
    Math Soc., Ser 2, 20, (1921), pp. 196-202.

[2] R. R. Draxler, <u>Determination of atmospheric diffusion parameters</u>,
    Atmos. Environ. 10, (1976), pp. 99-105.

[3] A. Venkatram, <u>The expected deviation of observed concentrations
    from predicted ensemble means</u>, Atmos. Environ. 13, (1979), pp.
    1547-1550.

[4] R. G. Lamb, <u>Air pollution modeling as a problem in statistics</u>,
    (1981) (available from the author).

[5] R. G. Lamb and D. R. Durran, <u>Eddy diffusivities derived from a
    numerical model of the convective planetary boundary layer</u>, Il
    Nuove Cimento 1C, (1978), pp. 1-17.

Statistical Evaluation
of Air Quality Simulation Models

K. P. MacKay* and R. D. Bornstein**

Abstract. Quantitative and qualitative statistical performance techniques used in the evaluation of air quality simulation models are reviewed. These techniques are used to evaluate the difference and correlation between observed and predicted air pollution concentrations.

Various sources of error, including model and instrument errors, are reviewed. In addition, possible improper uses of statistical techniques are reviewed, as these can lead to erroneous estimates of the actual error.

1. Introduction. Evaluation of air quality simulation models can consist of up to four phases: (1) a qualitative scientific evaluation as to whether model assumptions are reasonable and consistent with basic physical principles; (2) a one time tuning of model constants; (3) a sensitivity analysis of model dependence on input parameters; and (4) an operational evaluation for particular model applications.

Early evaluation efforts were reviewed by Hillyer et al. (1979), while previously utilized individual performance measures were summarized by Bencala and Seinfeld (1979), who also described a new assessment package called AQMAAP. Attributes of good model performance were identified and related to particular air quality issues by Hayes (1979).

The evaluation protocol developed for the Electric Power Research Institute (Bowne, 1980) included both operational evaluation and a sequential sensitivity analysis of each model module (e.g., transport, diffusion, and transformation). The performance assessment protocol of Ruff et al. (1980) contained loss functions for various types of poor model performance, while the protocol of Martinez et

---
*Department of Meteorology, San Jose State University, San Jose, CA 95192
**Department of Statistics, Stanford University, Stanford, CA 94305

al. (1980) discussed combining various performance measures into one "figure of merit". Such a figure could be either the worst or average evaluation statistic.

The recent American Meteorological Society (AMS) Workshop on Dispersion Model Performance (Fox, 1980, 1981) brought together model developers and users, regulatory personnel, and statisticians to develop an evaluation protocol for EPA. The resulting protocol included quantitative and qualitative techniques to evaluate the magnitude of the differences and correlations of the following observed and predicted concentrations (arranged in decreasing order of stringency): (1) paired (in time and space) concentrations; (2) paired (in various degrees of time and/or space) maximum concentrations; and (3) unpaired (in time) concentration cumulative frequency distributions.

Maximum (highest or second highest) concentrations are important in many health and regulatory situations. When comparing maximum observed and predicted concentrations, the following aspects are important: magnitude, downwind location (distance and direction), and time of occurrence (MacKay, 1980).

The current paper reviews quantitative and qualitative performance techniques recommended by the AMS Workshop, and reviews various sources of error and problems associated with the evaluation of air quality simulation models.

2. Quantitative Performance Measures. The AMS Workshop suggested quantitative estimates be made of the magnitudes of the difference and correlation between observed concentrations C_o and predicted concentrations C_p, as well as between maximum observed concentration $(C_m)_o$ and maximum predicted concentration $(C_m)_p$.

Four possible difference functions can be defined from $(C_m)_o$ and $(C_m)_p$ as shown in Table 1 (from Fox, 1980). The most stringent of these, $\Delta C_m(L,t)$, is computed from the difference between the observed maximum concentration at time t and the predicted concentration at that site L at that time. The next two are moderately stringent. The parameter $\Delta C_m(\Delta L,t)$ is computed as the difference between the observed and predicted maximum concentrations at time t, with these concentrations not necessarily at the same sites. The parameter $\Delta C_m(L,\Delta t)$ is computed as the difference between the observed maximum concentration and the predicted maximum concentration at that site, with these values not necessarily occurring at the same time. The final parameter $\Delta C_m(\Delta L,\Delta t)$ is the least stringent as it is computed from observed and predicted maximum concentrations occurring at any site and time.

TABLE 1

Possible difference functions defined using observed and predicted maximum concentrations paired in time t at location L. The quantities Δt and ΔL represent unpaired arguments.

Parameter	Paired in:
$\Delta C_m(L,t)$	time and location
$\Delta C_m(\Delta L,t)$	time only
$\Delta C_m(L,\Delta t)$	space only
$\Delta C_m(\Delta L,\Delta t)$	neither time or space

2.1. <u>Difference</u>. The concentration difference function $\Delta(\ )$ or residual is defined by

$$(1) \qquad \Delta(\ ) = (\ )_o - (\ )_p \ .$$

The residual is used in computation of the following quantitative estimates of difference: bias, noise, and gross error.

A model is biased if it consistently over or under predicts in some or all situations. The bias of the paired concentrations or the selectively paired maximum concentrations can be estimated by the average residual $\overline{\Delta(\ )}$ given by

$$(2) \qquad \overline{\Delta(\ )} = \frac{1}{N} \Sigma \Delta(\ ) \ ,$$

where N is the number of observations.

The bias of the unpaired frequency distributions can be estimated by use of t, z, Wilcoxon, or Mann-Whitney tests (Fox, 1980). The first two of these tests are parametric, while the latter two are nonparametric.

Noise is the root mean square error (RMSE) evaluated around the bias. For the paired concentrations and the selectively paired concentrations, it is estimated by the standard deviation of the residuals σ_Δ using

$$(3) \qquad \sigma_\Delta = \{\frac{1}{N-1} [\Delta(\ ) - \overline{\Delta(\ )}]^2\}^{1/2} \ ,$$

while the noise of the unpaired frequency distributions can be evaluated by use of the parametric F or χ^2 tests.

Gross error is estimated by measures in which over and under predictions do not cancel. For the paired concentrations and the selectively paired maximum concentrations, it can be estimated by either
the RMSE error evaluated around zero σ or the average absolute
error $|\overline{\Delta(\ )}|$, given respectively by

(4)
$$\sigma = \{\tfrac{1}{N} \Sigma [\Delta(\ )]^2\}^{1/2}$$

and

(5)
$$|\overline{\Delta(\ )}| = \tfrac{1}{N} \Sigma |(\ )_o - (\ )_p| \ ,$$

while the gross error of the unpaired frequency distributions can be
evaluated by use of the nonparametric χ^2 or Kolmogorov-Smirnov
tests (Fox, 1980).

Bias (first moment of a distribution) is related to noise (second
moment) and gross error by

(6)
$$\sigma \approx \{[\overline{\Delta(\ )}]^2 + \sigma_\Delta^2\}^{1/2} \ ,$$

where the approximation arises from the $N-1$ in (3). All information concerning normal distributions is in the bias and noise. In
addition, for normally distributed variables, the bias has a normal
distribution, the noise a chi-squared distribution, and the gross
error a bivariant or compound distribution.

Gross error can be given by

(7)
$$\sigma = (\overline{\Delta c})^2 + \sigma_o^2 + \sigma_p^2 - 2r\,\sigma_o\,\sigma_p \ ,$$

where σ_o and σ_p are the standard deviations of the observed and
predicted concentrations, respectively, and r is the correlation
coefficient between the observed and predicted concentrations. Brier
(1975) pointed out that (7) implies that the following must be satisfied to have perfect magnitude prediction

(8a)
$$\overline{\Delta C} = o$$

(8b)
$$\sigma_o = \sigma_p$$

(8c)
$$r = 1 \ .$$

2.2. Correlation. Evaluation of the correlation between observed
and predicted concentration values involves evaluation of temporal

correlation and/or spatial alignment determined using temporal or
spatial correlation coefficients (Table 2).

TABLE 2

Correlation coefficients for paired concentration data and selectively
paired maximum concentrations (from Fox, 1980). See text for explanation of entries.

Correlation Data for	Temporal	Spatial	Space-Time
ΔC	$r(\tau)$	r_s	r
$\Delta C_m(L,t)$	$r_m(\tau)$	-	-
$\Delta C_m(\Delta L,t)$	$r_m(\tau,\Delta L)$	$\Delta D(\Delta L)$	-
$\Delta C_m(L,\Delta t)$	Δt_m	-	-
$\Delta C_m(\Delta L,\Delta t)$	Δt_m	$\Delta D(\Delta L,\Delta t)$	-

Three types of correlation coefficients can be calculated using
observed and predicted paired concentration values. The cross-cor-
relation (temporal) coefficient $r(\tau)$ is calculated using values at
one site at all positive and negative time lags τ from the general
definition of the correlation coefficient. The spatial correlation
coefficient r_s is calculated using values at a zero time lag at a
given time using data from all sites together. The Pearson correlation coefficient r is calculated using all values at a zero time
lag for all times and for all sites together.

Given the definitions of the maximum concentration difference functions in Table 1, it is only appropriate to calculate correlation
coefficients for the temporal case for $\Delta C_m(L,t)$ and $\Delta C_m(\Delta L,t)$
according to Fox (1980). As shown in Table 2, $r_m(\tau)$ and $r_m(\tau,\Delta L)$
use the same maximum concentration data used to evaluate $\Delta C_m(L,t)$
and $\Delta C_m(\Delta L,t)$, respectively.

The above statistics can be used to define the time lag τ that
yields the highest correlations. However, zero time lags are generally
used in evaluation studies.

Time and space differences can be used in some of the cases where
correlation coefficients are inappropriate. The time difference between observed and computed maximum concentrations Δt_m (Table 2)

can be used with the data utilized in evaluating $\Delta C_m(L,\Delta t)$, i.e., data from a single site, but at any time. When Δt_m is computed using data associated with $\Delta C_m(\Delta L,\Delta t)$, it is calculated with data from anywhere in the region and at any time.

Instead of spatial correlation coefficients, vector differences (of distance and direction) between locations of observed and predicted maximum concentrations are used. When evaluated in conjunction with data associated with $\Delta C_m(\Delta L,t)$, it is determined using maximum predicted and observed concentrations at a given time anywhere in the region, but with data associated with $\Delta C_m(\Delta L,\Delta t)$, it is evaluated with data from anywhere in the temporal and spatial fields.

Correlation coefficients are generally evaluated in conjunction with a linear regression analysis in which

(9)
$$C_o = b_0 + b_1 C_p ,$$

where b_0 is the intercept and b_1 is the slope, given by

(10)
$$b_1 = r \frac{\sigma_o}{\sigma_p} .$$

Thus, for perfect correlation it is necessary that (8b) and (8c) be satisfied, as well as

(11a)
$$b_0 = 0$$

and

(11b)
$$b_1 = 1 .$$

3. Qualitative Analysis Techniques. Qualitative analysis techniques such as histograms, cumulative frequency plots, isopleth analysis, transections, and scatter diagrams can provide information on differences and/or correlation.

3.1. Difference. Histograms and cumulative frequency plots give information on differences between observed and predicted concentrations. Specific data sets to be used in these analyses are shown in Table 3.

A frequency distribution plot of the distance (in number of grid cells) from each observation site at which predicted concentrations first equaled observed values was used by Tesche et al. (1979).

TABLE 3

Quantities to be summarized in histograms and cumulative frequency plots.

Attribute / Data	Bias	Noise	Gross Error
Paired (in time and space) C	ΔC	$\Delta C - \overline{\Delta C}$	$\lvert \Delta C \rvert$
Selectively paired C_m	ΔC_m	$\Delta C_m - \overline{\Delta C_m}$	$\lvert \Delta C_m \rvert$
Unpaired in time, but paired in space	C_o & C_p	-	-

3.2. Correlation. Spatial correlation can be demonstrated by use of transections and/or isopleth analyses in the horizontal (at the surface or aloft) or in the vertical (in a plane perpendicular or parallel to the mean wind) for point or urban sources. Temporal correlation can be illustrated by the use of time series plots, while space-time correlation can be demonstrated by the use of scatter diagrams. Specific data sets to be used in these analyses are shown in Table 4.

TABLE 4

Qualitative analyses techniques for correlation studies.

Correlation / Data	Temporal	Spatial	Space-Time
Paired (in time and space) C	Time series of ΔC at a site	Isopleths and transections of ΔC at a time	Scatter diagrams of C_p or ΔC vs. C_o
Selectively paired C_m	Time series of ΔC_m for region	-	Scatter diagrams of $(C_m)_p$ or $(\Delta C)_m$ vs. $(C_m)_o$

Contingency tables, which function as quantitative scatter diagrams, were used by Roberts et al. (1970) and Zannetti and Switzer (1979) to evaluate air quality simulation models. The appropriate single valued performance measure to use in conjunction with such tables is the percent of incorrect or correct calculations (MacKay, 1981).

4. <u>Error Analysis</u>. Air quality simulation models have two sources of error according to Brier (1975), i.e., model errors and instrument error. In addition, improper use of statistical techniques can lead to erroneous estimates of the actual error.

4.1. <u>Instrumentation</u>. Instrument error leads to inaccuracies in measured concentrations. The magnitude of instrument error can be estimated by duplicate air quality monitoring instruments at individual sites (Brier, 1975). A quantitative analysis of instrument error was carried out by Anderson et al. (1977), who also supplied error bands for the maximum probable instrument error.

4.2. <u>Model Error</u>. Model error is composed of: (1) errors due to input data or from results from submodels used as input, and (2) errors due to deficiencies in the model itself.

Input error can be identified by the use of both case studies and sensitivity analysis, in which the effect of varying a single parameter is investigated. Such parameters include input parameters (e.g., pollutant emission strength, meteorological factors, and C_o), forecast length, forecast period (e.g., time of day, day of week, or month of year), and location (horizontal or vertical position).

Input model errors associated with pollutant emission rates arise from uncertainties in the spatial distribution of sources, both in the horizontal and vertical. This last effect was investigated by Koch and Thayer (1970) who performed a sensitivity analysis by changing a uniform stack height to a distribution of stack heights. Another source of input model error is concerned with area source emission grid size. For example, Shieh et al. (1970) performed a sensitivity analysis which demonstrated that a small emission grid gave a more detailed concentration field than a large grid. Peak values of predicted concentration were also increased with the smaller grid.

The temporal variation of pollutant source strength is normally parameterized by a single meteorological variable, i.e., temperature. However, Shieh and Shir (1976) found systematic errors when they plotted observed and predicted SO_2 values against air temperature. This parameter does not directly appear in the model formulation, but enters through parameterization of area source emission rates. Thus, it was concluded that the given functional relationship between area source emissions and temperature was not accurate for extreme temperatures.

To formulate a better area source emission algorithm, it was reasoned that the area source emissions should depend on wind speed as well, as heat loss from a home increases as this parameter increases in value. When this correction was applied to the area source emission formulation, systematic errors disappeared.

Similar results were found by Koch and Thayer (1971), who also carried out a complete sensitivity study involving other meteorological variables such as mixing depth and wind direction. The location of maximum predicted concentrations was extremely sensitive to small errors in this last parameter. A small error in input wind direction can result in a well predicted concentration pattern being shifted in location, resulting in a poor model evaluation. This is more of a problem with sharp gradients associated with narrow point source plumes, as opposed to the more uniform concentration fields associated with area source urban plumes. This is likewise more of a problem with primary pollutants, as opposed to secondary pollutants, for the same reason. Another problem with observations of point source plumes is the large number of zero values.

The probability of observing the maximum concentration is thus also lower for point source plumes and primary pollutants than for area source urban plumes and secondary pollutants. This is also true for relatively sparse observational networks associated with "real world" applications, as opposed to those of large scale research projects.

A final input parameter which can be a source of error is background concentration. Observed concentrations used by Mills and Stern (1975) were corrected for this effect before comparison to predictions from a large point source.

Sensitivity analysis must not be confused with "model tuning", in which constants within the model are adjusted to match observed and predicted concentrations to within a desired degree of accuracy (Bowne, 1980). Once this process is completed, the model formulation should be "frozen", and only data sets not used in the tuning process should be used in the evaluation process.

Output model errors arise due to deficiencies in the model itself in association with either parameterization of physical processes affecting concentration (such as diffusion parameters, linear decay and removal rates, and plume rise algorithms) or due to numerical approximations (e.g., artificial diffusion associated with modeling transport processes).

A theoretical mathematical analysis of instrument, input, and model errors was carried out by Brier (1975). However, he did not apply any of the suggested performance measures.

4.3. _Statistical Errors._ Statistical aspects of model evaluation processes can lead to erroneous estimates of model errors. Statistical

errors are related to inappropriate data and to improper use of statistical techniques.

In order to obtain appropriate data care must be taken in the design
of air quality monitoring networks with repect to the number and place-
ment of sites, as well as sampling frequency. In addition, during
statistical analysis, effects of intercorrelations between sites must
be accounted for.

Another such problem arises as pollutant observations are point
values, while predicted values from many models are volume-averaged.
Another aspect of this problem is that large differences exist between
predicted rooftop and observed urban canyon concentrations (Johnson et
al., 1970). They also discussed the need to relate these two concentrations via wind and traffic density data. Large (factor of two)
variations in concentration were found by Johnson et al. (1971) within
an urban canyon at the intersection of two streets due to the complex
microscale circulation pattern within the canyon.

Problems arise, according to Bowne (1980), when statistics are estimated with more than one-third of the values missing. To reduce the influence of a few outliers on the variance, Brier (1975) suggested trans-
forming the distribution of observed concentration to its logarithm or
to itself raised to some power. Another approach is the use of robust
(resistant) statistics such as the average absolute error instead of
σ.

A basic averaging time of one hour should be used in all calculations
(Fox, 1980). These values can then be used to compute the longer term
three, eight, and twenty-four hour averages of the air quality standards.

Statistical problems arise when running averages are used to smooth
data (Bowne, 1980), logarithmic plots are used (Bornstein, 1980), background concentration is removed from C_o (Fox, 1980), and C_o and/or
C_p are nondimensionalized by various combinations of C_o and/or C_p
(Fox, 1980). However, nondimensionalization is frequently useful in
presenting data, and various forms have been used by Hilst (1970),
Roberts et al. (1970), Hayes (1979), and Rao et al. (1980).

Statistical problems also arise if zero predicted values are not
eliminated before the cumulative frequency distribution is compared to
that of the observed values (Bowne (1980). One method of eliminating
zero values is by use of difference values.

Both Bowne (1980) and Brier (1975) discussed the need for symmetry
(i.e. normality) in the distributions of C_o and C_p, e.g., it is
assumed in many statistical tests. While the distribution of ΔC
values will be more normal than those of C_o and C_p, the AMS Workshop

recommended using an exponential or logarithmic transformation of C_o and/or C_p to achieve normality. However, Brier (1975) suggested using robust statistics such as: (1) $|\overline{\Delta(\ )}|$ instead of $\overline{\Delta(\ )}$; (2) the median error instead of σ; (3) looking at the percentage of time a particular concentration is exceeded; and (4) looking at the high end of the frequency distribution of concentrations, as percentage error is more important there than at the low end of the distribution.

The problem of time correlations within data sets can be overcome using autocorrelation techniques to determine their magnitude (Fox, 1980). Once such trends are removed, data will have been converted to random variables, more easily analyzed by statistical techniques. Another technique is to use only some values, e.g., every n-th observation.

While r^2 is equal to the explained portion of the variance, correlation coefficients only indicate whether the "trend" is properly simulated. They do not provide quantitative estimates of the magnitude of the error, e.g., if the model always overpredicts concentrations by a constant factor, the correlation will be perfect. In addition, when observed data possess an exponential distribution (at a fixed location) or a log normal distribution (with respect to a moving coordinate system), logarithmic correlation coefficients should be computed (Shir and Shieh, 1976).

Nonlinear correlation coefficients could be used when appropriate and median, as opposed to mean, temporal and spatial correlation coefficients were reported by Duewer et al. (1978). In four of five cases, temporal correlation coefficients were higher than their corresponding spatial coefficients. Similar results were also found by Nappo (1974) in a comparison of nine multisource urban air quality simulation models. Only one of the models simulated mean spatial correlations better than mean temporal correlations. Finally, Brier (1975) has noted the necessity for the variance of the departures from the linear regression line to be constant.

Since, as discussed above, small errors in input wind directions cause well simulated concentration patterns displaced in space, spatial correlation coefficients are frequently poor. Thus MacKay (1981) cautions against using this technique and suggests instead the use of graphical techniques to demonstrate spatial correlation.

5. <u>Conclusion</u>. This paper has summarized various statistical techniques and performance measures used to evaluate predictions made by air quality simulation models. Various sources of error and practical problems associated with model evaluation were also discussed.

The suitability of the statistical testing of appropriate null hypotheses by evaluation studies is an area needing clarification. A statistical test investigates the hypothesis that observed and predicted concentrations come from the same population. A test statistic is then calculated and compared with critical values, and the hypothesis is either rejected or accepted on the basis of this comparison. This approach was recommended by the AMS Workshop (Fox, 1980 and 1981).

An alternate argument is that the observed and estimated populations are assumed different and that small differences in their populations are statistically significant with large data bases. Thus, the appropriate question is whether or not these differences are significant in terms of a decision making process. It is therefore more informative to state confidence limits about the values of the performance measures. The AMS Workshop (Fox, 1981) recommended use of interval statements in evaluation studies and as an initial step in establishing future model performance standards.

A semi-qualitative analysis of the limitations of short term predictions due to the stochastic nature of concentration data was presented by Venkatram (1979). He proposed a method for estimating the difference between measured average concentrations and model predictions (which correspond to ensemble averages). The method involves computing the ratio between the observed maximum concentration during some time period and the predicted concentration. Details can be found in his paper, and it is hoped that future collaborations between air quality models and statisticians will help in determining the theoretical limiting accuracy of air quality simulation models.

Acknowledgement. This work was supported by SIAM Institute for Mathematics and Society (SIMS) and by EPA through its cooperative agreement with the AMS on air quality models.

REFERENCES

1. G. E. Anderson et al., Air Quality in the Denver Metropolitan Region, 1974-2000. SAI report to EPA, SAI No. EF77-222, 460 pp. (1977).

2. K. E. Bencala and J. H. Seinfeld, An Air Quality Performance Assessment Package, Atmos. Environ. 13, pp. 1181-1185 (1979).

3. R. D. Bornstein, Survey of Statistical Techniques Used in Validating Air Quality Simulation Models, Unpublished, 33 pp. (1980).

4. G. W. Brier, Statistical Questions Relating to the Validation of Air Quality Simulation Models, Report to EPA, No. EPA-650/4-75-010, 21 pp. (1975).

5. N. E. Bowne, Validation and Performance Criteria for Air Quality Models, 2nd Joint AMS/APCA Conference on Applications of Air Pollution Meteorology, March 24-27, 1980, New Orleans, La., pp. 614-622 (1980).

6. W. H. Duewer, The Livermore Regional Air Quality Model, J. Appl. Meteor., 17(3), pp. 273-399 (1978).

7. D. G. Fox, Judging Air Quality Model Performance, AMS Manuscript: 39 pp. (1980).

8. D. G. Fox, Review of the Woods Hole Dispers on Model Performance Workshop, Preprint Volume, AMS Fifth Symposium on Turbulence, Diffusion, and Air Pollution, March 9-13, 1981, Atlanta, Ga., pp. 14-16 (1981).

9. S. R. Hayes, Performance Measures and Standards for Air Quality Simulation Models, Report to EPA from SAI, Inc., No. EPA-450/4-79-032: 146 pp. (1979).

10. M. J. Hillyer et al., Procedures for Evaluating the Performance of Air Quality Simulation Models, SAI Report to EPA, No. EPA-450/4-79-032: 146 pp. (1979).

11. G. R. Hilst, Sensitivities of Air Quality Prediction to Input Errors and Uncertainties, Proceedings of Symposium on Multiple-Source Urban Diffusion Models, October 27-30, 1969, Research Triangle Park, NC, pp. 7.1-7.24 (1970).

12. W. B. Johnson et al., Development of a Practical, Multi-Purpose Diffusion Model for Carbon Monoxide, Proceedings of Symposium on Multiple-Source Urban Diffusion Models, October 27-30, 1969, Research Triangle Park, NC, pp. 5.1-5.38 (1970).

13. W. B. Johnson et al., Field Study for Initial Evaluation of an Urban Diffusion Model for Carbon Monoxide, SIR Report, Project #8563: 144 pp. (1971).

14. R. C. Koch and S. D. Thayer, Validation and Sensitivity Analysis of the Gaussian Plume Multiple-Source Urban Diffusion Model, Geomet. Report to EPA for Contract No. CPA 70-94: 181 pp. (1971).

15. K. P. MacKay, Proposed Rationale for Evaluating the Performance of Air Quality Simulation Models, EPA Staff Report (Draft), Research Triangle Park, NC: 21 pp. (1980).

16. K. P. MacKay, The Utility of Measures Proposed for the Evaluation of Photochemical Grid Model Performance, Preprint Volume AMS Fifth Symposium on Turbulence, Diffusion, and Air Pollution, March 9-12, 1981, Atlanta, Ga., pp. 165-166 (1981).

17. J. R. Martinez et al., Development and Application of Methods for Evaluating Highway Air Pollution Dispersion Models, Preprint Volume, 2nd Jouns AMS/APCA Conference on Applications of Air Pollution Meteorology, March 24-27, New Orleans, La., pp. 1-6 (1980).

18.   M. T. Mills and R. W. Stern, Model Validation and Time-Concentra-
      tion Analysis of Three Power Plants, Report to EPA from GCA Corp.,
      No. EPA-450/3-76-002: 139 pp. (1975).

19.   C. J. Nappo, Jr., A Method for Evaluating the Accuracy of Air
      Pollution Prediction Models, Preprint Volume, AMS Symposium on
      Atmospheric Diffusion and Air Pollution, Santa Barbara, Ca.,
      September 9-13, 1974, pp. 325-329 (1974).

20.   S. T. Rao et al., An Evaluation of Some Commonly Used Highway
      Dispersion Models, J. Air Pollut. Control Assoc., 30(3), pp. 239-
      246 (1980).

21.   J. J. Roberts et al., An Urban Atmospheric Dispersion Model,
      Proceedings of Symposium on Multiple-Source Urban Diffusion
      Models, October 27-30, 1969, Research Triangle Park, NC, pp.
      6.1-6.72 (1970).

22.   R. E. Ruff et al., Development and Application of a Statistical
      Methodology to Evaluate the Realtime Air Quality Model (RAM),
      Preprint Volume 2nd Joint AMS/APCA Conference on Applications of
      Air Pollution Meteorology, March 24-27, 1980, New Orleans, La.,
      pp. 663-669 (1980).

23.   L. J. Shieh and C. C. Shir, Evaluation of an Urban Air Quality
      Model with Respect to Input Parameters, IBM Technical Paper
      #6320-3351: 48 pp. (August 1976).

24.   L. J. Shieh et al., A Model of Diffusion in Urban Atmospheres:
      SO_2 in Greater New York, Proceedings of Symposium on Multiple-
      Source Urban Diffusion Models, October 27-30, 1969, Research
      Triangle Park, NC, pp. 10.1-10.39 (1970).

25.   T. W. Tesche et al., Recent Verification Studies with the SAI
      Urban Airshed Model in the South Coast Air Basin, Preprint Volume
      Fourth Symposium on Turbulence, Diffusion, and Air Pollution,
      January 15-18, 1979, Reno, Nevada, pp. 307-312 (1979).

26.   A. Venkatram, A Note on the Measurement and Modeling of Pollutant
      Concentrations Associated with Point Sources, Boundary-Layer
      Meteor., 17, pp. 523-536 (1979).

27.   P. Zannetti and P. Switzer, Some Problems of Validation and Test-
      ing of Numerical Air Pollution Models, Preprint Volume, Fourth
      Symposium on Turbulence, Diffusion, and Air Pollution, January 15-
      18, 1979, Reno, Nevada, pp. 405-410 (1979).

A Review of the Application
of Probability Models
for Describing Aerometric Data

David T. Mage*

Abstract. Probability models are often used for describing
aerometric data, and these models may become the bases for estimating
the emissions reduction required to meet National Ambient Air Quality
Standards at various locations. This paper reviews the history of the
applications of probability models to aerometric data and a critical
evaluation is made of some of the different probability modeling techniques which have been applied to these data. The Law-of-Proportional-
Effect which has been proposed as a theoretical basis for the lognormal
distribution is discussed, and a related development from the equation
of continuity of mass is presented which leads to the consideration of
bounded distributions as models for air quality data. The usage of
these bounded models is recommended for aerometric data analysis.

Introduction. The control of air pollution in the U.S.A. is
based upon national ambient air quality standards (NAAQS) and State
Implementation Plans (SIPs) to reduce emissions in order to meet the
NAAQS. The present trend, as standards are revised to reflect new
scientific knowledge, is to base the revised standards on an expected
number of observed pollutant concentrations above the NAAQS. This
shift from observed numbers to expected numbers often requires the
analyst to make probability models of the observed data so that a
probability statement can be made for the future. Because the choice
of different probability models leads to different extreme value
distributions, there is a need for a basis for choosing probability
models which could provide some uniformity in preparation and review
of SIPs.

This paper reviews the literature on probability models applied
to air quality data, theoretical relationships that have been proposed
for the generation of air quality data, and probability models which
describe the results of these processes. A general equation for
simulating the generation of sequences of air quality data is developed
and one possible solution process is shown to lead to a class of
bounded distribution models.

*For further information contact David T. Mage, U.S. EPA, Environmental
Monitoring Systems Laboratory, MD-56, Research Triangle Park, N.C.
27711. Telephone: 919/5412231.

Literature Review. The two-parameter lognormal (LN2) distribution
has a long history of application in the field of small particle statistics (1). Analyses of the dust generated by industrial grinding processes have shown the LN2 model to be a good descriptor of the size
distribution of these particles. It was logical to expect that this
work would be extended to describe the distributions of particles in
the atmosphere. The LN2 model was applied to air pollution particle
statistics (2); and later concentrations of total suspended particulate
(TSP) in both urban and nonurban ambient atmospheres were described as
approximately LN2 (3). Although it was noted that there were some
marked deviations from lognormality, it was concluded that "... in
general, concentrations of particulate matter are lognormally distributed" (3). Larsen extended the application of the LN2 model from TSP
to the gaseous air pollutants, and he stated that carbon monoxide and
oxidant concentrations in the Los Angeles area "... indicate that the
variables tend to be logarithmically distributed" (4). He later
expressed the suitability of the LN2 model for air quality data in
general terms: "Air pollutant concentration data usually fit the bell
(Gaussian) shape, if concentration is plotted on a logarithmic scale"
(5) and "... concentrations are approximately lognormally distributed
for all pollutants in all cities for all averaging times" (6). Larsen
applied the LN2 model to a variety of pollutants and cities and further
refined his "averaging time model" so that the LN2 parameters and
maxima could be calculated for any averaging time (7). In a 1971
report, Larsen presented the averaging time model in considerable
detail and concluded: "Pollutant concentrations are lognormally distributed for all averaging times" (8).

Some authors attempted to explain the apparent lognormality of air
quality data in theoretical terms. Several papers containing theoretical terms were presented at a symposium on statistical aspects of
air quality data (9). The explanations usually are based either on
statistical theory or on properties of the meteorological data. The
statistical explanations usually involve the central limit theorem and
the diffusion law, while the meteorological explanations assume that
one of the meteorological variables, such as wind speed, is lognormally
distributed. A large number of applications of the LN2 model to air
quality data had been undertaken by the mid-1970's, but few authors
had examined the goodness-of-fit of the model to the data or had considered other candidate models. The first comprehensive comparison of
the LN2 model with other models was made by Lynn (10) who analyzed TSP
data from Philadelphia and examined the suitability of the normal, LN2,
and three-parameter lognormal (LN3) probability models, along with the
Pearson Types I and IV distributions and the Gamma distribution. It
was concluded that "... the two-parameter lognormal does overall
slightly better than the three-parameter and, in fact, does the best of
all four distributions (LN2, LN3, Gamma, and four-parameter Pearson)."
This result was unexpected, because the LN2 model really is a special
case of the LN3 model for which the LN3 third parameter is zero.

    Although Lodge and West (11) challenged the a priori assumption of
lognormality, the near-unanimous acceptance of the LN2 model continued
until 1974 when it was demonstrated that the LN3 model was superior to
the LN2 model for every air quality data set considered, provided that
the model is censored at zero when the third parameter is negative (12).
This lack of censorship may explain why the LN3 model was not superior
to the LN2 model in Lynn's comparison study (10). Almost all air quality data sets when plotted on logarithmic probability paper appear as
convex curves which are not modeled well by the straight line LN2 model.
Because the LN3C model plots as a convex curve, it usually provides a
significantly better fit to these data than the LN2. Therefore, the
(censored) three-parameter lognormal LN3(C) model was recommended as a
general-purpose model which could represent air quality frequency
distributions in a large number of circumstances (13, 14). In 1977,
Larsen adopted the LN3 and LN3C models and recommended their use over
the standard LN2 model for analysis of air quality data (15). Several
other investigators also applied goodness-of-fit criteria to the models,
and upon careful inspection, were finding that the LN2 model did not
fit air quality data especially well. The LN2 was applied to Bulgarian
air quality data and it was rejected by the Kolmogorov-Smirnov goodness-
of-fit criterion, and in some cases, the normal probability model exhibited a goodness-of-fit that was superior to the LN2 model (16). Using
the exponential model as a reference, Curran and Frank analyzed the
"tails" of distributions of air quality data (17). They found that, in
general, the cumulative frequencies of the data approached unity more
rapidly than the cumulative distribution function (CDF) of the exponential probability model. They called this property "light tailed."
They showed that the LN2 was "heavy tailed" since its CDF approached
unity more slowly than the exponential model. They reasoned that a
light-tailed distribution, such as the Weibull probability model,
should be considered for fitting light-tailed data sets. The Weibull
distribution was applied to environmental data and it was reported that
ozone data appear better suited to the 2-parameter Weibull model than
to the LN2 model (18). Bencala and Seinfeld applied the Weibull, Gamma,
LN2, and LN3 distributions to air quality data and compared their relative goodness-of-fit (19). Although they state that the LN3 model
gives the best fit of all candidate models, they concluded that the air
quality data are approximately LN2 in distributional form.

    The four-parameter lognormal probability (LN4) model, also known as
the S_B distribution has been applied to air quality data (20,21). The
fourth parameter allows inclusion of a finite maximum concentration
which is approached asymptotically as the CDF approaches unity. A Box
Cox power transform was applied to CO air quality data to test whether
various power functions, such as the square root or the cube root, are
more suitable than the normal (untransformed) distribution (22). The
extreme value distribution also has been proposed for application to air
quality data (23). Its use seems especially well suited to situations
in which the maxima of air quality data sets are compared with environmental standards. Although the gamma distribution was reported to not
perform as well as the LN2 and LN3 models (10,19), Trajonis analyzed NO_2

data and observed the gamma distribution was better suited to representing these NO_2 data than the heavy-tailed LN2 model (24).

At the present time, there appears to be a growing consensus that the data analyst should not automatically choose any one probability model (such as the LN2 model) to the exclusion of others, but, rather, that he should carefully evaluate the problem he is addressing and the data at hand before selecting a probability model (25). For this purpose, a program (MAXFIT) is available that statistically tests six probability models (Normal, LN3, S_B, Weibull, Gamma, Beta) fit to any data set by the method of maximum likelihood (26).

Models for Generating Skew Distributions of Air Quality Data. An early model for generating skewed distributions was proposed by Kapteyn to account for the skewed distributions which arise for the characteristics of members of a biological species (27). The model, called the Law of Proportional Effect (LPE), assumes that the change in growth in each successive time period is proportional to the previous level attained, times some random 'shock" term (R´).

For example, assume that the length of a tree leaf on Day 1 is L_1. On Day 2, the length of the leaf will be L_2. The change in length will be $\Delta L = L_2 - L_1$, and the ratio of the change to the previous length will be $R_1´ = \Delta L/L_1$. If we assume that the Ratio R´ varies from day to day in a random fashion due to such factors as sunlight, wind, moisture, and rainfall, then it may be treated as a positive random variable, and the following general equation may be written:

(1) $L_{i+1} - L_i = R_i´ L_i$
     for i=1, 2,......,n

    L_i = length of a leaf in the ith time period,

    $R_i´$ = random "shock" term, $R_i´ \geq 0$

To find a general expression for the length L in n successive time periods, we first solve equation (1) for L_{i+1}:

(2) $L_{i+1} = L_i (R_i´+1)$

We shall denote $R_i = R_i´+1$ as a new random shock term. Note that successive terms in this model can then be written as $L_2 = R_1 L_1$, and

(3) $L_n = L_1 \prod_{i=1}^{n-1} R_i$.

By mathematical induction, we see that a general expression for length L_n in n successive time periods is written as the product of L_1 and n-1 random shock terms. Another way to write equation (3) is to take logarithms of both sides:

$$(4) \quad \ln L_n = \ln L_1 + \sum_{i=1}^{n-1} \ln R_i$$

Thus, the logarithm of the nth value is the sum of a constant, $\ln(L_1)$, and n-1 random shock terms. If we assume that each random shock term is a member of a set of independent identically distributed random variables (i.i.d.r.v.) with finite variance, then the Central Limit Theorem will apply to the summation in equation (4). That is, as n becomes large the summation will asymptotically approach a normally distributed random variable. If the mean of the distribution of n R_i is assumed to be $\bar{R}_i$ and its variance is σ^2, then the summation approaches a normal distribution of mean $n\bar{R}_i$ and variance $n\sigma^2$. Thus all the lengths of living leaves on a tree on day n might be expected to constitute such a lognormal population.

Knox and Pollack presented an LPE explanation for apparent logarithmic pollutant concentration distribution (28). Their development for time variation of concentration C follows from the continuity equation:

$$(5) \quad \partial C/\partial t + \Delta \cdot (UC) = \nabla \cdot (D\nabla \cdot C) + S + P$$

where U is the wind velocity vector
       D is the eddy diffusivity vector
       S is the emission source term
       P is the chemical reaction term.

This equation was manipulated to represent a finite difference box model formulation which concerned the concentration averaged over a box which is surrounded by several other boxes. They restricted their analysis to the case where the source and sink terms S and P are significantly smaller than the advection and diffusion terms and the equation (5) reduced to a form similar to equation (1).

$$(6) \quad C_{i+1} - C_i = R_i' C_i + E_i$$

where R_i' is a random variable independent of C_i and E_i is a random "error" term, independent of C_i.

The assumption was then made that the error term E_i has a zero mean and therefore the summation of the third term will be zero since the "positive and negative terms will cancel each other." They stated: "This argument implies that equation (6) is consistent with the law of proportional effect," and consequently C would be lognormally distributed. On closer inspection, this analogy with the LPE does not hold since what is lognormal in the LPE leaf process is not the time-series of the length of a single leaf, but the lengths of many leaves on a tree, all of the same age. In the time-series applications of the LPE by Knox and Pollack (28), Kahn (29), Gifford (30), and Mage and Ott (31), the variance of the concentration must increase without bound as n increases which is not a characteristic of air quality time-series. Consequently, the simple LPE analogy is not a sufficient condition to establish lognormality of consecutive values in a time series. However, if the positive and negative terms of E do not cancel each other, which is the general case, Soong (32) provides an exact solution for the expected value of C and the autocorrelation function of C in a process for which the variance of C does not have to increase without bound. The following section demonstrates how equation (6) leads to a class of bounded distributions which have the same positive skewness associated with air quality data.

Bounded Distributions. Some of the possible distributions generated by equations (5) and (6) constitute a class of bounded distributions which are related by the distributions of the random variables R_i' and E_i and their autocorrelations and crosscorrelations. The term E_i is a forcing function (usually positive) related to nonconcentration dependent variables, and the term R_i' is a damping factor (usually negative) due to concentration dependence. The bounds to the distributions can be determined by finding the extreme conditions where $dC/dt = 0$, or from equation (6), where $C_{i+1} = C_i$. Solving equation (6) for this condition

$$C_i = E_i/(-R_i')$$

The upper bound of C exists when E is at its maximum and $-R'$ is at its minimum, $C_{max} = (E)_{max}/(-R')_{min}$. Conversely, the lower bound exists when E is at its minimum and $-R'$ is at its maximum, $C_{min} = (E)_{min}/(-R')_{max}$. If $(E)_{min}/(-R')_{max}$ is negative, then $C_{min} = 0$ and a finite number of zero values can occur since concentrations can never be negative. The constraining value of C_{max} is generally related to the maximum pollution levels occurring when the sources are maximized and the atmosphere is calm and stable. A secondary constraint on C_{max} exists from the nature of diffusion, such that the plume concentrations of emitted pollution tend to decrease, and a concentration greater than the maximum concentration of emitted pollution will not be observed. A legislated constraint on C_{max} can also exist through emission controls that require E to be reduced whenever C reaches an established "emergency" level.

Soong (32) shows that no single probability distribution, such as lognormal, is predicted from equation (6), and depending upon the autocorrelation and cross correlation functions of the random variables, R_i' and E_i, different probability distributions may be generated which could have common properties of bounded distributions. In many cases where the process is nonstationary, it may be necessary to use time series modeling to adequately describe the sequence of concentration values (33, 34).

<u>Applications</u> <u>of</u> <u>Probability</u> Models. In general there are many purposes
for applying probability models to a data set $G_1(X)$ which constitutes
a realization from an underlying process with a CDF $F(X)$. Two common
purposes are as follows:

1. The first purpose is to provide a parsimonious description of the
   n observations in the data set $G_1(x)$ by an analytical expression
   which contains only a few parameters. For this purpose any probability model can be used, with the choice up to the user for a
   criterion of how closely an acceptable model needs to fit the
   observations. Several procedures for choosing between models to
   fit a series of observations are available (26, 35). If necessary,
   a nonparametric analysis of the probability density function can be
   used to describe these data.

2. The second purpose is to provide a model of the underlying process
   with CDF $F(X)$, from which the realization $G_1(X)$ was drawn with this
   model to be used to predict the statistical properties of future
   realizations, $G_i(X)$ where $i \geq 2$.

The analyst must be clear in distinguishing between these two purposes. Fitting an empirical frequency distribution model, $G(X)$ to a
given set of observations, (purpose 1) is very different from choosing a
probability model, $F(X)$, in order to make probability statements about
independent sets of future realizations $[G_2(X), G_3(X), ..., G_M(X)]$. It
would be incorrect to assume that the next sampled distribution $G_2(X)$
will be a sample from $G_1(X)$ and not a sample from $F(X)$. There appears
to be a great deal of confusion in the air pollution literature on
this distinction since some authors make predictions about future realizations based upon an empirical model of $G_1(X)$ as if it were a Bayes
estimator of $F(X)$.

In practice the underlying distribution, with CDF $F(X)$, is unknown.
However, the examination of the mass balance equation (6) with allow-
ances for sources, chemical reactions, diffusion, and advection leads
to the conclusion that concentration, C, should be treated as a bounded
variable. If we transform C as follows,

(7) $y = (C - C_{min})/(C_{max} - C)$; $o < y < \infty$

then y can be modeled as a positive variate by the standard techniques.
For example, if ln y is normally distributed, then C has an S_B distribution. In the event that the autocorrelation of these y data and
their nonstationary behavior might prevent the analyst from making a
valid simplifying assumption concerning independence of consecutive
samples of y, then the time-series method of Soong (32) may be a preferable choice. The time-series approach which involves the fitting of
a solution to equation (6) to the measured time series of $G_1(X)$ and
determining the time-series parameters of E_i and R_i' would provide an

estimate of $F(X)$. This process, $F(X)$, ideally satisfies a set of boundary conditions (X_{max} and X_{min}) in such a manner that it is not rejected by a statistical test as a possible parent distribution of the realization $G_1(X)$. Then the future realizations, $G_i(X)$, may be predicted from a total process which has characteristics of the joint atmospheric and emission processes which lead to the concentration distributions observed in nature.

In summary, the analyst should carefully consider the purpose for which the model is to be applied. When predictions are to be made concerning future air quality measurements, the analysts should consider using a member of the class of bounded distributions which could be generated by atmospheric and emission processes as described by equation (6).

REFERENCES

(1) J. AITCHISON and J.A.C. BROWN, The Lognormal Distribution, Cambridge Univ. Press, NY, (1966).

(2) E.D. HARRIS and E.C. TABOR, Statistical considerations related to the planning and operation of a national air sampling network, Proceedings of the 49th Annual Meeting of Air Pollution Control Association, Buffalo, N.Y. (1956).

(3) C.E. ZIMMER, E.C. TABOR, and A.C. STERN, Particulate pollutants in the air of the United States, J. Air. Poll. Control Assoc., 9, (1959), p. 136.

(4) R.I. LARSEN, A method for determining source reduction required to meet air quality standards, J. Air Poll. Control Assoc., 11, (1961), p. 71.

(5) R.I. LARSEN, Determining basic relationships between variables, Symposium on Environmental Measurements, PHS Publication No. 999-AP-15, Sanitary Engineering Center, Cincinnati, Ohio, (1964), pp. 251-263.

(6) R.I. LARSEN, Determining reduced-emission goals needed to achieve air quality goals--a hypothetical case, J. Air Poll. Control Assoc., 17, (1967), p. 823.

(7) R.I. LARSEN, A new mathematical model of air pollutant concentration, averaging time, and frequency, J. Air Poll. Control Assoc., 19, (1969), p. 24.

(8) R.I. LARSEN, A mathematical model for relating air quality measurements to air quality standards, Publication No. AP-89, U.S. Environmental Protection Agency, Research Triangle Park, N.C. (1971).

(9) Proceedings of the symposium on statistical aspects of air quality data, edited by L.D. Kornreich, U.S. Environmental Protection Agency, Research Triangle Park, N.C., No. EPA-650/4-74-038 (1974).

(10) D.A. LYNN, Fitting curves to urban suspended particulate data,
     U.S. Environmental Protection Agency, Research Triangle Park, N.C.,
     No. EPA-650/4-74-038, (1974), pp. 13-1 to 13-27.

(11) J.B. LODGE, JR. and P.M. WEST, Discussion, J. Air. Poll. Control
     Assoc., (1971), p. 979.

(12) D.T. MAGE, On the lognormal distribution of air pollutants,
     Proceedings of the Fifth Meeting of the Expert Panel on Air
     Pollution Modeling, NATO/CCMS N.35, Roskilde, Denmark,
     June 4-6 (1974).

(13) D.T. MAGE and W.R. OTT, An improved model for analysis of air
     and water pollution data, International Conference on Environmen-
     tal Sensing and Assessment, Volume 2, IEEE No. #75-CH 1004-1
     ICESA, September (1975), p. 20-5.

(14) W.R. OTT and D.T. MAGE, A general purpose univariate probability
     model for environmental data analysis, Comput. and Ops. Res., 3,
     (1976), p. 209.

(15) R.I. LARSEN, An air quality data analysis system for interrelat-
     ing effects, standards, and needed source reductions: Part 4,
     A three-parameter averaging-time model, J. Air Poll. Control
     Assoc., 27, (1977), p. 454.

(16) W. KALPASANOV and G. KURCHATOVA, A study of the statistical
     distributions of chemical pollutants in air, J. Air Poll.
     Control Assoc. 26, (1976), p. 981.

(17) T.C. CURRAN and N.H. FRANK, Assessing the validity of the log-
     normal model when predicting maximum air pollutant concentrations,
     Paper No. 75-51.3, presented at the 68th Annual Meeting of the
     Air Pollution Control Association, Boston, Mass. (1975).

(18) T. JOHNSON, A comparison of the two-parameter Weibull and log-
     normal distributions fitted to ambient ozone data, Proceedings,
     Quality Assurance in Air Pollution Measurements, New Orleans,
     LA, edited by the Air Pollution Control Assoc., March 11-14,
     (1979), pp. 312-321.

(19) K.E. BENCALA and J.H. SEINFELD, On frequency distributions of air
     pollutant concentrations, Atmos. Environ. 10, (1976), p. 941.

(20) D.T. MAGE, Data analysis by use of univariate probability models,
     Paper No. 1-G/75, Symposium on Air Pollution Control, Ministry of
     Health and Social Affairs, Seoul, Korea (1975).

(21) D.T. MAGE, An explicit solution for S_B parameters using four
     percentile points, Technometrics, 22, (1980), p. 247.

(22) J. LEDOLTER, G.C. TIAO, G.B. HUDAK, J.T. HSIEH, and S.B. GRAVES,
     Statistical analysis of multiple time series associated with air
     quality data: New Jersey CO data, Technical Report No. 529,
     Dept. of Statistics, Univ. of Wisconsin, Madison, WI (1978).

(23) E.M. ROBERTS, Review of statistics of extreme values with applications to air quality data, Part 1, Review, J. Air Poll. Control Assoc., 29, (1979), p. 632.

(24) J. TRAJONIS, Empirical relationships between atmospheric nitrogen dioxide and its precursors, U.S. Environmental Protection Agency, Research Triangle Park, NC, No. EPA-600/3-78-018 (1978).

(25) D.T. MAGE and W.R. OTT, Refinements of the lognormal probability model for analysis of aerometric data, J. Air Poll. Control Assoc. 28, (1978), p. 296-795.

(26) T.R. FITZ-SIMONS and D.M. HOLLAND, The maximum likelihood approach to probabilistic modeling of air quality data, U.S. Environmental Protection Agency, Research Triangle Park, N.C. No. EPA-600/4-79-044 (1979).

(27) J.C. KAPTEYN, Skew frequency curves in biology and statistics, Agronomical Laboratory Groningen, Noordhoff (1903).

(28) J.B. KNOX and R.I. POLLACK, An investigation of the frequency distribution of surface air pollutant concentrations, U.S. Environmental Protection Agency, No. EPA-650/4-74-038, (1974), pp. 9-1 to 9-17.

(29) H.D. KAHN, Note on the distribution of air pollutants, J. Air Poll. Control Assoc. 23, (1973), p. 973.

(30) F.A. GIFFORD, JR., The form of the frequency distribution of air pollution concentrations, U.S. Environmental Protection Agency, Research Triangle Park, N.C. No. EPA-650/4-74-038, (1974), pp. 3-1 to 3-6.

(31) D.T. MAGE and W.R. OTT, An improved statistical model for analyzing air pollution concentration data, Paper No. 75-51.4 presented at the 68th Annual Meeting of the Air Pollution Control Association, Boston, MA (1975).

(32) T.T. SOONG, Random Differential Equations in Science and Engineering, Academic Press, NY (1973).

(33) J. HOROWITZ, Extreme values from a nonstationary stochastic process: an application to air quality analyses. Technometrics 22, (1980), pp. 469-478.

(34) W.S. CEVELAND. Challenging assumptions in time series models - discussion of extreme values from a nonstationary stochastic process: application to air quality analysis, by J. Horowitz. Technometrics 22, (1980), pp. 479-481, n.b. Response by J. Horowitz. Technometrics 22, (1980), p. 482.

(35) D.T. MAGE, T.R. FITZ-SIMONS, D.M. HOLLAND, and W.R. OTT, Techniques for fitting probability models to experimental data, Proceedings, Quality Assurance in Air Pollution Measurement, New Orleans, LA, edited by the Air Pollution Control Association, Pittsburgh, PA, (March 11-14, 1979), pp. 304-311.

Transition to
Statistical Ambient Air Quality Standards

T. C. Curran*

Abstract. During the 1970's, there was a transition in the form used for the National Ambient Air Quality Standards (NAAQS). These national standards specify upper limits for ambient concentrations of various pollutants in the United States and are established by the United States Environmental Protection Agency (EPA). The change that occurred in the form of these standards during the decade of the 70's becomes apparent when the initial NAAQS, which were promulgated by EPA in 1971, are contrasted with the revised NAAQS for ozone which were promulgated in 1979. Although many different considerations were involved in the revision of the ozone standard, this paper is primarily concerned with the statistical aspects of the change in the form of this standard. The basic form of the revised standard is discussed and a probabilistic model is developed for the attainment test associated with this standard. Comparisons with the previous form of the standard are examined and the possible effect of serial correlation is considered.

1. Background. The initial 1971 NAAQS included short-term standards that were specified in terms of an upper limit concentration not to be exceeded more than once per year.(1) From an intuitive viewpoint, the initial "once per year" form of the short-term standards is appealing. For example, the initial standard for photochemical oxidant specified an hourly average of 160ug/m3 not to be exceeded more than once per year. Obviously, if a site has two or more hourly averages above 160 ug/m3 in the same year, then it has failed to meet the standard. With this type of standard, attainment decisions only need to consider the second highest value for the year. If it exceeds the level of the standard then the site fails to meet the standard. If the second highest value is less than or equal to the level of the standard, then the number of exceedances cannot be greater than one and the standard is met.

Although simplicity is desirable, there are certain inherent disadvantages to this form.(2) The most obvious is that there is no allowance for the number of measurements made in the year. Carried to the extreme, a site with only one measurement per year cannot have more than one exceedance per year and therefore attains the standard by default. This

---

*Environmental Protection Agency (MD-14), Research Triangle Park, North Carolina 27711

would obviously be viewed as inadequate monitoring, but the point is
that as the number of measurements taken decreases there is less chance
of failing to meet this "once per year" type of standard. One possible
approach to this problem is to require a certain minimum number of
observations for the year. However, this still means that a site that
barely satisfies the minimum has less chance of being declared nonattainment than another site with identical air quality but no missing data.
This approach also requires some type of decision rule for those sites
that fail to meet the minimum observation requirements.

A second problem with the "once per year" form of the standard is
that there is no convenient framework for accommodating an unusual year.
Attainment of the standard was judged on the basis of more than one year
so that the worst year during a multi-year time period must meet the
standard.(3) If a year is obviously atypical in terms of meteorology
or emissions it is difficult to justify simply ignoring its occurrence.
It would be more convenient to be able to weigh its impact according
to the likelihood of its reoccurrence.

2. The EPA Ozone Standard. To partially remedy these problems EPA
proposed that the new ozone standard be stated in terms of the expected
number of times per year that the level of the standard is exceeded.(4)
In reality the expected number is not known and decisions must be made
on the basis of estimates. To some degree, unless the criterion is
vacuous, there is always some risk of exceeding a decision rule based
upon a statistic computed from a finite amount of data. However, for
this problem the risk should be reduced by using more than a single year
of data. Based upon certain practical considerations, EPA indicated
that compliance with the new standard would be determined on the basis
of a three year moving average of the number of annual exceedances. The
term "exceedance" refers to a value that exceeds the level of the standard. In 1979 EPA promulgated a National Ambient Air Quality Standard
for ozone which replaced the previous photochemical oxidant standard and
instituted this new form of an ambient air quality standard.(5) This
paper develops a probabilistic model of the three year attainment test
associated with the new standard and contrasts the results with those
for the earlier form.

3. Development of the Model. Attainment of the new ozone standard
is demonstrated if the three year moving average of the number of annual
exceedances does not exceed 1. In practice, a correction is introduced
to account for the effect of missing data, however in this discussion
complete sampling is assumed. This is equivalent to requiring that the
total number of exceedances during any three consecutive years is three
or less. Therefore a total of four or more exceedances in three consecutive years may be viewed as a failure. If a site has no exceedances
then the probability of failure during the next three years is the
probability of four or more exceedances during this period. A probability model for the first three years of this process was developed by
Javitz.(6) In this initial phase, the probability of failure is simply
the probability of having a total of four or more exceedances during the

three year period. Over time, however, the process becomes more complicated because the probability of failure depends not only upon how many
exceedances a particular site has accumulated but also upon the years
in which they occurred.

A probability model for this process may be conceptualized in terms
of a state space. The following notation is convenient in describing
the model. A site will be said to be in state $SN_{t-2}N_{t-1}N_t$ at time t
if it has not yet failed and it had N_{t-2} exceedances in year t-2, N_{t-1}
exceedances in year t-1, and N_t exceedances in year t. Because a site
with four or more exceedances in three consecutive years is considered
a failure, S4 is used as a single state to denote failure.

For example, a site that has not failed the standard would be in
state S010 at time t if it had zero exceedances in year t-2, one exceedance in year t-1, and zero exceedances in year t. If this particular
site were to have zero exceedances in year t+1 then it would be in state
S100 at time t+1. Similarly if it had one exceedance in year t+1 it
would enter state S101 while if it had two exceedances in year t+1 it
would enter state S102. If this site in state S010 at time t has three
or more exceedances in year t+1 then it is considered to have failed to
meet the standard and is said to be in state S4 at time t+1.

If the probabilities of zero, one, two, and three exceedances during
year t+1 are known then it is possible to indicate the transition probabilities from one state to another during year t+1. Let f_0 (t+1), f_1
(t+1), f_2 (t+1), and f_3(t+1) denote the probabilities of 0, 1, 2, and 3
exceedances respectively during year t+1 and let f_4 (t+1) denote the
probability of 4 or more exceedances during year t+1. Then, for example,
the probability of a transition from state S010 at time t to state S101
at time t+1 is f_1 (t+1). Similarly the probability of a transition from
state S010 at time t to state S4 at time t+1 is f_3 (t+1)+f_4 (t+1) i.e.
the probability of three or more exceedances during year t+1.

In this framework it is apparent that the transition probabilities
depend upon only the state that the site is in at time t and not on how
the site reached that state. Therefore the model is a Markov process
and may be described by the transition probability matrix.(7) Although
in principle the exceedance probabilities may vary from year to year,
for this discussion they are assumed to be constant and the model
reduces to a time invariant Markov process. The state space and associated transition probability matrix are presented in Figure 1. As shown,
there are twenty-one states in the model. State S4 represents failure
and is an absorbing state because once a site enters state S4 it is
considered to remain in state S4 for all future time.

FIGURE 1   TRANSITION PROBABILITY MATRIX FOR EPA'S OZONE STANDARD

4. Application of the Model. With this framework, if the probability of 0, 1, 2 and 3 exceedances in a year are known then it is possible to determine the probability of failure under various conditions. For this application, the various exceedance probabilities are obtained by assuming a certain probability of one exceedance and using the binominal distribution to compute the probabilities of zero, one, two, three, or more exceedances for a year. This, of course, is somewhat of a simplification in that it assumes independence of day to day values but this type of approach has frequently been used in air quality data analysis and should provide a useful first approximation. A computer program was written to perform the calculations presented in this paper.

The level of the ozone standard is 0.12 ppm and therefore a site with exactly one expected exceedance per year of this level will be considered. Exceedances are not actually counted unless the concentration equals or exceeds 0.125 ppm so that there is an approximate 5% leeway built into the three year attainment test.(8) Assuming that the probability of exceeding 0.120 ppm is 1/365, the probability of exceeding 0.125 ppm is somewhat less. Exactly how much less depends upon the underlying distribution. Weibull distributions with shape parameters ranging from 1.0 to 2.0 have been used to approximate daily maximum ozone measurements.(9) As the shape parameter increases the probability of failure decreases which is what would be expected as the distribution becomes lighter tailed.

One situation of interest would be a site that is exactly on the borderline with respect to attainment. For such a site the expected number of exceedances of 0.120 ppm is 1 which, using the terminology of Gumbel(10), is equivalent to saying that the characteristic largest value is 0.120 ppm. Another consideration is how these results vary for sites that are above or below the standard. In doing this a Weibull distribution with shape parameter equal to 1.5 and annual expected exceedances of 0.120 ppm equal to 1.0 was used as the reference point. Four new Weibull distributions were constructed with characteristic largest values 10% lower, 5% lower, 5% higher, and 10% higher than 0.120 ppm and the same shape parameter of 1.5. The results for these distributions are shown in Figure 2 and indicate that while the probability of failure for the site 10% below the standard remains relatively low even after 10 years, a site that is 10% higher than the standard is very likely to fail. It should be noted that the expected number of exceedances of 0.120 ppm for the site 10% higher than the standard is 2.2 per year indicating that sites with annual exceedance rates of two or more have little chance of going undetected.

5. Comparisons with the Previous Form. Also of practical interest are comparisons between the new form and the previous "once per year" format. Under the old format, a failure occurred when two or more exceedances were recorded in a single year. Therefore the probability that the first failure occurs at time t is the joint probability of zero or one exceedance during each of the first t-1 years and the probability of two or more exceedances in year t.

Figure 2.   Failure probabilities for selected Weibull
            distributions (c denotes characteristic high)

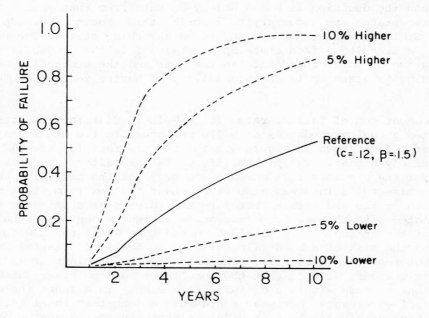

Figure 3.   Failure probabilities under the old and new form
            for a Weibull distribution with shape parameter
            1.5 and characteristic high of 0.12 ppm

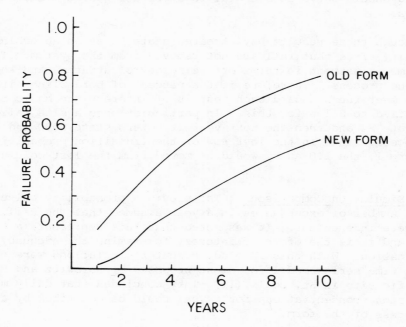

Alternatively, the previous form of the standard may also be viewed as a Markov process. In this case, a site either passes or fails each year and the decision is based solely on data from that year. Therefore only two states are necessary to describe this process i.e. Sp and Sf. Again Sf is viewed as failure and is an absorbing state. The probability of a transition from state Sp to state Sf is the probability of having two or more exceedances in the year and the probability of remaining in state Sp is the probability of having zero or one exceedance.

A comparison of failure rates for a Weibull distribution with expected annual exceedances of 0.120 ppm equal to 1.0 and a shape parameter of 1.5 is shown in Figure 3. The failure rate for the old form is appreciably higher. The probability of failure after five years was 0.56 for the previous form compared to 0.29 for the new form. While the median time to failure was nine years under the new form it is only five years under the old form. Therefore the three year attainment test associated with the new form represents an improvement over the previous form of the standard. It should be noted that while the new form reduces the risk of a borderline site being declared nonattaining it does not result in zero risk. The practical constraints of an air quality standard dictate that the compliance test be clear-cut and that decisions be made within a definite time span. In a sense the expected number of exceedances per year represents a long-term ideal while the three year attainment test provides an estimate of the status of a site based upon shorter term realizations of the process. This model serves as a means of quantifying the risk of failing the three year attainment test and should serve as a useful tool for air quality management problems.

Although these results have treated state S4 as an absorbing state, in reality sites that fail are not removed from the system. They may make some adjustment in terms of their control strategy and then re-enter the process. Therefore if the percent of borderline sites that fail to meet the standard each year is of interest the basic model can be modified to allow for this. In particular once a site fails it enters state S4 and then the next year it enters state S000 and continues the process. Thus in the last row of the transition probability matrix in Figure 1, the 1.0 entry would be moved from the last column to the first.

6. <u>Simulation Comparisons</u>. The previous probability calculations for the number of exceedances in a year assumed that the daily measurements were independent. It was noted that this represents a simplification and it is therefore of interest to examine the adequacy of this approximation. With this in mind, computer simulations were examined using a time series model for ozone proposed by Horowitz and Barakat for a specific site in St. Louis.[11] They concluded that daily maximum 1-hour ozone concentrations for a year could be described by a stochastic process of the form:

Log x(t) = f(t)+e

where x(t) is the daily maximum ozone on day t

f(t) is a second degree polynomial in t

and e represents a stationary, first order auto-regressive process.

The concentrations predicted by this model were scaled so that the average yearly exceedances of 0.120 ppm were approximately equal to 1.0. The time to failure was computed for 1000 trials using the IMSL random number generator GGNORM.(12) Results for both the old and new form of the standard are displayed in Figure 4. Figure 4 also illustrates the comparison between the simulation results and those obtained from the Markov process model under the assumption of independence. For both forms the maximum difference was 3% between the failure probability by a particular year resulting from the simulation and predicted by the Markov model. This agreement between the simulation and the previous model computations suggests that the results are not appreciably altered by the simplifying assumption of independence.

Figure 4.   Comparison of Markov model results assuming
            independence with those from a time series
            model simulation.

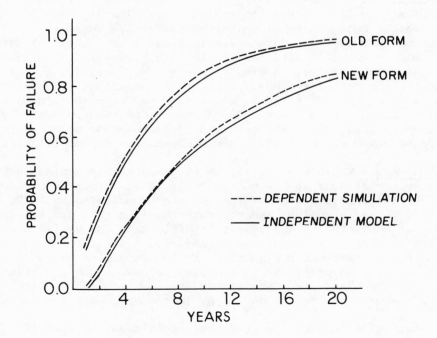

7. <u>Design Value Considerations</u>. For both the old and new form, attainment decisions are concerned with how often the standard level is exceeded. A second concern is by how much the standard level is exceeded. If a site has been determined to be nonattainment for an air quality standard then a certain amount of improvement is necessary to bring the site into attainment. This introduces the concept of a design value. The design value is the concentration value that must be reduced to the level of the standard in order for the site to just attain the standard. For the new expected exceedance form of the standard, the design value is the concentration that has an expected exceedance rate of one per year. If this were exactly equal to the level of the standard then the site would just meet the standard.

There are a variety of acceptable approaches that may be used to estimate the design value for the expected exceedance type of standard.(8) These would include a simple plot of the cumulative frequency distribution and then reading off the value that corresponds to an expected frequency rate of once per year. Another alternative would be to use a statistical distribution to approximate the air quality data and to use this approximation to determine the design value. A simple table look-up procedure can also be constructed so that the rank order of the observation to be used as the design value is given as a function of sample size. This is merely a simplification of the empirical frequency plot.

A more general approach that could be potentially useful is based upon conditional probabilities. Suppose, for example, that the distribution of air quality concentrations was approximately known for various meteorological categories, or emissions patterns. Then, if the frequency of occurrence of these categories is known from historical data, it is possible to use a conditional probability framework to estimate an appropriate design value. A simple, but quite practical, use of this approach is now done for ozone. Because of the strong seasonality present in ozone concentrations, monitoring may be discontinued during the colder months of the year under certain conditions. Design value estimation in these cases assumes that no exceedances occurred during this period which is an implicit use of conditional probabilities.

8. <u>Summary</u>. While the initial short-term NAAQS promulgated by EPA in 1971 were stated as levels not to be exceeded more than once per year, the revised ozone standard, which was promulgated in 1979, stated that the expected annual exceedance rate should not be greater than one. From an air quality data analysis viewpoint, this change is intuitively appealing in that it incorporates an adjustment for incomplete sampling and provides a framework for quantifying the impact of an unusual year, particularly in the development of design values. From a statistical viewpoint, this change represents a transition from the simple use of observed measurements to the use of estimates of underlying parameters.

The statistical consequences of this transition are twofold. While this change broadens the opportunity for the application of statistical techniques, it also presents the challenge of developing appropriate statistical procedures for real world situations. At the present time, standard statistical distributions are routinely used to approximate air quality data but because the upper tail is of the most practical importance there is an obvious need for fitting procedures and goodness of fit criteria that reflect this concern. There is also a need to go beyond models that merely describe the data to those that explain the data so that the parameters relate to physical realities in the underlying process. In this way, the parameters could be varied to examine the effect of alternative control strategies.

In addition to increasing the possible applications of statistical techniques, the transition to an expected exceedance standard affords more opportunity for the use of statistical concepts. For example, the number of exceedances observed during a certain number of days could be used to compute the probability that a site is nonattainment. Therefore while the new form of the standard is relatively consistent with the previous form it presents a framework that is more amenable to a statistical treatment.

REFERENCES

(1) National Primary and Secondary Ambient Air Quality Standards, Federal Register 36, (1971), pp. 8186-8187.

(2) T. C. CURRAN AND W. M. COX, Data Analysis Procedures for the Ozone NAAQS Statistical Format, J. Air Poll. Con. Assoc. 29, (1979), pp. 532-534.

(3) National Ambient Air Quality Standards, Federal Register 43, (1978), pp. 8962-8964.

(4) National Ambient Air Quality Standards for Photochemical Oxidants, Federal Register 43, (1978), p. 26970.

(5) National Ambient Air Quality Standards for Photochemical Oxidants, Federal Register 44, (1979), pp. 8202-8221.

(6) HAROLD S. JAVITZ, Statistical Interdependencies in the Ozone National Ambient Air Quality Standard, J. Air Poll. Con. Assoc. 30, (1980), pp. 58-59.

(7) WILLIAM FELLER, An Introduction to Probability Theory and its Applications, Vol. 1, John Wiley and Sons, Inc., New York (1950).

(8) T. C. CURRAN, Guidelines for Interpretation of Ozone Air Quality Standards, U.S. Environmental Protection Agency, Research Triangle Park, N.C. (1979).

(9) TED JOHNSON, Precision of Quantile and Exceedance Statistics, Proc. Am. Soc. Qual. Con., Milwaukee, WI. (1980).

(10) E. J. GUMBEL, Statistics of Extremes, Columbia University Press, New York (1958).

(11)   J. HOROWITZ AND S. BARAKAT, <u>Statistical Analysis of the Maximum</u>
       <u>Concentration of an Air Pollutant: Effects of Autocorrelation</u>
       <u>and Non-stationarity</u>, Atmos. Environ. 13, (1979), pp. 811-818.

(12)   <u>The IMSL Library</u>, International Mathematical and Statistical
       Libraries, Inc., Houston, Texas, (1975).

Stochastic Processes
in the Analysis
of Environmental Data

Paul Switzer*

Abstract. The statistical requirements for the analysis of environmental data, the design of environmental sampling programs, the regulation of environmental quality, the modelling of environmental systems, and the assessing of environmentally related health effects are stimulating special and important developments of statistical theory and methodology. This paper reports on some of these developments with particular emphasis on recent work at Stanford University's Statistics Department, particularly in the area of stochastic processes. By means of the few examples given here the scope of this activity is illustrated. The discussion has been divided into a part dealing with geographic or spatial problems and a second part dealing with temporal problems.

Spatial Environmetrics. The interpolation or mapping of air pollution fields from available station data can be viewed as a relatively standard problem in spatial processes. The pollutant concentration assigned to an unobserved geographic point x is generally taken to be some weighted combination of the observed nearby station concentrations. The principal problem is not how to do the weighting (resulting maps are insensitive to choice of weighting schemes), but rather how to associate a meaningful magnitude to the interpolation error at each x. The approach taken in [1] is to model the average squared concentration difference between two geographic points as a function of the vector joining the point-pair. The model is fitted using observed concentration differences between stations and then, via a complicated but standard calculation, a mean-squared interpolation error can be assigned to each x which depends on its position relative to the monitoring network.

Specifically, let $Z(x)$ denote the pollutant concentration field. The time dimension is suppressed here so that $Z(x)$ may be considered as either an instantaneous field or a time-averaged field. Now suppose stations are located at positions denoted by $x_1, x_2, \ldots, x_N$. The interpolated field may be written

*Department of Statistics, Sequoia Hall, Stanford University, Stanford, CA 94305

$$(1) \qquad \hat{Z}(\underset{\sim}{x}) = \sum_{i=1}^{n} w_i(\underset{\sim}{x}) \cdot Z(\underset{\sim i}{x}) \ ,$$

where the w's are weights chosen to minimize mean-squared interpolation errors, i.e. to minimize

$$(2) \qquad V(\underset{\sim}{x}) = E[\hat{Z}(\underset{\sim}{x}) - Z(\underset{\sim}{x})]^2 \ .$$

The error above is expressed in terms of an expectation so some probabilistic description of the concentration field is needed to calculate the error. This description can be decomposed as

$$(3) \qquad Z(\underset{\sim}{x}) = m(\underset{\sim}{x}) + \varepsilon(\underset{\sim}{x}) + \delta(\underset{\sim}{x}) \ ,$$

where $m(\underset{\sim}{x})$ is a deterministic mean field; $\delta(\underset{\sim}{x})$ is a zero-mean random field which combines measurement error and variability on a very short geographic scale, $\varepsilon(\underset{\sim}{x})$ is generally a white noise field; $\delta(\underset{\sim}{x})$ is a zero-mean spatially autocorrelated random field.

All three component fields need to be parametrized in such a way as to be estimable from the available station data. To some extent one can trade off complexity in the mean field $m(\underset{\sim}{x})$ for complexity in the autocorrelated random field $\delta(\underset{\sim}{x})$. The representation of $\delta(\underset{\sim}{x})$ is often in the form of a stationary "variogram", i.e.

$$\gamma(\underset{\sim}{u}) = \text{Variance}[\delta(\underset{\sim}{x+u}) - \delta(\underset{\sim}{x})]$$

$$= E[\delta(\underset{\sim}{x+u}) - \delta(\underset{\sim}{x})]^2$$

$$= 2\sigma^2[1 - \rho(\underset{\sim}{u})]$$

where $\rho(\underset{\sim}{u})$ is the autocorrelation function of the $\delta(\underset{\sim}{x})$ field.

In a simple application the mean function $m(x)$ is taken to be constant and the variogram is taken to have an isotropic gaussian form

$$(4) \qquad \gamma(\underset{\sim}{u}) = 2\sigma^2(1 - e^{-c|u|}) \ .$$

For this variogram model the squared concentration differences between station values provide estimates of model parameters, viz.

(5) $$E[Z(\underset{\sim}{x}_i) - Z(\underset{\sim}{x}_j)]^2 = \sigma_0^2 + \gamma(\underset{\sim}{x}_i - \underset{\sim}{x}_j)$$

where σ_0^2 is the measurement error variance, i.e. $\sigma_0^2 = Variance[\varepsilon(\underset{\sim}{x})]$.
Since the error criterion $V(\underset{\sim}{x})$ for unbiased linear interpolations can
be expressed in terms of the estimated parameters σ_0^2, σ^2, c, one can
"optimize" the weighting scheme (1), with the side condition that
$E[\hat{Z}(\underset{\sim}{x})] = m(\underset{\sim}{x})$. [With a constant mean function, the side condition
is $\Sigma w_i(\underset{\sim}{x}) = 1$.] Examples of interpolated fields for seasonal average
concentrations of ozone have been extracted from [1] and are shown
below. The two contour maps are constructed using the same station
data for the San Francisco Bay Area with different models for the mean
field.

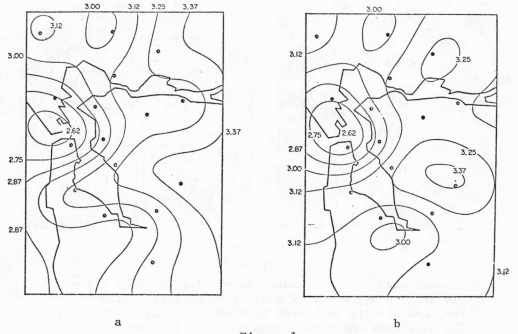

a   b

Figure 1

Interpolated seasonal ozone averages for the San
Francisco Bay Area. The interpolations are "optimal"
linear combinations of station values. The map on
the left employed a constant mean function; the map
on the right employed a linearly trending mean function. Station locations are indicated by dots.

Fortunately, the error criterion is not sensitive to departures
from optimal weighting, but the estimation of the error itself is model
dependent, particularly as one moves further away from the station

data. A crude check on the average model-calculated value of V(x)
is obtained by interpolating actual station values from surrounding
stations and calculating the actual average squared interpolation
error. The sensitivity of model-calculated error estimates to the
choice of probabilistic constructs and to geographic inhomogeneity
has been discussed to some extent in [2].

   One may calculate an interpolation mean-squared error V(x) at
each geographic point x and thereby produce an error map. Such maps
will show small errors near station values (not necessarily zero
errors) and larger errors elsewhere and are an aid to station network
design problems. A hypothetical example taken from [3] is shown below.
The error map on the left results from "optimum" interpolation on a
six-station network with a specific variogram model; the error map on
the right is produced the sam way with an added seventh station at the
bottom left.

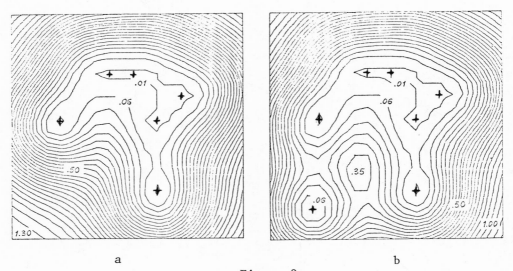

a   b

Figure 2

   Contour maps of mean squared interpolation error for a
   six station hypothetical monitoring network (left) and
   the same network augmented by a seventh station (right).
   The same stationary variogram was used to compute both
   maps. The interpolation algorithm is described above.
   Station locations are indicated by crosses.

   The effect on the interpolation error at a point x due to addition or deletion of a station can be described quite succinctly in the
current framework. Suppose the position of the candidate station is
x_0. Let e(x) denote the actual interpolation error at x using the
existing network and let $e^*(x)$ be the corresponding error for the
augmented network. Then the relative reduction in the calculated mean-
squared interpolation error is given by

(6) $\qquad \dfrac{E[e^{*}(\underset{\sim}{x})]^{2}}{E[e(\underset{\sim}{x})]^{2}} = \dfrac{V^{*}(\underset{\sim}{x})}{V(\underset{\sim}{x})} = 1 - \text{correlation}[e(\underset{\sim}{x}),\ e(\underset{\sim}{x}_{0})]\ .$

The above correlation may be expressed directly in terms of the variogram.

A related spatial problem is to estimate the areal frequency distribution function of a pollutant concentration at a given time point or
time-averaged interval. Denote by $F(z)$ the areal proportion of the
air basin where levels exceed z. In [4] a class of weighted estimators
of $F(z)$ is considered, viz.

$$\hat{F}(z) = \sum_{i=1}^{N} w_{i}(z) \cdot I[Z(\underset{\sim}{x}_{i}) \geq z]$$

where, as before, $Z(\underset{\sim}{x}_{i})$ is the observed concentration for the station
located at $\underset{\sim}{x}_{i}$, and $I[S] = 1$ if S is true and $I[S] = 0$ if S is
false. When $w_{i}(z) = 1/N$ for all stations then $\hat{F}(z)$ is the usual
empirical distribution function estimator.

To know how well the station data can estimate the distribution
function and, secondarily, to optimize the choice of station weights
w_{i}, one can estimate the mean-squared error criterion

$$U(z) = E[\hat{F}(z) - F(z)]^{2}\ .$$

The estimation of $U(z)$ requires the estimation of a spatial autocorrelation function of the dichotomized concentration field, separately
for each level z.

In [4] a method is outlined for deriving the required dichotomous
autocorrelations from the spatial autocorrelation function or variogram
function of the raw concentration field. The method was used to estimate areal distribution functions of concentrations of suspended particulates based on a 14-station monitoring network in the San Francisco
Bay Area. In optimizing the error criterion U some stations received
negligible weight, indicating that a subset of the network would perform
almost as well as the full network.

A potentially useful variant of the areal distribution function
would be a population-weighted areal distribution function, i.e. $F(z)$
would be interpreted as the fraction of the population exposed to pollutant levels greater than z. Each geographic point $\underset{\sim}{x}$ would then
be weighted by an estimate of the population density at $\underset{\sim}{x}$, say $p(\underset{\sim}{x})$.

Then an integral representation of the distribution function F(z) is given by

$$(7) \qquad F(z) = \int_{\underset{\sim}{x}} I[Z(\underset{\sim}{x}) \geq z] \; p(\underset{\sim}{x}) \; d\mu(\underset{\sim}{x}) / \left[\begin{array}{c}\text{total} \\ \text{population}\end{array}\right] .$$

Extensions of the estimation procedures discussed in [4] to this population-weighted case would be possible, if not straightforward.

    Temporal Environmetrics. Environmental data are frequently in the form of time series. An understanding of the statistical characteristics of such series underlies the monitoring, regulation, and prediction of environmental quality, the detection of changes in quality over time, and the inferring of health effects in panel studies.

    An example of a prediction problem is given in [5] where historical data are used to estimate a stationary joint distribution of pollutant concentrations at times t and t+k, conditioned on weather factors at time t. Rather than combine weather factors in a linear model, say, there was sufficient data to estimate pollutant distribution parameters separately for each of 50 weather syndromes.

    Specifically, suppose Z_t denotes the current pollutant level and that W_t denotes the current weather. The objective is an estimator $\hat{Z}_{t+k}$ of the pollutant level k periods ahead which makes use of the current and historical weather and pollutant data. The estimator proposed in [5] has the following form:

$$(8) \qquad \hat{Z}_{t+k} = m_k(W_t) + \frac{\sigma_k(W_t)}{\sigma_0(W_t)} \cdot [Z_t - m_0(W_t)]$$

where $m_k(W)$ = mean pollutant level k time periods ahead, when current weather is W;

        $\sigma_k(W)$ = covariance between pollutant levels separated by time lag k, when current weather is W.

The above expression is in the form of the optimal estimator of a future pollutant level which is a linear function of the current level, conditional on the current weather.

    For every desired lag k and every possible weather description W, the available historical data must be used to estimate the pair of model parameters $m_k(W)$ and $\sigma_k(W)$. In the application described in [5], there appeared to be sufficient data to estimate parameters

separately for 50 different W descriptions. In the absence of substantial amounts of historical data, the possible W descriptions
would be collapsed into fewer categories. [An alternative, which seems
less desirable, would be to fit arbitrary mathematical models which
express $m_k(W)$ and $\sigma_k(W)$ as simple functions of the numerically
expressed components of W.]

Figure 3 shows the performance of the predictor applied retrospec-
tively to hourly ambient carbon monoxide data from St. Louis described
more fully in [5]. This performance is compared with predictors using
substantially collapsed W descriptions as well as with predictors
which make no use of weather data at all.

The fitting of models to hourly time series of pollutant concentrations is discussed in [6] where hour-to-hour autocorrelations are very
high. This study attempted to illustrate the relation between mean
concentration, the probability of exceeding a threshold during any hour
of a day, and the distribution of the number of hours above a threshold.

Suppose Z_{dh} denotes the pollutant concentration level on day d
at hour h. The model described below was used to analyze summer ozone
data at San Jose, California where high ozone levels are encountered
almost exclusively during a six-hour mid-day period. Because of the
diurnal pattern of ozone concentrations, it is reasonable to decompose
the concentration into daily and hourly variance components. Specifically, one has

(9) $\log Z_{dh} = m_h + \lambda_d + \varepsilon_{dh}$ where

$\quad m_h$ = mean level for hour h over all days

$\quad \lambda_d$ = zero-mean random day effects with variance $(\lambda_d) = \sigma_\lambda^2$

$\quad \varepsilon_{dh}$ = zero-mean random autocorrelated hour effects with
$\qquad$ variance $(\varepsilon_{dh}) = \sigma_\varepsilon^2$ and correlation
$\qquad (\varepsilon_{dh}, \varepsilon_{dh'}) = \rho^{|h-h'|}$,

and all other correlations are taken to be zero.

The above model is a generalization of a random-effects model to
allow for autocorrelation of hourly values, and it is a generalization
of a first-order autoregressive model to allow for day-to-day variability and a nonconstant mean function. The estimation of the fixed
hourly means m_h was straightforward, but the estimates of σ_λ^2, σ_ε^2,

and ρ were highly correlated although, strictly speaking, all model parameters are separately identifiable.

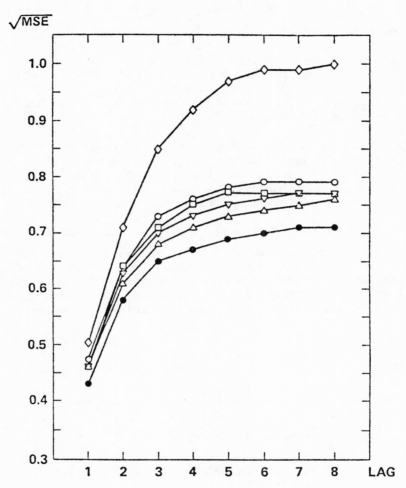

●   The model described in (8) with 50 weather descriptions.

△   The same model (8) using a log-transformation of the concentration data.

▢   The same model (8) with 8 collapsed weather descriptors.

▽   The same model (8) with 6 collapsed weather descriptors.

○   A first order autoregressive model ignoring weather descriptors.

◊   A persistence model ignoring weather descriptors.

Figure 3

Root mean squared prediction errors (actual) plotted against forecasting lag k for various forecasting models.

The objective, however, was to estimate the distribution of the number of hours in a day which exceed a threshold pollutant level. This
distribution is a complicated function of the model parameters and was
derived by simulation. Fortunately this distribution was insensitive
to the collinearity of the parameter estimates. The table below shows
the empirical distribution derived from the data series compared with
that given by the model above using parameter values estimated from the
data series.

TABLE 1

	Level x = .085 ppm		Level x = .125 ppm	
No. of hours exceeding x	Actual Distribution	Predicted Distribution	Actual Distribution	Predicted Distribution
0	.49	.48	.78	.77
1	.09	.08	.05	.06
2	.08	.07	.06	.05
3	.08	.08	.03	.04
4	.08	.09	.03	.03
5	.07	.10	.04	.03
6	.11	.10	.01	.02
	1.00	1.00	1.00	1.00

In [7] another kind of time series problem is addressed where the
objective is to relate the maximum observed pollutant concentration
over a period of time to the pollutant sampling frequency. This work
required several extensions of classical extreme value theory and produced an approximation for the probability distribution of the difference between two maxima calculated over the same time interval but based
on different sampling frequencies.

Once again, if Z_t denotes the pollutant concentration at time t
then the series maximum observed for N consecutive time periods is
denoted by

$$M_N = \max Z_t , \quad t = 1, 2, \ldots, N .$$

If the series is observed only at every kth time period then the maximum
of the reduced data over a total time interval of equivalent length N
is denoted by

$$M_N(k) = \max Z_{k \cdot t} \quad \text{for} \quad t = 1, 2, \ldots, N/k .$$

In the monitoring of particulates there has always been interest in reducing the sampling frequency. Of course, this will cause the maximum concentration to be frequently underestimated unless some correction for sampling frequency is applied, i.e., $M_N(k)$ cannot exceed M_N and will usually be less than M_N.

In [7] a probabilistic correction is developed for the case where the time series can be transformed to a stationary Gaussian series with autocorrelations which do not persist over a substantial part of the series. This correction is given in the form of an asymptotic probability statement about the magnitude of the difference $M_N - M_N(k)$, viz.

$$(10) \qquad \mathrm{Prob}\{M_N - M_N(k) \le c\sigma\} \underset{N}{\to} [1 + (k-1)\, \nu_N^c]^{-1}$$

$$\text{where} \quad \nu_N = \exp\{-1/\sqrt{2\ \ln\ N}\}$$

and σ is the standard deviation of the series. As an example, consider the probability that the two maxima differ by less than one standard deviation (c=1) when $N = 400$. This probability is estimated to be 0.57 when observations are made every third time period and estimated to be 0.21 when observations are made every sixth time period, using the above approximation.

Another problem related to monitoring pollutant concentrations is to infer the difference between the maximum of time-averaged concentrations and maximum of continuous records, sometimes called the "peak" concentration over a time period of length N. These time-averaged continuous maxima have been related for pollutant series which have been transformed to a standardized Gaussian process.

Suppose $\bar{Z}_i$ denotes the average concentration for unit time period i and suppose Z_i^* is the maximum momentary concentration during this same time period. Define the maxima of interest by

$$\bar{Z}^* = \max_i \bar{Z}_i \quad \text{for} \quad i = 1, 2, \ldots, N\ ,$$

$$Z^* = \max_i Z_i^* \quad \text{for} \quad i = 1, 2, \ldots, N\ .$$

Z^* is more aptly interpreted as the maximum momentary concentration over the whole time period of interest. Clearly $Z^* \ge \bar{Z}^*$.

For large N, both $\bar{Z}^*$ and Z^* will have Gumbel distributions provided the autocorrelation function $\rho(\Delta)$ of the pollutant series is not too persistent; but the scaling constants will be different. In [8] the following probabilistic relationship between the two maxima is demonstrated:

$$\text{Prob}\{a(\bar{Z}^* - b) \leq u/s\} \doteq \text{Prob}\{a(Z^* - d) \leq u\}$$

where

(11)
$$a = \sqrt{2 \ln N}$$

$$b = a - [\ln a + .92]/a$$

$$d = a - 1.84/a$$

$$s = 2 \int_0^1 (1 - \Delta)\, \rho(\Delta)\, d\Delta \ .$$

As an example, suppose the normally transformed series has mean μ and standard deviation σ. If $N = 400$ consecutive unit time periods and the autocorrelation remains close to unity over a single time period, then the median of the $\bar{Z}^*$ distribution would be estimated by $\mu + 2.7\sigma$ while the median of the Z^* distribution would be estimated by $\mu + 3.1\sigma$.

REFERENCES

[1]   R. FAITH, The interpolation of air pollution: A stochastic approach, SIMS Working Paper No. 5, Department of Statistics, Stanford University, 1976.

[2]   R. FAITH and R. SHESHINSKI, Misspecification of trend in spatial random function interpolation with application to oxidant mapping, SIMS Technical Report No. 28, Department of Statistics, Stanford University, 1979.

[3]   A. CABANNES, Estimation of random fields from network observations, SIMS Technical Report No. 26, Department of Statistics, Stanford University, 1979.

[4]   P. SWITZER, Estimation of spatial distributions from point sources with application to air pollution measurement, <u>Bull. Intn'l. Statist. Inst.</u>, 1977, pp. 123-137.

[5]   P. SWITZER and P. ZANNETTI, Some problems of validation and testing of numerical air pollution episode forecasting, <u>Proc. Fourth Symp. on Turbulence, Diffusion, and Air Pollution</u>, 1979.

[6]   CHEN-HUI FOO, Probability modeling and estimation for hourly var-
       iation of air pollution concentrations, SIMS Technical Report No.
       31, Department of Statistics, Stanford University, 1979.

[7]   Y. MITTAL, Maxima of partial samples in Gaussian sequences, Ann.
       Prob., 1978, pp. 421-432.

[8]   M. R. LEADBETTER, On extreme values of sampled and continuous
       stochastic data, SIMS Technical Report No. 10, Department of
       Statistics, Stanford University, 1977.

WATER QUALITY

Wastewater Treatment: A Review
of Statistical Applications

P. M. Berthouex,* W. G. Hunter** and Lars Pallesen#

Abstract. Millions of measurements are made each year on the performance of wastewater treatment plants. Intelligent analysis of
these data requires application of a range of statistical
methods from simple informal graphical procedures to complicated quantitative techniques. Statistical difficulties include
large measurement errors, missing and aberrant data, serial correlation among observations, and non-normal distributions of observations.
Furthermore, data often come from observational studies rather than
designed experiments. These problems are discussed. Some methods of
analysis, including the use of time series models and simple charts,
are illustrated with actual data.

1. Introduction. Every day each of the more than 20,000 municipal
wastewater treatment plants in United States typically measures from
5 to 100 values on performance, not counting data that are recorded
continuously. This sea of data floods record storage files in
regulatory agencies and treatment plants. Although it is unknown
how much of this information is analyzed carefully, it is known that
more than half the existing treatment plants, including many new
plants, fail to meet effluent guidelines. It is also known that many
regulatory agencies have no organized way of dealing with data. Moreover, effective quality assurance programs are often lacking, so the
data they get are often poor.

*Civil & Environmental Engineering Department, University of Wisconsin-
Madison, Madison, Wisconsin 53706
**Statistics Department and Engineering Experiment Station, University
of Wisconsin-Madison, Madison, Wisconsin 53706
#Institute of Mathematical Statistics and Operations Research,
Technical University of Denmark, Lyngby, Denmark 2800

This paper considers the use of statistical methods to analyze performance data from single plants; not the management of statewide, or larger, data banks, or the study of collections of data that comprise a group of treatment plants. The discussion is primarily expository rather than mathematical. Literature cited highlights certain important points and does not provide a complete survey. One objective is to see how some statistical methods have been used. Another objective is to draw attention to common difficulties such as those listed in Table 1, which often frustrate straightforward application of methods found in basic textbooks.

TABLE 1
Some Characteristics of Environmental Data

1. Large quantities of data.
2. Aberrant values – either bad data or unusual occurrences.
3. Large measurement errors, both random and systematic.
4. Missing data.
5. Serial correlation (autocorrelation) among observations.
6. Seasonal fluctuations.
7. Complex cause and effect relationships.
8. Lurking variables – those that exert an influence but are not measured.
9. Non-normal distribution of observations.
10. Observational data rather than data from designed experiments.

In most municipal wastewater treatment plants, the flow follows a generally predictable pattern; at night it is low and during the day it ordinarily peaks in the morning and again in late afternoon or evening. Normally, when the flow increases, the strength of the wastewater, measured as the 5-day biochemical oxygen demand (BOD), suspended solids (SS), ammonia, etc., also increases. Thus, the mass loading (product of flow and concentration) is more variable than either flow or concentration (1,2,3). The effluent pattern may not be as regular. Industrial discharges which may vary widely within a day, or from day to day, or over longer periods, may strongly affect patterns of influents and effluents. Environmental factors, such as temperature and rainfall, influence patterns in waste volume and quality, and they may affect treatment in more subtle ways.

Despite the existence of variable loadings, design engineers have traditionally used steady state models and empirical loading factors, derived from historical experience, that are somehow supposed to reflect typical fluctuations in loading. This steady state philosophy of design seemed satisfactory so long as all treatment plants used technology that had a proven history of performance and effluent limits were not strict. Today, however, increasing use is being made of statistical methods to study the dynamics of wastewater treatment plants in an attempt to build more realistic models. The elucidation of cause-and-effect relationships is difficult because they are apparently complex, controlled experiments sometimes cannot be done, and measurements that characterize process performance are often inexact in two ways: (a) measurement errors, both random and systematic, tend to be large, and (b) the measurements are coarse in that they lump together details that scientists know can be important. Consider, for example, the measurements of suspended solids and biochemical oxygen demand that characterize conventional secondary treatment plant performance. Suspended solids are defined as solids captured by filtration under standard laboratory conditions. The measurement, therefore, includes solids that are too small and too light to be removed by gravity sedimentation; furthermore, the test gives no information about the distribution of particle sizes in the sample or the chemical composition of the particles. Although the standard BOD test gives useful information about the destruction of organic compounds in the wastewater by microorganisms, it gives no indication of whether the organic compounds are carbohydrates, proteins, fats, or complex synthetic organics.

Wastewater treatment, then, is a complex, dynamic process that operates under varying conditions and is characterized by inexact measurements. The basic mechanisms that govern performance are not well understood. In this paper we indicate how statistical methods can contribute to better understanding of these systems.

2. Data Quality and Quality Assurance
The United States spends a lot for data of dubious quality, and the examples below illustrate this point. Hunter (4) has written persuasively on the urgent need for quality assurance in environmental laboratories.

   2.1 Wisconsin Study. As part of a large study in Wisconsin by Weber (5), five samples were taken over three months from a particular small Wisconsin treatment plant. These samples were split for analysis by a commercial laboratory (CL), which usually did such analyses for this plant, and the State Laboratory of Hygiene (SLH). The results are shown below. The effluent limits for this treatment plant are 20 mg/l for both BOD and SS, so the discrepencies between the CL and SLH readings are, indeed, serious. Presumably, the State Laboratory of Hygiene is more reliable, but how can we be certain? In broader terms, how accurate are the data being reported by commercial and municipal laboratories?

Sample	BOD (mg/l)		SS (mg/1)	
	SLH	CL	SLH	CL
1	3.7	19	3	8
2	4.3	12	1	12
3	8.2	49	7	26
4	4.9	21	4	32
5	5.1	29	1	10

In Wisconsin, in 1978, about half (324 out of 634) plants with discharge permits did their own testing; the others sent samples to commercial laboratories or other municipal plants. Weber (5) studied 25 of 48 major municipal labs, 113 of 275 minor municipal labs, all 11 major commercial labs, and 3 of 10 minor commercial labs. From each plant supplying samples, five split samples were sent to each of the 152 participating laboratories. The study was done by sending one-half of a split sample to these laboratories and the other half to the State Laboratory of Hygiene. The samples were entered into the work stream so analysts were unaware that they were part of a special study.

The work of a laboratory was judged acceptable if it met the following criterion: 80 percent of the lab's results fell within two standard deviations ($\pm$2s) of the SLH results. The values used for the standard deviation were those given in Standard Methods for the Examination of Water and Wastewater. For BOD measurements, s = 15%, so a laboratory's results were acceptable if they were within 30% of the SLH results. The value of s for suspended solids (SS) ranges from 33% at 15 mg/l to 15% at 100 mg/l. The SLH was sent "blind" samples prepared from Environmental Protection Agency (EPA) reference standards in order to gauge the accuracy of its work, which was a vital step because the State lab was to be the benchmark for the comparative study. The results of the BOD quality assurance study are shown in Figure 1. The average SLH measurement was 87.7% of the theoretical reference sample value. The SLH measurements, therefore, seemed to be satisfactory even though they tended to be biased downward somewhat. Figure 2 shows the split sample results for a major municipal laboratory. The solid and dashed lines show the limits on acceptability for BOD and SS. This lab would be judged unacceptable on BOD analyses and acceptable on SS analyses.

Weber (5) concluded that 72% of the minor municipal, 80% of the major municipal, 100% of the minor commercial, and 60% of the major commercial laboratories produced unacceptable BOD data. A review of laboratory procedures revealed eleven different kinds of procedural errors in measuring BOD. About 30% of all laboratories produced unacceptable suspended solids data.

2.2 EPA Study. Similar problems exist with other kinds of measurements, even in national laboratories. Trying to avoid the measurement problems of the BOD test by using a different measure of organic strength; for example, an instrumental method like Total Organic Carbon (TOC),which does not rely on fickle biological responses, does not necessarily reduce measurement errors, and it does not reduce the need for careful calibration and routine quality assurance. For example, two different methods of operating an activated sludge process were studied at an EPA pilot plant (6). Method A was used August 1-5, 1976, and method B was used April 25-28, 1976. TOC data were obtained on-line and separately in the laboratory. Using these TOC data, the on-line measurements indicate that method B is better, but the lab measurements indicate the reverse. (BOD data, incidentally, showed the performance of both methods to be about the same.) This

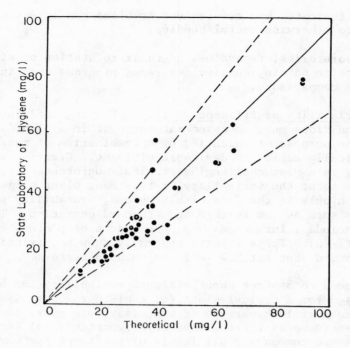

Figure 1.

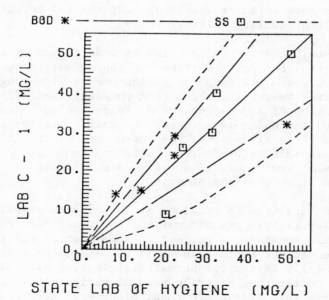

Figure 2.

example illustrates how measurement problems can inject serious confusion into otherwise useful studies.

All laboratories, regardless of their reputation or size, should
participate in ongoing quality assurance programs that involve inter-
laboratory comparisons.

3. Variability of Effluent Quality. Varying influents and environmental conditions must be taken into account in a plant's operating
policy, the purpose of which is, by a combination of manipulations,
to economically achieve a desirable effluent. Creating a good operating policy is a most challenging problem. Unfortunately, most published reports about the variability of treatment plant effluent contain
information only in the form of histograms, probability plots, and
statistics such as the average and standard deviation. They usually
fail to include information about the inputs or process control inter-
ventions (7-20). These reports typically show how existing plants
have performed, but not how well they should perform.

What seems to be true about effluent variability can be summarized
as follows. For a typical plant (a) a histogram that describes daily
performance over long periods of time (say, one year) is skewed toward
high values (some exceptions have been reported); (b) such skewed
histograms are common for all levels of treatment (primary, secondary,
and tertiary) and for many kinds of processes (activated sludge,
phosphorus precipitation, etc.); (c) a logarithmic transformation
often makes such histograms nearly symmetrical; (d) long term records
of daily data show definite weekly cycles; and (e) serial autocorrelation in effluent quality exists.

Skewed distributions tend to arise because of one of these two
factors (13): (a) the error variance is approximately constant on a
percentage basis and the response varies over a wide range, or
(b) the observed values lie close to a physical limit (for example,
the concentration of a metal cannot be less than zero but it can be
close to zero) and there is a finite probability of large values
occurring. In these situations, the log-normal distribution is a
logical model. Kolmorogov-Smirnov tests on cumulative probability
distributions of environmental quality data indicate that it is
adequate more often than any other.

Some scientists seem to consider it cheating to simplify a problem
by making a logarithmic transformation. Or, they feel that the
Normal distribution is more correct in some statistical sense. These
attitudes are without merit. There is no natural or statistical law
that unequivocally favors the Normal distribution over all other
distribution models that describe natural variability. Anyway, even
if effluent readings from a treatment plant were normally distributed
when the process were operating at a fixed mean level, a plausible
mechanism exists by which a skewed distribution would be expected to
occur in practice. Suppose a treatment plant operates at two or more

different mean levels; low ones when it is operating properly, and high
ones when it is in an upset condition. Suppose, further, that it
switches among these levels, spending a certain proportion of time at
each level. If results for this process are simulated by drawing random
samples from two or more normal distributions (alternatively one
could consider other forms of these distributions), it is easy to obtain
resulting histograms that have a skewed appearance.

Although a histogram is useful in showing the range, central ten-
dency, and skewness of data, it obscures information about cyclic
changes, shifts in level of performance, and autocorrelation. The
value of statistical time series analysis and simple plots of data in
time is that they reveal rather than conceal such information.

4. Monitoring. Monitoring is watching in order to learn and to
make decisions (21), (22), (23). Monitoring frequently is flawed
because (a) the reason for monitoring is not understood, (b) data are
not plotted and displayed, and (c) inappropriate statistics are
calculated. The reason for monitoring may be for (i) gaining an
understanding of the process, (ii) surveillance and checking compliance
with environmental standards, or (iii) measuring process performance
against expected behavior. It would be a terrible waste to sample an
effluent merely to document failure. Such data contain clues about
how performance can be improved and realistic goals can be set.

What does it mean to say that a treatment process is "out of control"? It does not mean simply that it fails to meet the standards
of effluent quality. It means that there is a high probability that
some factor has intervened and caused the process to behave in an
unusual (but not always undesirable) way. If the intervening factor
can be identified, then, depending on the circumstances, it would either
be removed from or incorporated into normal operation. Monitoring is
done to decide when the situation is unusual enough for us to search
for the cause with the idea of trying to improve performance.

If a treatment plant consistently fails to meet effluent standards
because of overloading, monitoring to decide whether the plant is in or
out of control has no meaning if the level of the violated standard is
used as the quality control limit. A quality control limit that would
have meaning is the level of performance that the plant can achieve if
all the inputs and operating conditions are at their normal levels.
This level can be discovered by statistical analysis of effluent
records. Cusum charting and time series analysis have been useful
tools for doing this (8), (21).

Performance might be measured by one or more kinds of averages:
long-term average, monthly average, weekly average, moving average,
and exponentially weighted moving average. The long-term average is
relevant to a pollutant that is bioaccumulative or causes chronic
toxicity. A short term average, perhaps as short as a few hours, is
relevant to monitor acutely toxic effluents. A 30-day average is

convenient for record keeping; e.g., to summarize a monthly report, but may not represent the environmental response to a pollutant. A pollutant that can be metabolized, detoxified, or excreted by an organism might be monitored best by a statistic that forgets the past and puts emphasis on the present. The exponentially weighted moving average is this kind of a statistic.

5. Useful Graphical Methods. It is shameful that so many environmental quality data are simply put into filing cabinets. These data are a wasted resource. Anyone who collects environmental quality data should, as the first and most important step, plot the data on a chart that is displayed in a frequently visited part of the plant, say, the entrance lobby or lunchroom. Publicize the performance record. Permit operators to evaluate the results of their work. Encourage frequent comparison of the present with past performance and with the target level of performance.

Many types of plots are useful (9). Plotting effluent BOD on a logarithmic rather than linear scale as a function of time tends to make extreme values more prominent by making the variation of the usual background random disturbances more homogeneous. A 30-day moving average gives equal weight to all 30 values, which means that the value thirty days past is numerically as important as today's data point. A 30-day average, which attenuates the differences between weekends and weekdays and other short-term fluctuations, is more sluggish than a 7-day moving average. The number of days incorporated into the average is determined by the features the statistic is intended to reveal.

The exponentially weighted moving average (EWMA) forgets the past at a rate determined by the value of w in the equation used to calculate the new average $\bar{Z}_i$ from the most recent average $\bar{Z}_{i-1}$ and the newest observation y_i, $\bar{Z}_i = w\bar{Z}_{i-1} + (1-w)y_i$, where $0 < w < 1$. As the value of w increases, the smoothing power increases and the quickness of response decreases. The EWMA is easy to calculate and its interpretation is easier than the ordinary moving average because it more closely tracks the daily performance.

A cusum plot displays the cumulative sum of deviations from a reference level of performance. The reference level may be the level specified in the discharge permit or the actual long-term average level. If performance varies randomly about the reference level, the deviations will be randomly distributed about zero and the expected value of cumulative sum will be zero. If the level of performance shifts from the reference level, a sequence of deviations with greater absolute value and with consistently positive or negative sign will result. The slope of the chart is the magnitude of the shift in level. The cusum plot is sensitive to small changes in level. Changes that are undetectable in the raw data often become clear on a cusum chart. This fact has been demonstrated by showing cusum plots to treatment plant supervisors.

We recommend the use of more than one kind of charting technique. Ordinary time plots can often be usefully augmented with plots of the cusum and a moving average. Together, these charts reveal many important features about the process. No difficult calculations are required. No special knowledge of statistics is required.

For those who are tempted to add quality control limits to these charts, we advise caution. The statistical assumptions needed for the justification of ordinary quality control techniques are almost always violated by environmental quality data. If limits are to be plotted, modification of standard procedures is required (22).

The habit of making monthly reports has given the monthly average undeserved popularity as a statistic in water pollution control work. For monitoring purposes, it is useless because there are only twelve monthly averages per year, while the 30-day moving average can be calculated 365 times per year if data exist for all days. Most standards and discharge permits contain language about 30-day averages, which is almost always interpreted to mean monthly average, though it would be preferable if it were interpreted to mean moving average.

6. <u>Sampling Frequency</u>. Most large plants sample daily and small plants less frequently; perhaps, three times a week. It has been argued that small plants cannot sample daily because they lack skilled manpower and money, and, since large plants represent a greater threat to the environment, they require more intensive monitoring. This is not necessarily true. For selection of an appropriate sampling interval, a careful analysis must take into account the natural variability of the process, the precision of control that is possible, the required uniformity of performance, the accuracy of measurements used to judge performance, the penalty for failing to detect bad performance, and the cost of sampling, laboratory work, and data analysis.

A qualitative assessment of these factors does not lead to the conclusion that small plants should sample less frequently than large ones. If small plants have less skilled manpower, they will tend to be less well controlled and their effluent quality will be more variable; thus, infrequent sampling is more likely to miss an extreme event. Furthermore, the wastewater loads on small plants are more variable than on large plants. The question of the best sampling frequency has been investigated quantitatively (23)(24)(25), and based on that work, it appears that daily sampling is excessive even though rather large financial penalties are assigned for having incomplete data. These studies should be extended. For example, they assumed the observations are independent in time, which is not the usual case. When the observations are serially correlated, the amount of information gained by sampling at a particular interval depends on the degree of autocorrelation.

One test of how much sampling is needed to capture the all important information in a record is simply to show people plots of data for different sampling intervals. Figure 3 shows three sequences obtained by sampling a daily record at 3-day intervals. Figure 4 compares a 30-day average calculated from daily data with a "30-day average" (actually 28-day) calculated from samples every fourth day. The people who have seen these plots have not felt that any damaging loss of information results from less than daily sampling. Time series analysis of daily data records and of the same records with different fractions of the data missing have led to the same conclusion: daily sampling is not substantially more effective than sampling every three or four days.

Sampling every fourth day is attractive for several reasons. In particular, it is preferable to three-day or five-day intervals, which would be almost equal in efficiency. Seven samples at a four-day interval cover 28 days, essentially a month, and this "monthly average" includes each day of the week once, so it is a fair average. If more intensive sampling is needed, intervals of two days doubles the number of samples and still gives data that are evenly spaced. The total work would still be less than daily monitoring requires.

7. Transfer Function Models. In wastewater treatment, simple first-order equations are often used to approximate the kinetics of BOD removal and oxygen consumption. These equations do not represent actual biochemical mechanisms for degradation of complex organic compounds, nor do they take into account the vast heterogeniety of the wastewater. In general, a useful model may be either empirical or mechanistic, or some combination of both. All common models of BOD removal are empirical and, yet, they are used in models of treatment process that are generally called mechanistic. Linear transfer function models are sometimes extremely useful in practice. A non-linear process does not need to be modeled by a nonlinear model if the degree of nonlinearity is slight, as it is, for example, when the range of performance is small.

The differential equation model for the change in concentration of a non-reacting substance in the effluent from a well-mixed tank is

(1) $T \dfrac{dY}{dt} = X - Y$

T is the time constant and Y and X are deviations from equilibrium at time t. This equation can be converted to the discrete model $T(Y_t - Y_{t-1}) = X_{t-1} - Y_{t-1}$, which can be written as

(2) $Y_t = \phi Y_{t-1} + \omega X_{t-1}$

where $\omega = 1/T$ and $\phi = (1-T)/T$ and the numerical approximation has been made tnat dY/dt equals $Y_t - Y_{t-1}$ Here the time interval Δt is taken as unity. (If the time interval is not unity, the same formula applies with t-1 replaced by $t-\Delta t$ and T replaced by $T/\Delta t$.)

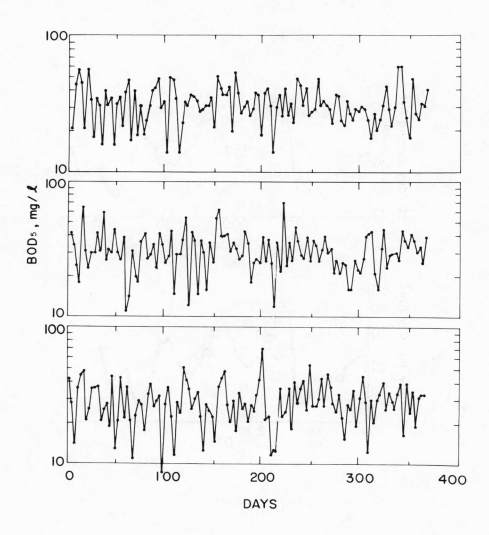

Figure 3.   3-Day Sampling Interval

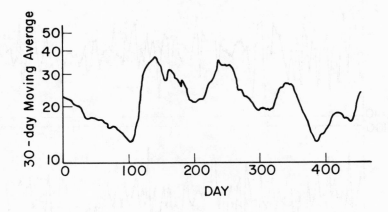

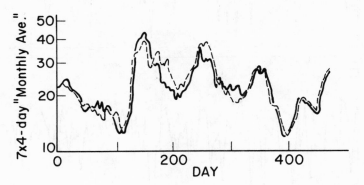

Figure 4.   Monthly Moving Averages

Consider how this discrete mechanistic model might need modification. First, to take into account that data are not perfect, a noise term N_t could be added to the right hand side. The two parts on the right side are, then, the mechanistic part of the model(the transfer function) and N_t is the noise(stochastic) part of the model. If it is found, after fitting (2) to the data, that the residuals are approximately white noise (random with mean zero and constant variance), there would be no reason to question the adequacy of the model (2). However, if the residuals exhibited a systematic pattern, the model would be suspect. Inadequacy may exist in either the transfer function or noise part. For example, one possible elaboration of the noise part would be to set $N_t = (1-\theta B)a_t$, where B is the backshift operator, θ is a parameter, and a_t is white noise.(3)

The form of the model that seems to fit the data may change under certain circumstances. For example, suppose the time constant T is large and the pertubations of X_t are so small that it is not possible to identify the influence of X_t on the level of Y_t. The last model then reduces to

$$Y_t = \phi Y_{t-1} + (1 - \theta B) \quad a_t$$

If this simple univariate model were adequate with respect to all statistical tests, one might be tempted to conclude that, since the value of the input is not included, the model is purely empirical, purely stochastic, and that the process has no transfer function. In fact, such an inference may be incorrect.

This example illustrates two important points. First, it may not be possible to estimate the parameters in a mechanistic model from a particular set of data because the response of the process is swamped by the noise. Second, even when the error is small, when the size of a perturbation is restricted, the data may not be useful for fitting and verifying the model. Consequently, complex mechanistic models may be difficult to verify. Models built from observational field data, on the other hand, often have simple empirical structures.

Model builders often seem to cling fondly to mechanistic models even if no data exist to support them. Empirical polynomial models seem to present no psychological stress for the modeler. If analysis shows that a coefficient is not statistically significant, the term is readily, even cheerfully, dropped because "it makes the model simpler". This same experimenter will not be so cheerful when the estimated value of a parameter in a mechanistic model is not significantly different from zero. Some experimenters in this situation hesitate to simplify the model. There are times when the process is so simple and well understood that we can say honestly that we know the model, but such processes are rare. If we must fall in love while doing statistics on environmental data, we had better fall in love with the data; not the model.

The variance of the effluent readings from a particular treatment

plant can be considered to be the sum of the variances attributable
to analytical measurement errors of the influent and the effluent,
the influent and other factors acting through the transfer function,
and other disturbances. Under certain circumstances, it is possible
to calculate the relative contributions of such sources of variance.

   7.1. Anaerobic sludge digestion process. Accounts of mechanistic modeling of anaerobic sludge digestion have been published (26),
(27). Most of the components of the models (which include substrate
reduction, methane gas formation, and chemical equilibria of organic
acids, alkalinity and carbon dioxide) have been validated in the
laboratory, and they are in accord with experience from full-scale
operation. Full-scale dynamic verification, however, has not been
accomplished, and there is some disagreement about some of the basic
mechanisms.

   A black box multiple-input/single output model was used with normal
operating records for a digester at Norwich, England, for the period
November, 1968, to February, 1969, and the difficulties of working
with "normal operating records" were discussed by Beck (28). The
complaint was not that they were filled with poor quality data but
that the noise to signal ratio of the output data was high and the
input perturbations were weak. Without an interval of considerably
reduced digester loading over the Christmas holiday (days 35 to 45
in Figure 5),all the data series would have been essentially white
noise and probably no definite conclusion about process dynamics could
have been made. Accordingly, Beck suggested that "perhaps public
holidays should be promoted as a natural means of dynamic experimentation with sewage treatment process plants"! The 29-day detention
time in the digester was long compared to the 1-day sampling interval.
The final version of the model was

$$y_t = 0.521\ y_{t-1} + 5.78\ x1_t - 2.15\ x2_t - 1.57\ x2_{t-2} + 0.431\ x3_{t-11} + n_t$$

where y = gas production rate, $x1$ = input feed rate, $x2$ =
volatile acids concentration in the digester, and $x3$ = alkalinity in
the digester.

   Figure 6 shows the response of the model and the data. The deterministic component of the model accounts for about 58% of the sample
variance of the output time series. Beck stated that the first two
terms of the model result largely from behavior during the first half
of the record and, in particular, the Christmas holiday period. Beck
offered no explanation of why gas production rate is affected by
alkalinity levels eleven days prior.

   Modeling wastewater treatment processes is difficult because of
(a) an inability to implement specialized experiments that perturb
process operations, (b) the characteristically low signal/noise ratio
of normal operating records, (c) the multivariate nature of the
process. Modeling waste is further hampered by the limited accuracy
of techniques for sampling and monitoring process variables. With

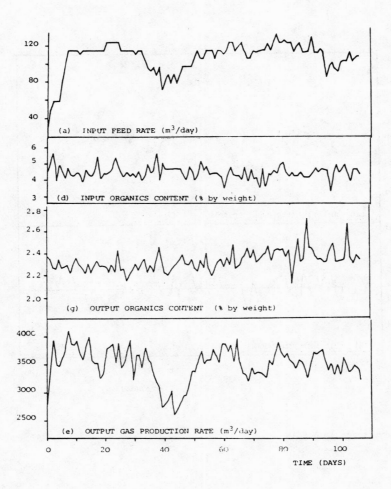

Figure 5.   Normal Operating Records (28)

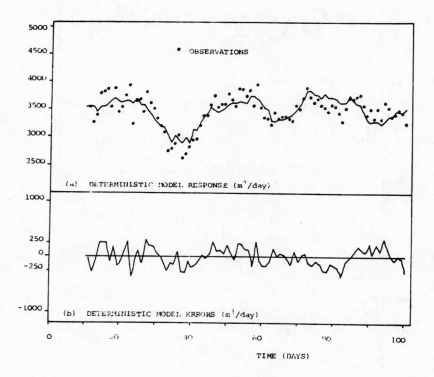

Figure 6.   Output Gas Production Rate Dynamic Model (28)

respect to the anaerobic digestion process, for instance, a one liter
sample of sludge may not be representative of a 140 m^3 batch, from
which it is taken, the measurement of volatile acids concentration
expressed as mg/l acetic acid gives no indication of the relative
proportion of acid types, and gas production rate measurement provides
no information about gas composition. Moreover, major time constants
may have widely different magnitudes. The anaerobic digester in (28)
had a time constant for gas production dynamics of 1.5 days and a
hydraulic time constant of 29 days, and some reactions within the
reactor may have had time constants of a few hours. Gustavsson's
guidelines (29) suggest an experiment lasting for 200-300 days. If
all process variables were measured every hour to observe the high-
frequency responses, no ordinary laboratory could do the work and the
cost of the experiment would be staggering. Clearly, experimental
design is not a trivial matter.

In summary, Beck said, "The black box model identified in this
study is a hypothesis about anaerobic digester dynamics. Like all
hypotheses it needs to be tested again and again, and modified where
it is found inadequate. For many reasons, the model cannot be
considered as in any way universal. It is a model which reflects
how one particular digester behaves under a unique set of conditions".
Beck has written other interesting papers about the difficulties of
process identification and verification (30), (31).

7.2. <u>Nitrification</u>. A factorial-type design was used by
Murphy, et al (32) for dynamic experimentation to identify stochastic
transfer function models to evaluate the effect of changing influent
conditions on combined and separate sludge nitrifying systems.

The authors did not describe the experimental design as such, but
it was essentially a 2^3 factorial design. The variables were flow
rate, feed/organic carbon, and total Kjeldahl nitrogen TKN (organic
nitrogen plus ammonia nitrogen) in the feed. The design and the
randomized sequence of applying the perturbations are shown in Figure
7. Designed experiments were used because "the high degree of correlation between input variables, typical of the daily input to wastewater
treatment plants, made it necessary to disturb the inputs artificially
in a designed manner". The two pilot plants used in the study could be
supplied wastewater in any desired hydraulic pattern. The feed wastewater was degritted municipal wastewater which could be supplemented
by additions of organics (dextrose) and inorganic nitrogen (NH_4Cl) to
create different combinations of hydraulic, organic, and inorganic
loadings.

On modeling with mechanistic and linear time series models, the
authors said, "By substrate and organism balances and the incorporation
of a description for the settler performance, a dynamical mathematical
model for the system could be developed. Such a representation
inherently would contain many simplifying assumptions. Because of
the averaging effect of the many growth and substrate removal functions,

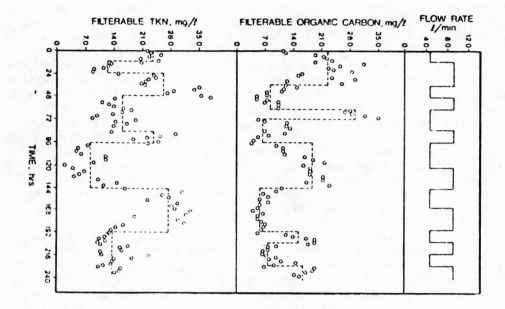

Figure 7.   Programmed Influent Series (32)

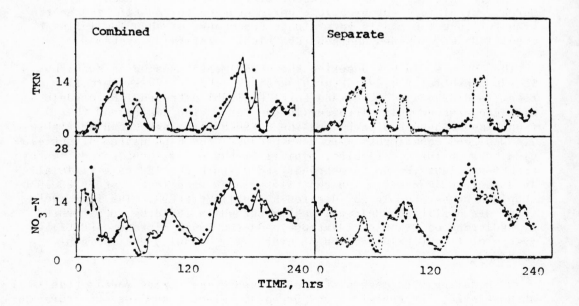

Figure 8.   Transfer Function Models for Effluent (32)

the processes may tend to act as linear systems; consequently, linear transfer function models should describe the time-dependent behavior of these systems adequately. Such models, together with linear time series models to account for the unexplained output variations, are used to describe the response of the combined and separate sludge systems to input variations...". The models and iterative model-building methods of Box and Jenkins (33) were used.

Figure 8 shows the effluent data and the modeled effluent quality. Both systems responded positively to variations in TKN loading but did not show any significant response to changes in filterable organic carbon concentration or loading. The effluent nitrate (NO_3) concentration responded positively to changes in TKN concentration and negatively to organic carbon loading. The model for nitrate had two parameters in the mechanistic part of the model and one parameter in the noise model; the TKN model had four mechanistic parameters and one parameter in the noise model. This well designed experiment, which should have excited the process dynamics and given a clear signal for modelling, leads to simple three and five parameter models. Given this, one must not expect to fit and validate complicated, many-parameter models from poorly designed or undesigned experiments.

Anyone who contemplates doing such experiments will be struck by the enormous work involved and that such studies cannot be done on full-scale treatment plants because the inputs cannot be regulated so nicely. Nevertheless, this is the kind of experimental design that should be used whenever it can be managed. More experiments of this high quality are needed.

7.3 Activated Sludge. References (34),(35),(36) by Olsson and co-workers contain excellent examples of perturbation studies on aeration systems. The time constants of the aerators have been estimated and opportunities for saving large amounts of money by aerator control have been demonstrated.

Studies in Madison, Wisconsin, on a full-scale activated sludge plant were done with the sludge recycle rate held constant over a two week study period while the input followed its undisturbed diurnal pattern (3). This is the normal method of plant operation. Local constraints prohibited using designed perturbations, so to identify all process dynamics was not the research objective but, rather, to evaluate how stable the process was under the normal dynamic growth. It was concluded that the process was inherently stable and that return sludge manipulation was not likely to improve the performance. For other references on dynamic process modeling of wastewater treat-ment, see (21) and (37) through (43).

8. Conclusion. With regard to the volumes of data collected from sewage treatment plants, there has been too much mindless tabulation and too little careful analysis. The number of articles on the use of statistical methods for such data is impressive mainly because it

96 P. M. Berthouex, W. G. Hunter and L. Pallesen

is so small. Standard statistical methods are often inadequate. Particularly troublesome problems include large measurement errors (both random and systematic); lack of reliable and standardized measurement methods for some important properties; frequent occurrence of aberrant data, whether bad data or manifestations of unusual events; missing data; colinearity among process input variables that makes it difficult to estimate separate effects of individual inputs; seasonal fluctuations; complex cause and effect relationships; important variables not being recorded, sometimes because they have not been recognized as important; slow process dynamics which may extend over more than one operating shift; distributions of observations that are non-normal; and data more often coming from observational studies than from designed experiments. In this paper we have discussed some of these problems and indicated how statistical methods have been used to deal with them.

For some problems, new methods will have to be developed. But, in the meantime, much progress can be made by the intelligent application of existing methods; especially, simple ones such as plotting data and displaying the resulting graphs in prominent places. The human mind is remarkably well-suited for the interpretation of graphical information, but it is remarkably ill-suited for the interpretation of tables of numbers. For more formal analysis, useful parsimonious models can be created by judiciously blending common sense, subject matter knowledge, and mathematical techniques. It is rare that the most complicated statistical methods provide the mind with results in a form most likely to reveal important information and to stimulate the generation of new ideas. The purpose for using statistics should not be to dazzle. The proper purpose of statistics is to help people effectively and economically learn from data.

REFERENCE

(1) N. WINNIKE and G. TCHOBANOGLOUS, Analysis of the variations in municipal flow rates and BOD and suspended solids mass loading rates, Proc. ASCE Envir. Engr. Specialty Conf., (1979), pp.223-230.

(2) J.C. YOUNG, J.C. CLEASBY, and E.R. BAUMANN, Flow and load variations in treatment plant design, J. Envir. Engr. Div., HSO, 104, (1978), pp. 289-303.

(3) P.M. BERTHOUEX, W.G. HUNTER, L. PALLESEN, and C.Y. SHIH, Dynamic behavior of an activated sludge plant, Water Research, 12, (1978), pp. 957-972.

(4) J.S. HUNTER, The national system of scientific measurement, Science, 210, (1980), pp. 869-874.

(5) S. WEBER, An evaluation of the accuracy of biochemical oxygen demand and suspended solids analyses performed in Wisconsin laboratories, M.S. Thesis, University of Wisconsin-Madison, 1978.

(6) T.K. KEINATH and B.S. CASTRION, Control Strategies for the Activated Sludge Process, EPA-600/2-80-131, August, 1980.

(7)   D.R. KENDALL, Evaluation and use of monitoring information
      obtained for determining compliance with environmental regulations,
      J. Envir. Sci. Health, A12, (1977), pp. 353-365.

(8)   A.L. DOWNING, Variability of the quality of effluent from waste-
      water treatment processes and its control, Prog. Water Tech.,
      8, (1976), pp. 189-200.

(9)   P.M. BERTHOUEX and W.G. HUNTER, Simple statistics for interpret-
      ing environmental statistics, Jour. Water Poll. Control Fed.,
      53, (1981), pp. 167-175.

(10) W.H. HOVEY, E.D. SCHROEDER, and G. TCHOBANOGLOUS, Activated sludge
      effluent quality distribution, Jour. Envir. Engr. Div., ASCE,
      105 (1979), pp. 819-828.

(11) P.M. BERTHOUEX, Some historical statistics related to future
      standards, Jour. Envir. Engr. Div., ASCE, 100, (1974), pp.423-437.

(12) R.B. DEAN and S.L. FORSYTHE, Estimating the reliability of
      advanced waste treatment, Water and Sewage Works (in 2 parts),
      (1976). June. pp. 87-89. and July. pp. 57-60.

(13) N.A. ESMAN and Y.H. HAMMAD, Log-normality of environmental sampl-
      ing data, J. Envir. Sci. Health, A12, (1977), pp.29-41.

(14) M.T. GARRETT, JR., Effluent variability in domestic wastewater
      treatment plants, Prog. Water Tech., 8, (1976), pp.183-188.

(15) D.G. HUTTON, Statistical Distribution of Biological Wastewater
      Treatment Plant Effluent Data, 34th Purdue Indust. Waste Conf.,
      (1979)

(16) S. NIKU, E.D. SCHROEDER, and F.S. SAMANIEGO, Performance of
      activated sludge processes and reliability-based design, J.
      Water Poll. Cont. Fed., 51, (1979), pp. 2841-2857.

(17) H.J. POPEL, A concept for realistic effluent standards, Prog.
      Water Tech., 8, (1975), pp. 69-89.

(18) R.V. THOMANN, Variability of waste treatment plant performance,
      J. San. Engr. Div., ASCE, 96, (1970), pp. 819-337.

(19) A.R. TOWNSHEND, Statical Analysis of the Effluent Quality of
      Biological Sewage Treatment Process, Proc. 3rd Canadian Symp.
      on Water Poll. Res., (1968).

(20) A.B. WHEATLAND, Statistical expression of effluent quality
      standards, Water Res., 6, (1972), pp. 339-340.

(21) P.M. BERTHOUEX, W.G. HUNTER, LARS PALLESEN, and C.Y. SHIH, The
      use of stochastic models in the interpretation of historical
      data from sewage treatment plants, Water Research, 10, (1976),
      pp. 689-698.

(22) P.M. BERTHOUEX, W.G. HUNTER, and LARS PALLESEN, Monitoring
      sewage treatment plants - some quality control aspects, J.
      Quality Control Tech., 10, (1978), pp. 139-148.

(23) P.M. BERTHOUEX and W.G. HUNTER, <u>Sewage treatment</u>
     <u>plant monitoring: a preliminary analysis</u>, J. Water Poll. Control
     Fed., 47, (1975), pp. 2143-2156.

(24) A.L. JENSEN, <u>Statistical analysis of biological data from pre-</u>
     <u>operational-post-operational industrial quality monitoring</u>,
     Water Res., 7, (1973), pp. 1331-1347.

(25) G.W. FOESS and W. ST. JOHN, <u>Industrial waste monitoring: a</u>
     <u>statistical approach</u>, J. Envir. Eng. Div., ASCE, 106, (1980),
     pp. 947-958.

(26) J.F. ANDREWS, <u>Dynamic model of the anaerobic digestion process</u>,
     J. San. Engr. Div., ASCE, 95, (1969), pp. 95 116.

(27) S.P. GRAEF and J.F. ANDREWS, <u>Stability and control of anaerobic</u>
     <u>digestion</u>, J. Water Poll. Control Fed., 46, (1974), pp. 666-683.

(28) M.B. BECK, <u>An Analysis of Gas Production in the Anaerobic Digest-</u>
     <u>ion Process,</u> (1976), Univ. of Cambridge, Dept. of Engr., CUED/F-
     CAINS/TRI 35.

(29) GUSTAVSSON, <u>Survey of applications of identification in chemical</u>
     <u>and physical processes</u>, Automatica, 11, (1975), pp. 3-24.

(30) M.B. BECK, <u>Identification and Parameter Estimation of Biological</u>
     <u>Process Models</u>, (1975), Cambridge Univ., Dept. of Engr.,
     CUED/F-Control/ TR 116.

(31) M.B. BECK, <u>Hard or Soft Environmental Systems</u>, (1980), WP-80-25,
     Int'l. Inst. for Applied Systems Analysis, Laxenburg, Austria.

(32) K.L. MURPHY, P.M. SUTTON, and B.E. JANK, <u>Dynamic nature of</u>
     <u>nitrifying biological suspended growth systems</u>, Prog. Water
     Tech., 9, (1970), pp. 279-290.

(33) G.E.P. BOX and G.M. JENKINS, <u>Time Series Analysis Forecasting</u>
     <u>and Control</u>, Holden-Day (1970).

(34) G. OLSSON and J.F. ANDREWS, <u>Estimation and Control of Biological</u>
     <u>Activity in the Activated Sludge Process Using Dissolved Oxygen</u>
     <u>Measurements</u>, Int'l. Fed. of Auto. Control Symp. on Envir. Eng.
     Systems Plan., Design, and Control, Kyoto, Japan (1977).

(35) G. OLSSON and O. HANSSON, <u>Stochastic Modeling and Computer Control</u>
     <u>of a Full Scale Wastewater Treatment Plant</u>, Report 7636 (c), Dept.
     Auto. Control, Lund Inst. of Tech. (Sweden)(1976).

(36) G. OLSSON and D. HANNSON, <u>Modeling and Identification of an</u>
     <u>Activated Sludge Process,</u> IFAC Symp. on Ident. and Syst.
     Parameter Est., (1976).

(37) P.M. BERTHOUEX, W.G. HUNTER, L.C. PALLESEN, and C.Y. SHIH, Modelling sewage treatment plant input BOD data, J. San. Engr. Div., ASCE 101, (1975), pp. 127-138.

(38) P. COACKLEY, J.M. CROWTHER, I.M. HAMILTON, and J.F. DALYRMPLE, Time Domain Techniques in the Study of Treatment Plant Performance, Chap. 4 in New Processes of Wastewater Treatment and Recovery, ed. G. Mattock, Ellis Harwood & Co., London, (1978).

(39) J. GANCZARCZYK, Evaluation of activated sludge treatment plant performance, Chap. 22, Statistical and Mathematical Aspects of Pollution Control, Ed. John W. Pratt, Marcel Dekker, Inc., New York, (1974).

(40) N.M.D. GREEN, Statistical concepts in the field of water pollution control, Chap. 3 in Mathematical Models of Water Pollution Control, ed. A. James, John Wiley & Sons (1978).

(41) P.V. KNOPP, Frequency Response Analysis of the Activated Sludge Process, Ph.D. Thesis, University of Wisconsin, (1967).

(42) K.C. LIN and G.W. HEINKE, Variability of temperature and other process parameters: a time series analysis of activated sludge plant data, Prog. Water Tech., 9, (1977), pp. 347-363.

(43) S.G. NUTT, J.P. STEPHENSON, and J.H. PRIES, Steady State and Non-Steady State Performance of the Aerobic Biological Fluidized Bed, Conf. on Bio. Fluidized Bed. Trt. of Water and Wastewater, Univ. of Manchester, England, (1980).

Some Nonparametric Statistics
for Monitoring Water Quality
Using Benthic Species Counts

C. B. Bell,* L. L. Conquest,** R. Pyke# and E. P. Smith**

Abstract. Some nonparametric statistical techniques for use in biological monitoring of water pollution are presented. The basic data for
these analyses is obtained through a reduction of the species count
vectors by a diversity, biotic/trophic or affinity measure. Ranks and
permutation procedures are discussed for regression-randomness, k-sample,
and autoregressive models of water pollution. The use of these procedures
is illustrated on data appearing in the water pollution literature.
Feasibility, goodness criteria and open problems related to the methodology are discussed.

1. <u>Introduction and Summary</u>. Biological monitoring of aquatic
environments is a useful method of assessing long term changes in water
quality. As aquatic organisms, in particular benthic macroinvertebrates
are exposed to pollutants in the water, they indicate possible effects
of those pollutants. By monitoring the benthic community for changes
associated with pollutants, one can detect trends in water quality and
hence measure effectiveness of pollution controls or detect violations.
In this paper, we present methodologies for using benthic organisms as
indicators of pollution.

The basic procedure we propose is to sample the water body at several
similar stations at various distances and/or times, consolidate each
sample into a single measure and look for changes of that measure
in either time or space. The methodology we suggest is based on permutation and ranking procedures, all of which are nonparametric.

In Section 2 we discuss further the basic methodology. Sections 3 and
4 are presentations of the statistical properties of the permutation and
ranking procedures, in particular ease of computation, power, approximations to test statistics and efficiency of the tests. Examples based on
several data sets of both polluted and nonpolluted waters are presented
in Section 5 to evaluate and compare methodologies. Section 6 is a
discussion relating to choice of measures and selection of species. In
Section 7 techniques for two types of dependent observations are discussed;
and in Section 8 some conclusions and unsolved problems are presented.

*Department of Biostatistics, University of Washington, Seattle, WA 98195.
**Center for Quantitative Science, Univ. of Washington, Seattle, WA 98195.
#Department of Statistics, University of Washington, Seattle, WA 98195.

2. <u>The Basic Procedures</u>. There are three significant steps that
should be taken when using organisms to assess pollution.   Since
the benthic community is represented by a large and diverse group of
organisms, as a practical matter, the first step in the analysis is
the choice of a representative set of appropriate pollution-sensitive
and pollution tolerant species as indicators for the habitats in
question.

The second step consists of selecting a univariate descriptor of the
indicator benthic community. This descriptor is typically a diversity
measure, a biotic/trophic measure or an affinity measure. It will be
referred to as an f-measure.

The third step involves choosing a statistic which suitably compares
the f-measures associated with different times and/or distances. The
idea here is that the value of f represents the response to pollution
and that these responses change with time or distance from a pollution
source.

<u>Example 2.1</u> Let $n_j = (n_{j1}, \cdots, n_{jk})$ be the count vector of
the indicator species at time t_j at a particular sampling
station of interest, i.e., n_{ji} is the number of species type
i present in the sample at time t_j. The data matrix is then

$$\underset{\sim}{n} = \begin{pmatrix} n_1 \\ n_2 \\ \vdots \\ n_L \end{pmatrix} = \begin{pmatrix} n_1 & \cdots & n_{1k} \\ \vdots & & \vdots \\ n_{L1} & \cdots & n_{Lk} \end{pmatrix}$$

and the time sequence of f-values is

$$(f_1, \cdots, f_L) = [f(n_1), \cdots, f(n_L)].$$

One measure of pollution change would be the correlation between the
f-values and time, or perhaps more properly, the regression coefficient
of $f(\cdot)$ versus time. The statistical distribution of this regression
coefficient depends on the generally unknown statistical distribution of
$f(n)_j$. In order therefore, to make practical use of the above ideas, one
is lead to a nonparametric approach, using a permutation statistic based
on the regression coefficient. Using this method, one arrives at the
statistic

$$h = h(\underset{\sim}{n}) = \sum_{j=1}^{L} t_j f_j$$

whose values are to be compared with h-values obtained when the times t_j
are permuted. These new values are called "permuted values" The
rationale (to be explained more precisely in the sequel) is that if
indeed there is no change in the indicator community with time, each
possible h-value would be equally likely. This means that with high
probability, the original h-value should fall somewhere in the middle of
the range of permuted values. If, on the other hand, the "structure" of
the benthic community has changed with time, the original h-value should

be at or near the extremes of the "permuted values". The degree of
extremeness will be a measure of the extent of pollution. The effectiveness of this procedure depends on how strongly the indicator species
respond to the pollutant and how well f measures that response.

Example 2.2 Consider seven comparable monitoring stations on a lake
and nine indicator benthic species. The data matrix (the matrix of
species counts) is:

$$\underset{\sim}{n} = \begin{pmatrix} \underset{\sim}{n}_1 \\ \vdots \\ \underset{\sim}{n}_7 \end{pmatrix} = \begin{pmatrix} n_{11} & \cdots & n_{19} \\ \vdots & & \vdots \\ n_{71} & \cdots & n_{79} \end{pmatrix}$$

Let $n_j = \sum\limits_{k=1}^{9} n_{jk}$ denote the total abundance at the jth station,

$p_{jk} = \dfrac{n_{jk}}{n_j}$ denote proportional abundance,

and take $f(\underset{\sim}{n}_j) = - \sum\limits_{k=1}^{9} p_{jk} \ln p_{jk}$ as the Shannon-Weaver "infor-

mation" measure. Let d_j denote the distance of the jth station
from an origin of pollution, e.g., the site of a plant suspected
of polluting a lake, etc. Here d_j may be interpretable as the mean
dilution rate at station j. In some situations, other forms (e.g.,
$1/d_j$) may be more reasonable.

The permutation statistic based on nonparametric regression
ideas would be

$$h = h(\underset{\sim}{n}) = \sum\limits_{j=1}^{7} d_j \, f(\underset{\sim}{n}_j).$$

Using the diversity measure to indicate pollution, we would look
for high values of h to indicate a pollution effect. We expect
diversity to increase with distance from the source of pollution.

Example 2.3 Consider a body of water which can be divided into
five comparable regions based on its past history of pollution.
Let the number of stations within the regions be denoted as c_1,
$c_2, \ldots, c_5$ respectively. For a given common set of indicator species, one has then five samples of f-values

$$(f_{11}, f_{12}, \ldots, f_{1c_1}); (f_{21} \ldots f_{2c_2}); \ldots (f_{51}, \ldots, f_{5c_5}).$$

Consider collecting species count data and computing f-values after
an extensive "clean-up" campaign; such as that for Lake Washington
in the early 1970's. If such a campaign is successful, the f-
values over the five regions should be identically distributed.
A "natural" permutation statistic for the problem is

$$h = \sum\limits_{j=1}^{5} c_i (\overline{f}_{i.} - \overline{f}_{..})^2 \quad \text{where}$$

$$\bar{f}_{i.} = \frac{1}{c_i} \sum_{j=1}^{c_i} f_{ij}$$ denotes the average of the f-values for the ith region.

$f_{..}$ = overall average of the f-values.

$N = \sum_{i=1}^{5} c_i$, the total number of samples.

Relatively large values of the k-sample statistic, h, would indicate significant differences in the five regions, and hence, that the effect of the clean-up is not equal in all regions.

3. <u>Some Pertinent Non-Parameter Techniques</u>. In Sections 3 and 4 we will discuss the statistical reasons for using permutation tests. If desired one may skip to Section 5, losing only the motivation for using these types of tests and related results.

Each of the permutation statistics in Section 2 is non-parametric (NP) in the sense that they enable one to make inferences about the pollution with very minimal assumptions about the underlying statistical distributions. Since only NP techniques will be used in this paper, it is necessary to clearly delineate some of the more important concepts.

The basic random variables here are the f-values, and it is usual to write the (combined) sample of f-values as

$$Z = (f_{11}, \ldots, f_{1c_1}, \ldots, f_{k1}, \ldots, f_{kc_k}) = (Z_1 \ldots, Z_N)$$

where $N = c_1 + c_2 + \ldots + c_k$.

A large number of NP procedures are based on the ranks $[R(Z_1), \ldots, R(Z_N)] = [R(f_{11}), \ldots, R(f_{kc_k})]$ of the data, which are in this case the f-values.

For instance, in Example 1 of the preceding section, one might consider ranking the times as well as the f-values and using the statistic $T^* = \sum R(t_j) R(f_j)$ which is based on the well-known rank correlation coefficient, and related to one of the statistics considered by van Belle and Fisher [13].

For Example 2 of the preceding section, the corresponding rank statistic would be $T^{**} = \sum R(d_j) R(f_j)$. Of course, the d's and the f's are not comparable and are, hence, ranked separately.

The rank concept is quite well-known and widely used. Pitman in 1937 introduced a different type of ranking related to permutations of the data.

<u>Definition 3.1</u> A statistic h , is a B-Pitman function with respect to a   family Ω' (of distributions) and a set S' (of permutations) if

$$P_F[h(\underset{\sim}{Z}) = h(\gamma(\underset{\sim}{Z}))] = 0 \text{ unless } \underset{\sim}{Z} = \gamma(\underset{\sim}{Z}).$$

This means that the function h(.) almost always assumes a different value for each permutation of the data.

Pitman's idea was to compare the h-value of the original data to the h-values of the permuted data. Formally, one has

<u>Definition 3.2</u> $R_h(z)$ is a B-Pitman statistic generated by h(.) if h(.) is a B-Pitman function, and

$$R_h(\underset{\sim}{z}) = \sum_{\gamma \varepsilon S'} \varepsilon \{h(\underset{\sim}{z}) - h(\gamma(\underset{\sim}{z}))\}$$

where $\varepsilon(u) = 1$ if $u \geq 0$ and $= 0$ if $u < 0$.

$R_h(\underset{\sim}{z})$ is, then, the rank of the h-value of the original data among the h-values of the permuted data. A usual test is to reject the null hypothesis if R_h is "too large" or "too small".

For the cases considered here the family Ω' consists of all continuous distribution functions. However, S' changes with the type of problem. This is illustrated in the table below.

TABLE 1.

	f-measure	"covariate"	h(.)	Ω'	S'
Ex. 1	Generic f(.)	time	$\sum_{j=1}^{L} t_j f_j$	continuous distributions	all L! permutations of (1,2,...,L)
Ex. 2	Shannon–Weaver	distance	$\sum_{j=1}^{7} d_j f_j$	as above	all 7! permutations of (1,2,...,7)
Ex. 3	Generic f(.)	sample number i.e., (1,2,...k)	$\sum_{i=1}^{5} c_i (\bar{f}_{i.} - \bar{f}_{..})^2$	as above	all $(\dfrac{N!}{c_1! \ldots c_5!})$ permutations between samples

As mentioned above, the corresponding rank statistic for Examples 2.1 and 2.2 is the rank correlation coefficient. It is also true that the rank statistic corresponding to the permutation statistic in Example 3, is the well known Kruskal-Wallis statistic.

The formula for the rank correlation coefficient is

$$r_s = 1 - \frac{6\Delta^2}{L^3 - L} \quad \text{where} \quad \Delta^2 = \sum_1^L [R(f_j) - R(d_j)]^2.$$

The formula for the Kruskal-Wallis statistic is

$$H = \frac{12}{N(N+1)} \sum_{i=1}^K c_i (R_{i.} - R_{..})^2 \qquad R_{..} = \frac{N+1}{2}$$

$$R_{i.} = \sum_{j=1}^{c_i} \frac{R(f_{ij})}{c_i} \qquad\qquad N = \sum_{i=1}^k c_i$$

One should note here that the rank tests are, in general, easier to perform than the permutation tests. However, in a variety of situations permutation tests have higher power. Hence, both types of tests should be considered.

4. <u>Goodness Criteria for NP Technique</u>.

a) <u>Ease of Computation of the Statistic</u>. As previously mentioned the rank statistics are generally easier to compute. If, for example, the number L of times, t_j, of Example 2.1 is 10, then the number of required permutations is $10! > 3.5 \times 10^6$.

b) <u>Accessibility of Tables</u>. For each of the rank statistics, one will need appropriate tables. For example, tables related to the rank correlation coefficient can be found in Hollander and Wolfe [5].

For the permutation statistics, no table is necessary since the null distributions are all discrete uniform. That is, the null distribution of each R_h has

$$P\{R_k = j\} = \frac{1}{k*} \quad \text{for } j = 1, 2, \ldots, k* \text{ where } k* \text{ is the number}$$

of relevant permutations.

c) <u>Power</u>. In general, the most powerful NP test against a specific alternative will be a permutation test and not a rank test (unless the sample sizes are quite small).

<u>Example 4.1</u>   Consider Example 1 of Section 2. If the benthic populations are not changing with time, one has a "$H_o: G_1 = \ldots = G_L$"

where G_j is the distribution function of f_j. In this case, the joint density of the (f_j) is

$$L_o(f_1, \ldots, f_L) = \prod_1^L g(f_j).$$ When the alternative is a simple

linear regression of f-values with time, the joint density of the f_j is

$$L_1(f_1, \ldots, f_L) = (2 \Pi \sigma^2)^{-\frac{L}{2}} \exp [- \frac{1}{2\sigma^2} \sum_1^L (f_j - \alpha - \beta t_j)^2].$$

In order to get the most powerful NP test against this simple alternative, one first follows the Neyman-Pearson principle and considers the likelihood ratio: L_1/L_o. To "nonparameterize" the test, one considers

permuting the f_j. In the present case L_o is constant, and the non-constant

part of L_1 is "$\beta \Sigma t_j f_j$". The permutation test is then to be based on

$h = \Sigma t_j f_j$. One rejects for "large" values of $R_h(z)$ if $\beta > 0$, and for small values of $R_h(z)$ if $\beta < 0$. In any event the function to be permuted is $h = \Sigma t_j f_j$. Following the logic of Neyman-Pearson's fundamental result, one has then

"Among all NP tests of randomness of the f_j against simple linear (normal) regression, the most powerful test is the one based on permuting $h = \sum_1^L t_j f_j$".

Once it is established that permuting $h = \sum_1^L t_j f_j$ leads to the most

powerful NP procedure against simple linear (normal) regression, one then asks is R_h "good" against other alternatives. Following the path of Koopman and Pitman relative to sufficient statistics, one finds that R_h generates the test that is uniformly most powerful (among all NP tests) against the following family of alternatives.

$$G_j(f,\alpha,\beta) = \exp [\beta d_j f + K (d_j,\alpha,\beta) + t(f,\alpha,\beta)].$$

The rank test most closely corresponding to the permutation test described above is that based on the previously mentioned statistic

$$T^* = \Sigma R_t(t_j) R_f(f_j).$$ This statistic is much easier to evaluate

than R_h, but of course, will not achieve the level of power of the most powerful NP test.

Faced with a trade-off between power and ease (and hence cost) of computation, one seeks approximations to the (most powerful) permutation test. A usual approximation is the normal approximation. In the case of the statistic:

$$h = \sum_{j=1}^{L} d_j f_j \text{ we have that } Z = \frac{h - E[h]}{\sqrt{V(h)}}$$

is approximately $N(0,1)$; where

$$E[h] = L \, \overline{d} \, \overline{f}$$
$$V(h) = (L - 1) \, S_d^2 \, S_f^2$$

with

$$S_d^2 = \sum \frac{(f_j - \overline{f})^2}{L - 1} \; ; \quad S_d^2 = \sum \frac{(d_j - \overline{d})^2}{L - 1}$$

(van Belle and Fisher [13]).

The formulas for $E[h]$ and $V(h)$ are based on the conditional expectation of h and h^2, where we condition on the observed data. The probability that f_i, the value of f at station i takes on some value $f \varepsilon \, (f_1, f_2, \ldots, f_L)$ is, under the null model, $1/L$. Now

$$E[h] = E[\Sigma d_j f_j] = \Sigma d_j E[f_j].$$

But

$$E[f_j] = \sum_{j=1}^{L} f_j \, P[f_j = f] =$$

$$\sum_{i=1}^{L} f_j \cdot \frac{1}{L} = \overline{f}$$

So

$$E[h] = \overline{f} \sum_{j=1}^{L} d_j = L \cdot \overline{f} \cdot \overline{d}.$$

The formula for $V(h)$ follows in a similar fashion.

For many of the situations of interest the sample sizes are quite large and, hence, (large sample) approximations such as the one above are quite good. Further, for comparison of test procedures the asympotic relative efficiency (ARE) becomes a more realistic measure of "goodness".

Consider the tests based on statistics T_1 and T_2, respectively, and $n(T_j;\alpha,\beta)$, the number of observations required to achieve error levels α and β against a specified family of alternatives. Then one calls

$$E = \frac{n(t_2;\alpha,\beta)}{n(t_1,\alpha,\beta)} \, , \text{ the relative efficiency of } T_1$$

with respect to T_2. If for example, T_1 requires more observations than T_2 to achieve the same error levels, then the ratio E is less than one, and T_1 is less efficient than T_2. Efficiencies can be computed in a variety of different situations. However, in many cases the exact calculations are quite cumbersome. A large number of statisticians prefer to use the ARE, which is

$$A(T_1, T_2) = \lim \frac{n(T_2;\alpha,\beta)}{n(T_1,\alpha,\beta)}$$ where the limit is taken as

the alternative becomes more and more difficult to detect, i.e., its distribution increasingly resembles the null distribution (of the f's, for example).

Of considerable interest to persons using nonparametric techniques, is the ARE of a nonparametric procedure with its "natural" parametric competitor. In the example considered above, one has the following situation:

The "natural" classical statistic in the normal case is

$$\hat{\beta} = \frac{\Sigma t_j f_j - n\,\overline{f}\,\overline{t}}{\Sigma(t_j - \overline{t})^2}$$; and the two NP competitors considered

above are R_h, where $h = \Sigma t_j f_j$, and $T^* = \sum_1^n R_t(t_j)R_f(f_j)$. A "Gaussianized"

NP statistic is

$$S^* = \sum_1^n R_t(t_j)\,\overline{\Phi}^{-1}\left(\frac{R_f(f_j)}{n+1}\right),$$ where $\overline{\Phi}(\cdot)$ is the standard

normal distribution function. (This latter statistic is an extension of the ideas of Nievergelt and van der Waerden [14]).

For simple linear (normal) regression with the slope parameter β tending to zero as the sample size increases, one has

$$0 < A(T^*,\hat{\beta}) < A(S^*,\hat{\beta}) = A(R_h,\hat{\beta}) = 1.$$

5. Examples
Example 5.1 Wise and O'Sullivan [16] describe the physical, chemical and biological water quality characteristics of Ross Bay, part of a lake in southwest Ireland which is undergoing eutrophication due to detergents and sewage. Seven samples were taken from stony habitats in the littoral zone during the summer of 1973. Data were summarized as biomass, diversity (Shannon), community similarity (Kendalls tau) and biotic quality (Chutter [3]). The biotic quality index was not considered in our data analysis as the sensitivity of the organisms was decided on after the data was collected, based on abundances at the stations.

Comparisons of several measures are given in Table 2. As can be seen
from hypothesis A, an analysis based on biomass would lead to erroneous
results. Since organic enrichment acts as food as well as a toxicant,
some organisms flourish in this environment and hence there is a greater
biomass than normal. This leads to a curvilinear response over distance
rather than a linear response. (See Figure 1).

Diversity detects the change but the strongest results are for the
community similarity measure. The change is also reflected by using the
number of species as an f. Use of inverse distance improves the test
slightly. Consistent results using phosphorous concentration instead of
distance supports the general approach.

Comparisons of the three approaches indicate that the permutation
significance is not as well estimated by the normal approximation as
expected. The rank correlation test is often close to the other methods
although in one case (D) it is quite disparate. The reasons for this are
discussed in the next example.

TABLE 2

Statistical Results for Various Alternative Hypotheses for Data From
Wise and O'Sullivan [16] Using Seven Sampling Stations. (Here
W_j is the average weight of species j, and S_i is the number of
species at station i.)

Alternate Hypothesis	f_i	Permutation Test	Spearman's Rank Correlation	Normal Approx. to Permutation
A. Biomass increases with increasing distance	$\sum_{j=i}^{k} W_j N_{ij}$	p = .615	rho = -.21 p = .669	z = -.3289 p = .629
B. Diversity (Shannon) increases with distance from source	$-\sum P_{ij} \log P_{ij}$	p = .012	rho = .96 p = .0014	z = 1.930 p = .027
C. The number of species increases with increasing distance	S_i	p = .031	rho = .51 p = .129	z = 1.863 p = .0314
D. The number of species decreases as a function of 1/distance	S_i	p = .018	rho = -.58 p = .079	z = -2.293 p = .0110
E. Community similarity decreases with increasing distance, Q is the number of concordant pairs	$1 - \dfrac{4Q_{i1}}{n(n-1)}$	p = .0002	rho = -1.0 p = .0002	z = 2.167 p = .015
F. Community similarity decreases with decreasing phosphorous	same	p = .0014	rho = .96 p = .0014	z = 2.406 p = .0082

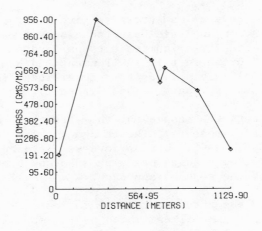

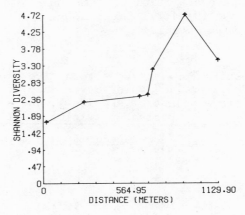

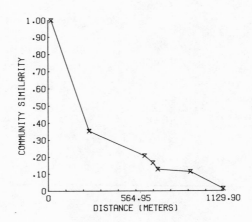

Figure 1

Graphs of Data from Wise and O'Sullivan [16] for
Hypotheses A, B and E.

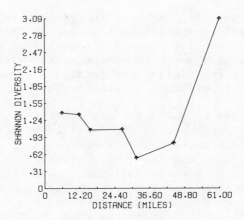

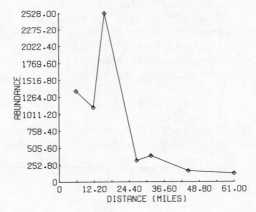

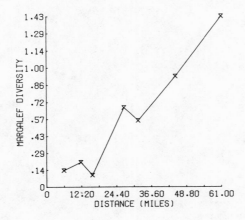

Figure 2

Graphs of Data from Wilhm [15] for
Hypotheses B, A and D.

Example 5.2. Wilhm [15] discusses the changes in the community structure of a benthic community in a stream in Oklahoma. Data are summarized for seven stations at various distances along the stream in the form of diversity measures (Shannon, Margalef), a biotic measure (ratio of insects to tubificids) and total abundance for several seasons. The type of pollution is organic waste.

Significant effects of pollution are indicated by using numerical abundance, the number of species and Margalef's index of diversity (Table 2). A biotic measure based on the ratio of insect abundance to Tubificidae abundance did not give a significant effect. As some insects are tolerant of organic pollution, this result is not unusual but represents a poor choice of measure. The Shannon measure gives differing results according to which test is used. The graph of Shannon diversity (Figure 2) indicates that the last point appears to greatly influence results. The permutation test gives larger weight to extreme valued points than the rank test which gives each point equal weight. This difference is made more evident by considering alternate hypothesis E, using the ratio of insect weight to Tubificidae weight (Table 4). As the last value is reduced, the permutation statistic approaches the rank statistic, indicating the greater sensitivity of the permutation statistic.

TABLE 3

Statistical Results for Various Hypotheses for Data from Wilhm [15]
Using Seven Sampling Stations (Summer Data)

Alternate Hypothesis	f_i	Permutation Test	Spearman's Rank Correlation	Normal Approx. to Permutation
A. The number of organisms decreases with distance	N_i	p = .017	rho = −.857 p = .012	z = −1.72 p = .043
B. Diversity (Shannon) increases with distance from source	$-\sum_{j=1}^{k} P_{ij} \log P_{ij}$	p = .065	rho = .321 p = .249	z = 1.68 p = .046
C. The number of species increases with distance from source	S_i	p = .003	rho = .875 p = .009	z = 2.29 p = .0110
D. The diversity (Margalef) increases with distance from source	$\dfrac{S_i}{\sqrt{N_i}}$	p = .0019	rho = .875 p = .009	z = 2.38 p = .0087
E. The ratio of insects to Tubificidae increases with distance from source I = insect group T = Tubificidae group	$\dfrac{\sum_{j \in I} n_{ij}}{\sum_{k \in T} n_{ij}}$	p = .341	rho = −.142 p = .609	z = .449 p = .326

TABLE 4

Difference Between Permutation and Spearman Rank
Correlation

Original Data							
Distance	6	12	16	27	32	45	61
Insect/ Tubificidae	.850	.80	.67	.16	.06	.41	1.32
Rank	6	5	4	2	1	3	7

		Permutation	Rank	Normal Approx to Permutation
1)	Tests on above data	p = .341	p = .609	p = .326
2)	Last value changed from 1.32 to 1.00	p = .528	p = .609	p = .527
3)	Last value changed from 1.32 to 0.90	p = .603	p = .609	p = .606

Example 5.3. Zeigelmeier [17] presents data on the German Bight for
nine stations averaged over a 24-year collection period. Zeigelmeier
indicates that although the nearby Elbe River is a possible source of
pollution, no indication of community changes is apparent from the data.
Most patterns in the community structure are related to environmental
factors. The number of species is related to depth, especially for
Bivalvia and Polychaeta. Two stations located near the coast are affected strongly by shifting sediments due to strong tidal currents.

Examples of tests are given in Table 5. With the exception of one
test, no strong associations with distance occur. The test using Shannon diversity does however indicate a significant relationship (A). The
measure is affected by the environmental conditions in particular, by
the low diversity at the stations affected by tidal conditions.

TABLE 5

Statistical Results for Various Alternative
Hypotheses for Data from Zeigelmier [18]
(Using nine stations.)

Alternate Hypothesis	f_1	Spearman's Rank Correlation	Normal Approx. to Permutation
A. Diversity (Shannon) increases with distance from the Elbe River	$-\Sigma p_{1j} \ln p_{1j}$	rho = .80 p = .007	z = 1.93 p = .027
B. Diversity (Simpson) increases with distance from the Elbe River	$1 - \Sigma p_{1j}^2$	rho = .316 p = .205	z = .768 p = .224
C. The number of species increases with distance from the Elbe River	S_1	rho = .500 p = .089	z = 1.27 p = .103
D. The number of Polychaeta decreases with distance from the Elbe River	n_{1p}	rho = .050 p = .560	z = -.017 p = .490

6. Choice of measure and indicator species.

6.1. Choice of f_j. There are a vast number of possible choices of
f, the measure of response to pollution. Diversity measures have been
used extensively in pollution studies and relate to changes in the number of species and how the abundances are distributed among those species.
Low values of diversity are often associated with possible pollution
stress. Biotic/trophic measures are weighted averages of a function of
abundance with the weights related to sensitivity or trophic position.
Affinity measures are often used to compare stations which are in an
unaffected area of pollution with those in an affected area. Examples
of possible measures are given in the above three applications.

At present, we recommend using several measures, possibly one of
each type. No single measure is adequate to represent the spectrum of
possible responses to pollutants. Measures may also be affected by
factors other than pollutants. For example, the Shannon-Weaver diversity measure is affected by seasonality, sampling method, and level of
taxonomic identification (Hughes [8]).

6.2 Selection of species. Experimental studies of pollution using
benthic organisms have varied considerably in the number of species used.
Howmiller and Beeton [6], for example use only eight taxa in their
study of pollution in Green Bay. The study of Zeigelmeier [17] on the
other hand was based on 145 species. Our feeling is that for pollution
assessment, large species lists are not necessary. If species are
selected a priori to include a wide variety of responses to pollutants, a
small list may be used. In using a smaller list, better inference may
be made for fixed cost as more stations can be sampled.

To make a list, one would choose species based on several sensitivity
categories. Analysis is then based on the abundance of these categories.
An example of this approach is given in Howmiller and Scott [7]   where
the abundant Oligocharte taxocene is subdivided into three sensitivity
groups (see Table 6) and analysis is performed on these groups. Sensitivity of organisms to organic type pollution has been widely documented with reviews in Pearson and Rosenberg [10] for marine environments and Hawkes [4] for stream riffle communities.

An alternate approach to using sensitivity to pollution is to use
trophic status or feeding behavior. Examples of analyses using this
approach are given in Word [17]   and Osborne et.al. [9].

TABLE 6

Sample List of Species Grouped By Sensitivity (Howmiller
and Scott [7].

Group 1. High sensitivity.
        Stylodrilus heringianus
        Peloscolex variegatus
        P. superiorensis
        Limnodrilus profundicola
        Tubifex kessleri
        Rhyacodrilus coccineus
        R. montana

Group 2. Slight sensitivity.
        Peloscolex ferox
        P. freyi
        Hyodrilus templetoni
        Potamothrix moldaviensis
        P. vejdovskyi
        Aulodrilus spp.
        Arcteonais lomondi
        Dero digitata
        Nais elinguis
        Slavina appendiculata
        Uncinais uncinata

Group 3. High tolerance
        Limnodrilus angustipenis
        L. cervix
        L. claparedeiannus
        L. hoffmeisteri
        L. maumeensis
        L. udekemianus
        Peloscolex multisetosus
        Tubifex tubifex

7. <u>Dependent</u> <u>Observations</u> <u>and</u> <u>an</u> <u>Autoregressive</u> <u>Model</u> <u>for</u> <u>Water</u>
<u>Pollution</u>. The preceding discussions and examples primarily concerned
nonparametric regression-randomness and k-sample approaches to water
pollution problems. In both of these approaches an inherent assumption
is the statistical independence of f-values.

In many real-world situations there is considerable dependence in the
data. A detailed treatment of the more important types of dependence is
beyond the scope of this paper. Some of these cases are treated in the
work of Bell and Donoghue [2] and that of Basawa and Rao [1].

In this section the authors briefly discuss two types of dependence
related to water pollution.

7.1 <u>Exchangeability</u>. The set of variables $(f_1, \ldots, f_L)$ is said to
be exchangeable if their joint statistical distribution is invariant
under all permutations $(i_1, \ldots, i_L)$ of the subscripts 1, 2, ..., L.
This type of dependence includes, for example, a modified Tukey-Gross-
Error dependence, where

$$L(f_1, \ldots, f_L) = p(2\Pi\sigma^2)^{-\frac{L}{2}} \exp\ [-\frac{1}{2\sigma^2} \sum_1^L (f_j-\mu_1)^2]$$

$$+ q(2\Pi\tau^2)^{-1/2} \exp\ [-\frac{1}{2\tau^2} \sum_1^L (f_j-\mu_2)^2].$$

One has for this type of dependence, the following proposition.

Proposition 7.1. Under exchangeability, both the rank statistics of
the form $\Sigma R(d_j)R(f_j)$ and the permutation statistics based on functions
of the form $\Sigma d_j f_j$, have the same distributions as in the independence
case.

This means that the "no-pollution-effect" behavior of the statistics
is the same under independence as under exchangeability. Their behaviors
under various types of pollution effects will in general tend to be
different.

7.2 <u>Markov Autoregressive Dependence</u>. Autoregressive models are
widely used in a variety of applications. To illustrate the use of this
model in a water pollution context, one considers a point source of
(suspected) pollution on a stream and data of $f_1, \ldots, f_L$, from successive
downstream monitoring stations. (As usual, the f's are the values of the
diversity measures of the count vectors of the benthic species.)

A NP first-order autoregressive relationship entails

$$f_1 = a\ f_0 + \varepsilon_1,\ f_2 = a\ f_1 + \varepsilon_2,\ \ldots,\ f_L = a\ f_{L-1} + \varepsilon_L,$$

where the ε's constitute a random sample from a continuous distribution G with median 0.

In this case

(1) "a = 0" corresponds to "no pollution effect", i.e, the f's are independent and identically distributed with distribution $G(.)$; and

(2) $0 < a < 1$ corresponds to a pollution effect decreasing with increasing distance from the point source. Let $\underset{\sim}{z} = (f_1, \ldots, f_L)$.

$$L_1(\underset{\sim}{z}) = (2\Pi\sigma^2)^{-\frac{L}{2}} \exp\left[-\frac{1}{2\sigma^2} \sum_1^L (f_j - a\, f_{j-1})^2 \right].$$

This L_1 is a B-Pitman function which is equivalent to

$$h_1(\underset{\sim}{z}) = 2a \sum_1^L f_j f_{j-1} - a^2 f_L.$$ The locally most powerful B-Pitman

function is then

$$h(\underset{\sim}{z}) = \sum_1^L f_j f_{j-1}$$ which is closely related to the empirical

serial correlation coefficient. It can be further proved (e.g., Bell and Donoghue, [2]) that not only is R_h locally most powerful among NP tests against L_1 above, but is also uniformly most powerful against the family of (dependent) alternatives of the form

$$L^*(\underset{\sim}{z}) = \exp\left[a(\theta) \sum_1^n f_j f_{j-1} + b(\theta,\underset{\sim}{z}) + \sum_1^n g(f_j) \right].$$

8. <u>Conclusions</u> <u>and</u> <u>Research</u> <u>Areas</u>. From the preceding discussions, examples, etc., and from a variety of references such as those listed, one can conclude the following.

8.1 <u>Biological monitoring</u> is in many situations quite feasible. In some cases it is more cost effective than the other types of monitoring, and in some sense it is almost always more interpretable to the layman.

8.2 <u>Nonparametric techniques</u> seem to be the most reasonable to use since exact distributional forms of the various bio-phenomena are generally unknown. These techniques are valid under very minimal assumptions. The major non-parametric statistics are (in general) easy to compute and relevant tables are readily available. Further, especially for large data sets (e.g., STORET), the appropriate NP statistics have efficiencies equal to those of their parametric counterparts. The techniques presented in this paper only scratch the surface of available NP procedures for applications in water pollution problems. There are many avenues of research in this area.

8.3 Choice of indicator benthic species in any given practical situation
is quite critical. One has to be aware of the myriad of benthic series
"native" to and/or adaptable to the regions in question. Further, effective
use of the statistical techniques requires some specialized knowledge of
the relative tolerances and sensitivities of the various species to a
variety of known pollutants. The authors' somewhat extended literature
search yielded at least one study utilizing eight benthic taxa and at
least one utilizing 145 benthic taxa. The number of relevant possibilities
is enormous, and will vary from region to region. Continuing research in
this area is highly desirable.

8.4 The choice of diversity (information, biotic/trophic or similarity)
measures is equally important to the effective utilization of the NP methods
of the type treated and mentioned above. This is because the basic data
of the analyses consists of the f-values of the benthic count vectors at
the various points in time and/or space. There is an extensive literature
on these measures. Some of the literature in this area is listed in the
references (Hughes [8] ; Pielou [11]). Research related to optimal choices
of these measures is ongoing, important and wide open.

8.5 Effective and/or generalized distance, suitably defined, is of
importance especially to the NP regression techniques. This is because
the currents, for example, in a body of water determine what is the
"natural" time ordering or distance ordering of the data points. Further,
factors such as the effluent pattern of an outfall determine whether
or not "distance-squared" or "reciprocal-distance" give more power against
certain realistic alternatives. Clearly, these effects vary from region
to region, and will require extensive study to achieve maximum "goodness"
in the use of NP techniques.

Finally, one might say that the fundamental paper of van Belle and
Fisher [13] has opened a gateway of new approaches to water pollution
problems. The current paper solidifies some of the possibilities in this
area. However, the area is quite extensive and there are many more unsolved
problems than solved ones.

REFERENCES

[1] I. V. Basawa and B. L. S. Prakasa Rao, Statistical Inference for Stochastic Processes, Academic Press, New York, N. Y. 1980.

[2] C. B. Bell and J. F. Donoghue, Distribution-free tests of randomness, Sankhya, Series A,31(2),157-176, 1969.

[3] F. M. Chutter, An empirical biotic index of the quality of water in South African streams and rivers. Water Res. 6, 19-30, 1972.

[4] H. A. Hawkes, Invertebrates as indicators of river water quality pp 2-1 to 2-47, in:Biological Indicators of Water Quality, A. James and L. Evison eds., Wiley and Sons, New York, N.Y., 1979.

[5] M. Hollander and D. A. Wolfe, Nonparametric Statistical Methods, John Wiley and Sons, New York, N.Y. 1973.

[6] R. P. Howmiller and A. M. Beeton, Biological evaluation of environmental quality, Green Bay, Lake Michigan, J. Water Poll. Cont. Fed. 42, 123-130, 1971.

[7] R. P. Howmiller and M. A. Scott, An environmental index based on relative abundance of oligochaete species, J. Water Poll. Cont. Fed. 48,802-815, 1977.

[8] B. D. Hughes, The influences of factors other than pollution on the value of Shannons index of diversity for benthic macroinvertebrates in streams, Water Research 12,359-364, 1980.

[9] L. L. Osborne, R. W. Davies and K. J. linton, Use of hierarchial diversity in lotic community analysis, J. Appl. Ecol., 17,567-580, 1980.

[10] T. H. Pearson and R. Rosenberg, 1978, Macrobenthic succession in relation to organic enrichment and pollution in marine environments Ocean. and Mar. Biol. A Rev. 16,229-311, 1978.

[11] E. L. Pielou, An Introduction to Mathematical Ecology, Wiley-Interscience, New York, N.Y., 1969.

[12] E. J. G. Pitman, Signifance tests which may be applied to samples from any population, J. Royal Stat. Soc. Supp. 4,119-130, 225-232, 1937.

[13] G. van Belle and L. Fisher, Monitoring the environment for ecological change, J. Water Poll. Cont. Fed., 49,1671-1679, 1977.

[14] B. L. van der Warden, Order tests for the two-sample problem and their power, Indagationes Math. 15, 303-316, 1953.

[15] J. L. Wilhm, Comparison of some diversity indices applied to populations of benthic macroinvertebrates in a stream receiving organic
wastes, J. Water Poll. Cont. Fed., 39,1673-1683, 1967.

[16] E. J. Wise and A. O'Sullivan, Preliminary observations on the benthic
communities of Ross Bay, a polluted area of Lough Lane, southwest
Ireland, Water Res., 14,1-31, 1980.

[17] J. Q. Word, Classification of benthic invertebrates into infaunal
trophic index feeding groups, in: Annual Report 1979, Coastal Water
Research Project, pp. 103-121, El Segundo, California, 1979.

[18] E. Zeigelmeier, Macrobenthos investigations in the eastern part of
the German Bight from 1950-1974, Rapp. P-v. Reun. Cons. int. Explor.
Mer. 172,432-444, 1978.

HAZARDOUS SUBSTANCES

Biologically Based Environmental Standards
for Time-Varying Exposures
to Hazardous Substances

Allan H. Marcus*

Abstract. The concentrations of hazardous substances to which
individuals are exposed are often highly variable over time. The
biological consequences of exposure thus often depend on the time-
scales of processes such as organ distribution, biotransformation,
and elimination of the substance, and on the accumulation and repair
of damage to tissues. Toxicokinetic models must thus include nonlinear physiological mechanisms, mechanisms depending on dose-rate or
concentration, tissue or protein binding, tissue damage and repair.
The following examples are discussed: (i) Carboxyhemoglobin from
carbon monoxide in the environment and in cigarettes; (ii) Continuous and intermittent exposures to nitrogen dioxide; (iii) Metabolism of cadmium; (iv) Body burdens of lead and alkaline earth
metals; (v) Metabolic processes affecting environmental carcinogens
or mutagens such as urethane and vinyl chloride. The first problem
is the identification of a kinetic model and estimation of its parameters. The second problem is the specification of statistical criteria for risk; in time-varying environments, stochastic criteria
such as first passage times and exceedances can be studied analyt-
ically and by computer simulation. We recommend that environmental
standards be formulated directly in terms of predicted exceedances of
biological hazard criteria.

Introduction

A more precise quantification of the adverse biological consequences of exposure of pollutants is needed to balance the costs
and benefits of environmental standards and their enforcement. Unfortunately, we are still saddled with older approaches to environmental regulation in which regulatory criteria are not sufficiently
precise or appropriately formulated to allow meaningful prediction of
biological effects. These environmental standards are often stated in
the form of permissible maximum or average concentrations (at a fixed
source or monitoring site) for a specified time interval such as
eight hours or one year. These standards virtually ignore the fact

---

*Department of Pure and Applied Mathematics, Washington State Univer-
sity, Pullman, Washington 99164

that concentrations of hazardous substances to which individuals are
exposed are often highly variable over time due to individual activity patterns and to time patterns in pollutant production and release.

In this paper we will review some models and biological response
to time-variable exposures for certain important environmental pollutants, including: carbon monoxide from the environment and from
cigarette smoking; nitrogen dioxide in continuous and intermittent
exposures; cadmium metabolism; lead metabolism; and exposures to carcinogenic chemicals and radiation.

Our study of these examples will show the importance of different
time scales of biological processes in relation to exposure patterns.
The processes will include: organ distribution and elimination
("toxicokinetics"); biotransformation by metabolic processes leading
to the activation or inactivation of a contaminant; accumulation of
tissue damage and repair. Toxicokinetic models may be affected by
nonlinear physiological processes, including: tissue or protein-
binding; concentration or dose-rate dependence; exogenous chemical,
physical, or biological stresses; saturability of some protective
mechanisms. Any of these processes can appreciably modify our interpretation of the experimental data for both low-dose and high-dose
extrapolations of hazard. It is thus essential that we try to under-
stand the biological kinetics of pollutants within the affect organism.

Biological and Regulatory Criteria

Stochastic process models combine the concepts of variability and
temporal kinetics. Define $C(i,t)$ as the concentration of pollutant
i at time t, external to the subject but possibly variable with his
location; $i = 1, ..., m$. Let $X(j,t)$ be the quantity of pollutant in
internal "compartment" j at time t; $j = 1, ..., n$. The general form
of a linear toxicokinetic model is then

$$(1) \qquad dX/dt = KX + AC$$

where $K = (k(i,j,t))$ is the n*n matrix of rate coefficients,
$A = (a(i,j,t))$ is the n*m matrix of absorption coefficients,
$X = (X(i,t))$ is the n-vector of state variables, and $C = (C(i,t))$ is
the m-vector of ambient pollution concentrations. Particular examples
of this model will be used throughout this paper.

One of the most important decisions is the choice of a hazard assessment criterion. My own preferences lean toward those criteria that
indicate how long an environment with acknowledged noxious substances
can be safely endured. Possible biological hazard criteria include:
$T(L)$, the first passage time of $X(i,t)$ to level $L(i)$ for specified i;
$Z(i,t,u)$, the maximum value of $X(i,t)$ during the interval from t to
$t + u$; and $Y(i,t,u)$, the average exceedance of $X(i,s)$ above level $L(i)$

during the interval t < s < t + u. For laboratory experiments the
response functions might include the percent mortality and number of
tumors or other indications of pathology in serially sacrificed animals.
In human populations, a useful criterion might be the expected reduction in length of life.

On the other hand, the regulatory criteria are usually expressed in
terms of acceptable maxima or other order statistics of moving averages
of C(j,t) over specified time intervals of length u; denote the moving
average of C(j,t) from t to t + u by C(j,t,u). The question is that of
relating exceedances of C(j,t) to excursions of X(i,t) measured by T(L),
Y(i,t,u) or Z(i,t,u). We will show how C(j,t,u) may not tell us enough
about T,Y or Z. In view of the occasional discrepancy between regulated average concentrations C and health effects indicators T, Y, Z,
it may thus be helpful to revise environmental standards so as to
directly reflect predicted health effects, at least for those pollutants about which enough is known to promote a biologically realistic
health effects model of general applicability. Several such pollutant
systems are described below. In most instances, the use of ambient
concentrations C to directly calculate T, Y, or Z directly by use of
mathematical models would add only a trivial additional computation to
the already computerized treatment of routine monitoring data. This
direct calculation of health effects indicators should simplify discussions about whether or not a particular pollutant source constitutes
an actual or potential health hazard. We strongly recommend such an
approach.

Carbon Monoxide

The concentration of carboxyhemoglobin COHb (CO bounded to hemoglobin in the blood) is by far the most important physiological indicator, although other body stores of CO may also be of some interest.
We may thus use a one-compartment model, but the model is intrinsically
nonlinear and its rate coefficients depend on time-variable ventilation
rates as well as individually variable physiological parameters [1].
Explicitly, the COHb fraction X(t) obeys

(2) $dX/dt = ALPHA + BETA(t)*C(t) - MU(t)*X/O2Hb(t)$

ALPHA is the endogenous CO production rate, BETA(t) is the rate of
absorption of ambient C(t) and MU(t) is the rate of elimination of
COHb. The oxyhemoglobin fraction O2Hb is that fraction of hemoglobin
bonded to oxygen. Since hemoglobin has a much higher affinity for CO
than for O2, most of the available CO will be absorbed in preference
to O2.

The rates BETA(t) and MU(t) depend on physiological parameters such
as the mean lung diffusion capacity, and on environmental variables
such as the atmospheric pressure; but by far the most important source
of variation is the individual's activity level and ventilation rate.
For healthy inactive individuals, typical values of the parameters are

ALPHA = 0.004/hr, BETA = 0.0015/ppm CO/hr, and MU = 0.2/hr; but over
a range of activities from sleep to heavy exercise, MU could vary from
0.15/hr to 0.5/hr and BETA proportionately.

O2Hb also varies in a nonlinear manner. There is relatively little
change in oxygen content of the blood as COHb increases from 0% to
about 3% or 4%, but at larger values of COHb, increased COHb is com-
pensated by decreased O2Hb. A more precise treatment using the inverse
oxygen dissociation curve is given in Collier [2].

The nonlinearities are not important in practice, but Ott and Mage
[3] and Marcus [4] have demonstrated the importance of ventilation rate
in modifying the time scale for uptake and elimination of CO. For
single brief exposures the shorter time scales are more hazardous
because more CO is absorbed, but for environmentally and occupationally
significant exposure patterns, such as continuous exposure or repeated
intermittent exposures to CO, the longer time scales are more hazardous
because there is less chance for COHb to wash out between exposures.
Thus COHb exceedances, e.g., X(t) > 2% = L may or may not correspond to
air quality violations, e.g., C(t, 8 hrs) > 9 ppm in a highly variable
environment [3]. Sources of highly variable CO exposure are motor
vehicles, heating systems, and cigarette smoking. Ott and his colleagues are combining personal monitoring and individual exposure
modeling [5].

It is convenient to assume that time patterns of exposure are continuous, or are implusive at regular intervals, or are impulsive at
completely random epochs (Poisson process model). Other patterns are
more likely in real life: (i) Scheduled regular releases of the
pollutant are subject to random variations in time and magnitude;
(ii) A criterion pollutant is monitored and is released to the environment only when the concentration of that pollutant drops below some
threshold value. After release the quantity of pollutant is controlled
so that the criterion pollutant concentration does not exceed some
upper threshold level. While the criterion pollutant is being controlled, concentrations of noncriterion pollutants with longer physiological residence times are building up in the body; (iii) Exposure
is governed by stages of some extrinisc process, e.g., the arrival of
a railroad tank car filled with some hazardous chemical, or the decision to drive home during a summer rush hour with the car window open.

One example of situation (ii) is the personal nasal monitoring of
irritating air pollutants such as ozone and nitrogen oxides— and
acrolein and hydrogen cyanide in cigarette smoke. A worker may remove
himself from these irritants for a time and then return to them when
their effects are diminished.

Cigarette smoking provides another example of situation (ii). In
cigarette smoking, the CO doses are self-administered in a time pattern
which is governed by opportunity as well as by psychological and physiological factors that are not well understood [6]. A better understanding of cigarette smoking behavior and exposure patterns is needed

to separate out the effects of ambient air pollutants from those self-administered by the smoker. Furthermore, cigarette smoking behavior is a useful model for controlled or self-monitored pollutant exposures.

The "nicotine maintenance" hypothesis for smoking uses nicotine as the criterion substance. A new cigarette is started when the blood level of nicotine drops below some threshold (opportunity permitting), but the cigarette is puffed only until a desired upper nicotine level is first exceeded. Nicotine is absorbed from cigarette smoke and reaches the brain within a few seconds, but thereafter seems to follow a compartment model with n = 2 or 3. A two-compartment catenary model (i = 1, blood; i = 2, other tissues) is shown in Fig. 1. We used the SAAM-27 least squares program to fit dX/dt to various data sets, obtaining parameter estimates $1/k(2,1)$ = 3 to 5 minutes, $1/k(0,2)$ = 50 to 100 minutes, $1/k(1,2)$ = 30 to 50 minutes for a number of adult male smokers, where $k(i,j)$ is the rate of transfer of nicotine from compartment j to compartment i. These rates are much faster than the rates for COHb elimination (4 to 6 hours in inactive people) so that COHb continues to build up even though nicotine may have achieved an equilibrium condition in both blood and other tissues.

A computer simulation model for nicotine and COHb is based on the two-compartment nicotine model described above. We have used an upper threshold in blood of 25 ng/ml, and a lower maintensance level of 3 ng/ml. The nicotine model is shown in Fig. 1, and the results of typical simulation runs in Figs. 2 and 3. The first passage time to 5% COHb is shown in Fig. 3 as $T(5\%)$, and the average of the shaded areas is $Y(0,8 \text{ hrs})$ for L = 5%.

A mathematical model for impulsive exposures such as cigarette smoking requires a point process $N(t)$ for exposures. The elimination process has a purely random component $dW(t)$. The differential equation analogous to (1) is:

$$(3) \qquad dX(t) = f(X(t))dt + g(X(t))dW(t) + \int h(X(t),d) \, N(dt,dD)$$

where $N(dt,dD)$ is the number of exposures occurring between t and t + dt whose dosage is between D and D + dD. We usually assume that N is a stationary process with mean

$$(4) \qquad E\{N(dt,dD)\} = \text{FREQ} \, dt \, dG(D)$$

where G is the cumulative distribution of D, and FREQ is the mean exposure frequency. If N is a Poisson process with completely independent doses, this stochastic integro-differential equation for X is easily converted into an equation for the moments of $T(L)$ [7,8]. Define $T(L,X(0))$ as the first passage time from an initial level $X(0)$ to threshold L $X(0)$, and

$$(5) \qquad M(n,X(0)) = E\{T(L,X(0))^n\}$$

128

Allan H. Marcus

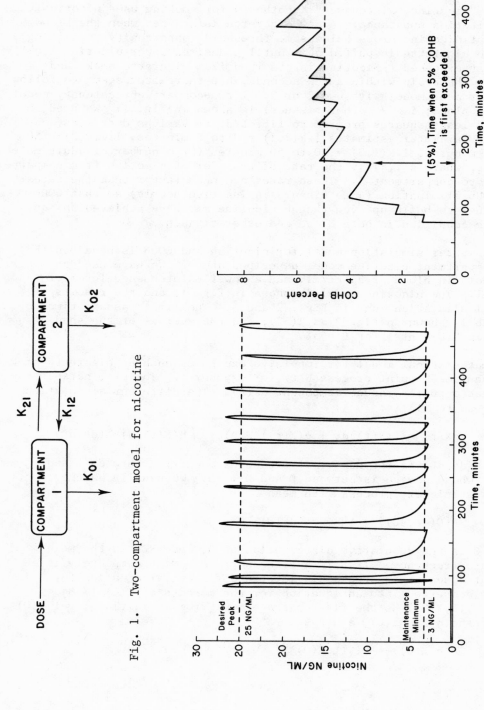

Fig. 1. Two-compartment model for nicotine

Fig. 2. Computer simulation of nicotine in compartment 1

Fig. 3. Computer simulation of carboxyhemoglobin

Then for n > 0,

(6)   FREQ*M(n,x) = f(x)M'(n,x) + (1/2)(g(x)^2)M"(n,x)

+ n M(n - 1,x) + FREQ $\int$ M (n,x + h (x,D)) dG(D)

where derivatives are w.r.t. x, and M(0,x) = 1. Explicit solutions
have been obtained for many cases, but only when D is constant or G
is exponential; the methods require expanding M(1,x) as a power series
in x, and then establishing recurrence relations for higher moments.
The washout functions include f(X) = -MU*X and f(X) = -MU*X/(1 - X).

In all cases, the longer time scales were more hazardous by all the
criteria, both in the computer simulation models and in the mathematical analysis of the point process model. We have also studied a "semi-
simulation" model. The real patterns of cigarette smoking shown in
Fig. 4 were used in place of the theoretical exposure from the pharmacokinetic model for nicotine maintenance, and in place of random or
purely regular patterns (we are grateful to Drs. N. Wald and S. Howard
for providing these data). Calculation of T(5%) and Y(8 hrs, 5%)
depends on the assumed value of the washout rate MU, and on the assumed
COHb increases or dose per cigarette— we used values of 1.5% and 2%
COHb. Again, the longer washout times (smaller MU) are more hazardous,
as seen in Figs. 5 and 6.

One physiological defense mechanism against extra CO burdens is an
increased red blood cell count, but the limits of such a mechanism are
shown by "smokers' polycythemia" [9].

In summary, we have enough knowledge at present to realistically
predict biological hazard indicators for the short-term effects of
carbon monoxide exposure based on carboxyhemoglobin levels, and should
consider reformulating short-term CO standards in terms of predicted
biological hazard. Long-term CO exposures still require study, particularly toward the development of an explicit dose-response relationship between COHb and cardiovascular disease.

Nitrogen Dioxide and Benzene

The effects of continuous and regularly intermittent exposures to
NO2 have been described by E.P.A. investigators and their Russian
colleagues [10-13]. The most important biological response criteria
for exposure to NO2 in mice were: (i) increase in mortality relative
to controls after challenge with streptococci; (ii) time required to
elicit 20% mortality after exposure. Several damage mechanisms may be
present and operating simultaneously at different time scales. In the
published results, intermittent exposures to high concentrations appear
to be more harmful than continuous exposures to lower concentrations of
NO2 even though the total exposure (concentration*time), i.e., long-
term average C(t,u) is the same in both cases. Recent experiments with
NO2 peaks superimposed on a base level show a more complicated situation (F. Miller, personal communication).

Time	PERSON A	Time	PERSON B	Time	PERSON C	Time	PERSON D
7 a.m.		7 a.m.		7 a.m.	←Wake up * cig	7 a.m.	
	←Wake up						←Wake up
8 a.m.	* cig	8 a.m.		8 a.m.	* cig * cig	8 a.m.	
			←Wake up				
9 a.m.	* cig * cig	9 a.m.		9 a.m.	* cig * cig	9 a.m.	* cig
			* cig				* cig
10 a.m.		10 a.m.	* cig	10 a.m.		10 a.m.	* cig
			* cig				* cig
11 a.m.	* cig * cig	11 a.m.	* cig	11 a.m.		11 a.m.	* cig
			* cig				
Noon	* cig * cig * cig	Noon	* cig	Noon	* cig * cig * cig	Noon	* cig * cig
			* cig				* cig
1 p.m.		1 p.m.	* cig	1 p.m.		1 p.m.	* cig
			* cig * cig				* cig
2 p.m.		2 p.m.	* cig	2 p.m.		2 p.m.	* cig
			* cig				* cig
3 p.m.	* cig * cig * cig	3 p.m.	* cig	3 p.m.	* cig * cig ←Stop	3 p.m.	* cig
	* cig		←Stop				* cig
4 p.m.	←Stop	4 p.m.		4 p.m.		4 p.m.	* cig ←Stop

Fig. 4.   Cigarette smoking times for four heavy smokers

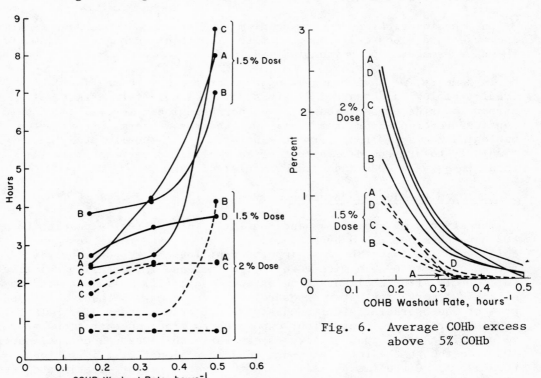

Fig. 5.   Simulations of first exit time above 5% COHb for smokers in Fig. 4

Fig. 6.   Average COHb excess above 5% COHb

The published data have been analyzed using log-linear regression
on the effective delivered dose, which was calculated using a one-
compartment model. The logit models were fitted to the actual counting
data published by Larsen [12] using the SAS NLIN program, which also
allowed several robust methods including trimming or Huberizing extreme
residuals. A large number of models were fitted. We used separate
"blocks" of experiments with both exposed and unexposed mice rather
than "excess mortality", since this formulation was more appropriate
to the regression framework.   However, common regression coefficients
were estimated for NO2 concentration C, exposure time T, the total
exposure C*T, and the dose D estimated from the one-compartment model

(7) $D = C*(1 - \exp(-T/MRT))*MRT$

where the nonlinear parameter MRT = $1/k(0,1)$ is the mean residence time
in the body of the mouse.

Results are shown in Table 1. One can omit either time T or total
exposure C*T and still get an adequate fit, but neither dose D nor
concentration C can be omitted without noticeably degrading the fit.
There is apparently an almost immmediate effect due to initial exposure to concentration C, and a longer-term effect with mean life
MRT of 4 to 6 hours due to extended exposure. We suspect additional
effects at longer times are also present.

TABLE 1

Residual Mean Squares for Logit Regression Model (d.f.)

Robust Methods - - -	Trimming	Huberizing
Model		
Blocks,Conc,Dose,Time,Conc*Time	0.964(27)	0.879(29)
Blocks,Conc,Dose,Time,*********	0.910(28)	1.070(30)
Blocks,Conc,Dose,****,Conc*Time	0.932(29)	0.866(30)
Blocks,Conc,****,Time,Conc*Time	3.79(21)	5.69(31)
Blocks,****,Dose,Time,Conc*Time	5.45(20)	1.276(30)
Blocks,Conc,Dose,****,*********	1.086(31)	1.036(31)
Blocks,****,Dose,****,Conc*Time	6.09(26)	1.249(31)

The choice of a regression model depends not only on goodness-of-fit
criteria, but also on substantive knowledge of underlying causal mechanisms outside the realm of statistics. We would therefore suggest
including the concentration-time product as a measure of cumulative
long-term effect and as a surrogate for damage from mechanisms with
long time scales, even when the time scales cannot be estimated as
precisely as those shown in Table 2.

TABLE 2

Mean Residence Time in Rat +/- Standard Error

Robust Methods - - -	Trimming MRT, hours	Huberizing MRT, hours
Model		
Blocks,Conc,Dose,Time,Co*Ti	4.62+/-2.43	4.49+/-0.77
Blocks,Conc,Dose,Time,*****	5.33+/-0.79	5.69+/-0.97
Blocks,Conc,Dose,****,Co*Ti	4.43+/-0.61	4.55+/-0.77
Blocks,****,Dose,Time,Co*Ti	0.84+/-1.08	3.61+/-0.81
Blocks,Conc,Dose,****,*****	5.70+/-0.95	5.60+/-0.90

The same methodology could be applied to intermittent exposure experiments in which the dose D is replaced by a mixture of exponential terms summing up the on-off exposure pattern. Explicitly, if P is the probability of onset of some physiological condition indicating NO2 damage (e.g., death) then we use

$$(8) \quad LOGIT = \log(P/(1 - P)) =$$

$$b0 + b1*\max C(t) + b2*T*C(T,T) + b3*D(T)$$

where the effective dose in compartment j after T hours of exposure is given by

$$(9) \quad D(T) = \int_0^T X(j, T - t) \, dC(t).$$

Parallel investigations for benzene and other organic chemicals have been carried out by Russian investigators [10,13]. The biological criteria were the times of onset of leukopenia and of an inverse ratio of muscle antagonist chronaxy in white rats. Under similar total doses, the intermittent exposures were less harmful. This can also be attributed to toxicokinetic factors, e.g., benzene washout or animal recovery between exposures.

It is thus clear that environmental standards for nitrogen dioxide, for benzene and for other air pollutants should recognize, as explicitly as possible, the different biological time scales associated with different possible modes and mechanisms for biological damage. We have shown for NO2 that at least some of the relevant time scales may be of comparable order of magnitude to patterns of occupational and environmental exposure. For a randomly variable environment we would then predict the maximum LOGIT from equation (8), or the first passage time of LOGIT to level L. The preceding analysis shows that such a proposal is feasible.

Cadmium

Cadmium is a toxic metal for which bone and kidney are the primary target organs. Detailed multicompartment toxicokinetic models have been fitted to mouse data [14,15], whole-body retention functions fitted to data on many animal species [16], and multicompartment models proposed for man [17,18] have been tested against autopsy data. At low concentrations in controlled laboratory settings, linear toxico-kinetic models for cadmium appear to be adequate. We discuss cadmium here because it exhibits two serious problems in the formulation of biologically based environmental standards. The first problem is that the mouse-to-man extrapolation may require much more complex compart-mental models than most investigators have so far cared to fit. The second problem is that the kinetic parameters for cadmium may be highly sensitive to the exposure patterns for other, non-criterion substances such as zinc, calcium, copper, iron, selenium, and other metals that may induce the formation of metal-binding proteins such as metal-lothionein in the liver or kidney. The implication here is that it will be necessary to keep track of different highly variable sources of exposure (food, water, cigarettes, air) for many different sub-stances simultaneously in order to make meaningful biological predic-tions of hazard.

Data sets and multispecies retention parameters are summarized by Thomas et al. [16]. These models, and those suggested for man [17,18] are aimed at long-term retention parameters such as the "biological half-life". This focus on long-term kinetics may not be completely justified: (i) short-term kinetic parameters may be needed to describe the absorption, organ distribution, and elimination of cad-mium in response to time-varying patterns of occupational and environ-mental exposures; (ii) kinetic parameters for cadmium are affected differently in different compartments by the presence of other metals, as we shall demonstrate below for zinc. The use of whole-body reten-tion functions alone does not allow accurate estimation of kinetic parameters by compartment.

Estimation of separate retention functions for each organ or com-partment is also inadequate. Many investigators fail to recognize that responses to pollutant exposures are determined by the entire ensemble of kinetic parameters $k(i,j)$. The cadmium content in "small" compartments cannot much affect the cadmium content in "large" compart-ments, but the converse is clearly not true. Thus, estimated half-lives for absorption and elimination in separate organs reflect not only the kinetic parameters of those organs, but also the entire pat-tern of cadmium circulation and recirculation in organs. For this reason, it is desirable to estimate all the kinetic parameters simultaneously.

The data set on cadmium in mice published by Shank et al. [14] was selected for analysis because of the large number of observed compart-ments (9), time points (5 for each of 3 intraperitoneal injections of

cadmium acetate), and presence of parallel studies with and without
zinc exposure. Shank fitted the 9-compartment "mammillary" model
shown in [14], with a central blood compartment and 7 peripheral
compartments. We tried to extend this treatment to the more complex
model for man suggested by Kjellstrom and Nordberg [17] which included
three blood compartments, and we also added peripheral compartments to
the kidney and liver. The separate pathway for fecal excretion from
the liver corresponds, roughly, to biliary excretion. Kjellstrom's
model is shown in [17], and ours in Fig. 7.

The SAAM-27 program was again convenient for analysis of repeated
doses and provided (at considerable expense) the reasonably convergent
solutions shown in Table 3. Some of the kinetic parameters clearly
depended on zinc exposure and some did not. The residual sum of
squares (error variance) of our model is roughly 1000 times smaller
than Shank's model, and some important parameters have reliable estimates that differ from Shank's estimates by a large factor. The
improvement in precision appears to justify the much more complex
model and its additional parameters.

We found reliable evidence for a peripheral liver compartment that
exchanged cadmium relatively slowly with a fast-moving liver compartment. Since Shank's data covered only 6 days, we could not reliably
estimate rate parameters $k(3,2)$, $k(2,3)$, or $k(6,3)$ for a third blood
compartment. While the arguments in favor of a long-lived kidney
compartment are very strong, we were not able to estimate the rates
$k(7,6)$ into or $k(6,7)$ out of the long-term compartment 7. There is
evidence to suggest time scales of 25 to 65 days, and 600 to 1400
days. We are tempted to attribute slow-exchanging compartments to
the presence of metal-binding proteins.

Statistically significant differences due to the zinc treatment
are marked in Table 3. Zinc appears to increase the rate of flow of
cadmium to slowly exchanging compartments in blood $k(2,1)$ and liver
$k(5,4)$, by at least a factor of two. Most other cadmium distribution
processes appear to be slowed by zinc exposure, particularly flows
from blood to liver, kidney, pancreas, and gastrointestinal tract.
The reverse flows are also slower, particularly liver, kidney, and
pancreas to blood. Fecal and urinary excretion rates appear nearly
unchanged.

An alternative approach to multicompartmental modeling and data
analysis for zinc is described by Foster et al. [19]. A separate
submodel is first fitted to blood serum and subsequently used as a
forcing function to the peripheral compartments. We believe this
approach should be used for cadmium as well.

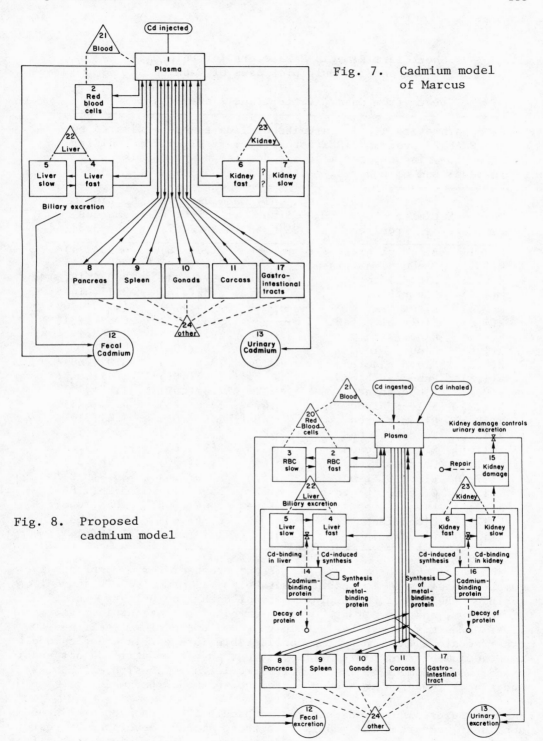

Fig. 7.   Cadmium model
of Marcus

Fig. 8.   Proposed
cadmium model

TABLE 3

Short-Term Kinetic Parameters for Male Mice
Exposed to Multiple Doses of Cadmium

(Data from Shank, Vetter, and Ziemer [14])

Rate parameters $k(i,j)$ in units of 1/days were estimated by
the SAAM 27 program. Statistically very significant differences for zinc exposed mice are denoted by *. SS is the
residual sum of squares.

| Parameter | Estimate From/to | Only Cadmium | | Zinc |
		Shank SS = 3688	Marcus SS = 2.67	Marcus SS = 3.38
k(2,1)	Blood plasma/cells	------	2.74(.78)	6.34(2.4)*
k(1,2)	Blood cells/plasma	------	24.9(.63)	26.0(.64)
k(4,1)	Blood/liver	950.4	397(8.31)	260.6(18.6)*
k(1,4)	Liver/blood	2.30	3.82(.14)	3.17(.14)*
k(5,4)	Liver fast/slow	------	5.34(1.0)	11.03(1.00)*
k(4,5)	Liver slow/fast	------	3.83(.94)	6.62(.75)*
k(6,1)	Blood/kidney	96.48	29.5(1.1)	22.67(1.34)*
k(1,6)	Kidney/blood	2.02	0.98(.02)	0.74(.02)*
k(8,1)	Blood/pancreas	43.2	13.5(.47)	8.92(.68)*
k(1,8)	Pancreas/blood	2.88	1.47(.05)	1.11(.04)*
k(9,1)	Blood/spleen	4.32	2.37(.09)	1.85(.14)
k(1,9)	Spleen/blood	5.47	5.18(.25)	4.57(.21)
k(10,1)	Blood/testes	3.60	1.62(.05)	1.41(.11)
k(1,10)	Testes/blood	3.02	2.42(.10)	2.95(.13)
k(11,1)	Blood/carcass	561.6	389(8.6)	396(29.2)
k(1,11)	Carcass/blood	6.05	7.03(.30)	7.78(.31)
k(17,1)	Blood/GI tract	345.6	99.0(1.6)	80.9(5.2)*
k(1,17)	GI tract/blood	8.64	5.94(.17)	5.26(.18)
k(12,4)	Liver/feces	------	.044(.006)	.063(.006)
k(12,1)	Blood/feces	1.04	6.74(.45)	7.00(.53)
k(13,1)	Blood/urine	0.14	1.18(.14)	1.18(.14)

The model sketched in Fig. 8 is our proposal for a comprehensive
compartmental model for cadmium metabolism in mammals. This model
includes the effect of cumulative renal damage on urinary excretion
of cadmium, and the effects of cadmium-binding proteins in kidney and
liver which may be synthesized in response to cadmium itself and to
other metals. There has been considerable interest in kinetic models
for cadmium-binding proteins [20,21] but as yet we still do not under-
stand the phenomena well enough for prediction of health effects.
Additional research is needed to define the model parameters.

A computer simulation model could handle the responses of linked
nonlinear compartmental models like those already developed by Foster
et al. for zinc, and that proposed in Fig. 8 for cadmium, in the face

of multiple sources of exposure to both cadmium and zinc. We would
then use the model to estimate, e.g., the length of time until the
cadmium concentration in the renal cortex first exceeds some value on
the order of L = 100 to 300 mg Cd/kg. wet weight, i.e., in Fig. 8,
$X(7,T) > L$ *(mass of cortex for that person). It is important to note
that the model structure and parameters cannot really be determined
experimentally for man, and that scale-up of such quantities from
other mammalian species requires a common structural model for all
analyses.

Lead

Lead is a toxic metal that damages the central nervous system.
Linear multicompartment models have been fitted to human data [22-25].
In such models the $X(i,t)$ are necessarily mixtures of exponential
functions of time. The long-term retention of lead may be better
described by a single power function rather than by an exponential
function, due to the retention of lead by bones and hard tissues
[26,27]. Power functions are also characteristic of the long-term
retention of other alkaline earth metals ("bone-seekers") in man and
other species [28,29]. Such models can be partially understood by
assuming the slow diffusion of lead out of the bone matrix. These
long-term parameters are needed to predict the total body burden of
potentially mobilizable lead. On the other hand, in highly variable
environments the short-term kinetic parameters play the major role in
the recirculation of lead among the organs and may be more important
for hazard prediction than are the long-term bone parameters. Both
short-term and long-term responses to changes in lead exposure have
been calculated in [22,23,25,27].

Two of the frustrating problems in developing a kinetic model for
lead are: (i) the lack of agreement on a common model structure:
(ii) the lack of a convenient mechanism for building power functions
rather than exponentials into a compartmental model structure like
equation (1). Two models are exhibited in Figs. 9-10. Fig. 9 shows
the 5-compartment model proposed by Batschelet et al. [23]. A
5-compartment model was used by Bernard [24] and a 3-compartment
model was used by Marcus [27]. It would have been preferable to use
a model at least as complex as that shown in Fig. 10, which includes
sensitive target compartments in brain and blood cells.

Only the Marcus model incorporated power-function kinetics. In
order to do this, we had to use a very different formulation, that of
the semi-Markov process. The motivation is the often-noted corres-
pondence between the differential equation for the occupancy probabilities of a Markov process and the differential equation (1) for the
compartmental system. In the Markov process formulation, each molecule of lead is assumed to move independently of each other molecule
from compartment to compartment according to a Markov chain with
transition probability matrix $P = (p(i,j))$, and to reside in compartment i for a random interval of time. The purely Markov model implies
that residence times are exponentially distribution with mean

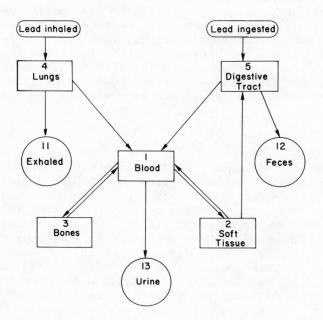

Fig. 9.   Lead model of
          Batschelet

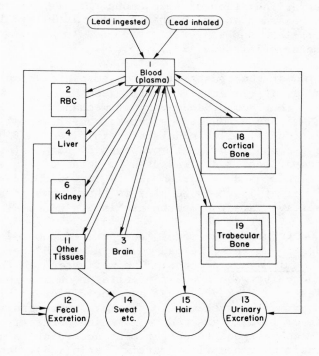

Fig. 10.   Proposed
           lead model

MRT(i) = -1/k(i,i). The transition probabilities p(i,j) =
-k(j,i)/k(i,i) are also calculated from the infinitesimal generator
of the process, the matrix K. Power functions are now obtained by
assuming residence time distributions with power-function tails, such
as the Pareto or skew-stable distributions. Unfortunately, the only
mathematically "neat" results for such systems involve matrices of
Laplace or Fourier transforms, but the systems are numerically tract-
able [29,31]. In Table 4 we present P and MRT values fitted to the
models in [23,24,27]. The differences in model parameters and
structures are not easy to interpret.

We see then that hazard criteria for lead could be expressed in
terms of exceedances of lead concentrations in blood or brain, e.g.,
X(1,t) > (blood volume)*L, where L = 40 to 80 ug/dl. The recirculation
of lead among other soft tissues and its long-term storage in bone and
hard tissues is also very important and needs to be included in the
model, since there appear to be relevant biological time scales comparable to fluctuations in lead exposure.

TABLE 4

Semi-Markov Parameters for Lead

Batschelet			Bernard			Marcus		
From (MRT,d)	To	Prob	From (MRT,d)	To	Prob	From (MRT,d)	To	Prob
Blood (27.7)	Tissue	0.308	Blood (1.7)	Kidney	0.233	Blood (30)	Tissue	0.308
	Bone	0.108		Liver	0.544		Bones	0.108
				Cort.	0.028			
				Trab.	0.051			
				Feces	0.072		Feces	0.292
	Urine	0.585		Urine	0.072		Urine	0.292
Tissue (35)	Blood	0.4	Liver (5.71)	Blood	1.0	Tissue (81)	Blood	0.625
	GI	0.4					Hair	0.375
	Hair	0.2	Kidney (228)	Blood	1.0			
Bone (28571)	Blood	1.0	Cort. (9479)	Blood	1.0	Bone (18000)*	Blood	1.0
			Trab. (2160)	Blood	1.0			
GI (0)	Blood	0.088						
	Feces	0.912						
Lungs (0)	Blood	0.347						
	Exhale	0.653						

*In the Marcus model, residence time is not exponential

Carcinogens and Mutagens

We can only point out a few of the applications of kinetic modeling to environmental carcinogens and mutagens. Repair of genetic damage before cell division and replication has been used by Neyman and Puri [32] in order to explain an observed dependence of the incidence of leukemia and reduction in mean life of experimental animals on radiation dose-rate rather than total "dose". This is somewhat analogous to the use of concentration C and dose D in the NO2 model proposed above, rather than total exposure C*T.

Neyman has also called attention to the effects of dose-rate (intermittent exposure to urethane) in the number of lung tumors in mice, in which a large single urethane exposure caused far more tumors than a large number of smaller exposures. A number of kinetic models have been advanced to explain these observations [33].

The importance of nonlinear kinetic models for carcinogens has been demonstrated by Gehring and Blau [34,35] for vinyl chloride. The use of a compartmental model like equation (1), but with linear terms $k(i,j) X(j,t)$ replaced by a nonlinear term

(10) $k(i,j) X(j,t)/(m(i,j) + X(j,t))$

for some compartments i,j and constants k,m, is physiologically realistic. This function produces nearly zeroth-order kinetics, i.e., saturation of the washout mechanism at high concentrations $X(j,t)$. The extrapolation of the percentage of angiosarcoma in rats from high experimental doses to low doses encountered in occupational exposure to vinyl chloride thus depends on a fairly precise knowledge of the metabolic transformation parameters, since the occurrence of angiosarcoma may depend on the presence of a vinyl chloride metabolite rather than on the concentration of the chemical itself. Thus, in highly variable environments, the saturability of these metabolic processes may be important. The extrapolation is sensitive to the dose-response model as well [36].

At Washington State University, a team of geneticists and statisticians is currently studying the use of barley pollen grains to detect the mutagenicity of chemicals such as sodium azide. We are finding that amount of chemical present at various stages of the cell division process (e.g., meiosis) may be of critical importance in determining the number of reverse mutations that occur [37]. That is, the dilution of the chemical and its biotransformation must be related to the biological time scale of the development of the pollen grains. Statistical models of the process and some methods for statistical analysis of pollen counts based on jackknife estimators will be described elsewhere.

Summary

The biological responses to pollutants may depend critically on the occasional high peaks in pollutant concentrations due to the variety of kinetic processes occuring with different time-scales. Pollutant criteria based only on long-term averages may thus be substantially in error in predicting the biological effects and potential hazards of time-varying exposures to the pollutants.

We recommend that, when the level of information is adequate to propose a realistic kinetic model, environmental standards should be formulated directly in terms of criteria for the predicted or esti-mated biological effect of exposure. This will require: (i) a generally accepted kinetic model (usually a compartmental model) whose parameters can be estimated for a variety of human types, especially the most vulnerable segments of the population; (ii) selection of a stochastic criterion for hazard, such as the time to exceedance of a threshold, or the average excess above the threshold, or the maximum concentration of the pollutant or one of its metabolites in some com-partment; (iii) the prediction of the hazard criterion using the compartmental model as a "filter" of the external pollutant concen-tration.

There is a fundamental question about the adequacy of a biological model for purposes of hazard prediction. One difficulty arises at the very beginning: Under many conditions, it may not be possible to identify even the structure of a linear compartmental model, much less estimate its parameters from a set of data. In general, we concur with Wagner [38]:

"(a) Most of the time we cannot determine which
model applies to one or more sets of data, but only which
class of model applies: (b) When linear pharmacokinetics
apply, it is usually not necessary to determine which model
applies: and (c) When nonlinear pharmacokinetics apply,
it is necessary to obtain a partial or complete model to
make accurate predictions."

There are also many unsolved problems in fitting nonlinear kinetic models with multivariate response data. More research is needed into nonlinear regression techniques such as robust estimation and the use of relatively model-free confidence regions for parameters, e.g., by jackknifing or "bootstrapping". Finally, the choice of acceptable stochastic hazard criteria is as much a matter of psychology, politics, and law as it is biology or mathematics; but we should be able to point out to the public which of these criteria are most reliable and statistically valid.

There does not appear to be any universally valid method for the "inverse" problem of relating the biological hazard criteria, in terms of stochastic exceedances of $X(t)$, to the acceptable patterns of

concentration C(t). But in an era in which microcomputers are becom-
ing very widely available, we ought to be able to assess the potential
hazardousness of a particular concentration process C(t), either
observed or predicted for hypothetical new sources of pollutants, by
the use of the mathematical models developed above.

REFERENCES

[1] R. F. COBURN, R. E. FORSTER, AND P. B. KANE, Consideration of the
    physiological variables that determine the blood carboxyhemoglobin
    concentration in man, J. Clinical Investigations 44, (1965),
    pp. 1899-1910.

[2] C. R. COLLIER, Oxygen affinity of human blood in presence of
    carbon monoxide, J. Applied Physiology 40, (1976), pp. 487-490.

[3] W. OTT AND D. MAGE, A computerized model for blood carboxyhemo-
    globin, J. Air Pollution Control Assoc. 28, (1978), pp. 911-916.

[4] A. H. MARCUS, Mathematical models for carboxyhemoglobin, Atmos.
    Environ. 14, (1980), pp. 841-844, and letters to appear in
    Vol. 15, (1981).

[5] W. OTT, Models of human exposure to air pollution, SIMS
    Technical Report 32, Department of Statistics, Stanford
    University, 1980.

[6] M. A. H. RUSSELL AND C. FEYERABEND, Cigarette smoking: dependence
    on high-nicotine boli, Drug Metabolism Reviews 8, (1978), pp.
    29-57.

[7] A. H. MARCUS AND S. CZAJKOWSKI, First passage times as environ-
    mental safety indicators: carboxyhemoglobin from cigarette
    smoke, Biometrics 35, (1979), pp. 539-548.

[8] A. H. MARCUS, Pharmacokinetic models for cigarette smoking and
    self-administration of drugs, in Proceedings of the Summer
    Computer Simulation Conference, Seattle, WA, (1980), pp. 677-681.

[9] J. R. SMITH AND S. A. LANDAW, Smokers' polycythemia, New Engl. J.
    Med. 298, (1978), pp. 6-10.

[10] D. E. GARDNER, D. L. COFFIN, M. A. PINIGIN, AND G. I. SIDORENKO,
     Role of time as a factor in toxicity of chemical compounds in
     intermittent and continuous exposures, Parts I-II, J. Toxicol.
     Environ. Health 3, (1977), pp. 811-828.

[11] D. E. GARDNER, F. J. MILLER, E. J. BLOOMER, AND D. L. COFFIN,
     Influence of exposure mode on the toxicity of NO2, Environ.
     Health Perspective 30, (1979), pp. 23-29.

[12] R. I. LARSEN, D. E. GARDNER, AND D. L. COFFIN, An air quality
     data analysis system for interrelating affects, standards, and
     needed source reductions: Part 5. NO2 mortality in mice,
     J. Air Pollut. Control Assoc. 29, (1979), pp. 133-137.

[13] G. I. SIDORENKO AND M. A. PINIGIN, Predicting toxicometric para-
     meters on the basis of studying the concentration-time dependence,
     Environ. Health Perspectives 30, (1979), pp. 19-21.

[14] K. E. SHANK, R. S. VETTER, AND P. L. ZIEMER, A mathematical model
     of cadmium transport in a biological system, Environ. Res. 12,
     (1977), pp. 209-214.

[15] A. H. MARCUS, Kinetic models for cadmium, I: Effects of zinc on
     cadmium retention in male mice, submitted for publication (1981).

[16] R. G. THOMAS, J. S. WILSON, AND J. E. LONDON, Multispecies
     retention parameters for cadmium, Environ. Res. 23, (1980),
     pp. 191-207.

[17] T. KJELLSTROM AND G. NORDBERG, A kinetic model of cadmium
     metabolism in the human being, Environ. Res. 16, (1978), pp.
     248-269.

[18] C. C. TRAVIS AND A. G. HADDOCK, Interpretation of the observed
     age-dependency of cadmium body burdens in man, Environ. Res. 22,
     (1980), pp. 46-60.

[19] D. M. FOSTER, R. L. AAMODT, R. I. HENKIN, AND M. BERMAN, Zinc
     metabolism in humans: A kinetic model, Amer. J. Physiol. 237,
     (1979), pp. R340-R349.

[20] F. N. KOTSONIS AND C. D. KLASSEN, The relationship of metal-
     lothionein to the toxicity of cadmium after prolonged oral
     administration to rats, Toxicol. Appld. Pharmacol. 46, (1978),
     pp. 39-54.

[21] R. J. COUSINS, Metallothionein synthesis and degradation:
     Relation to cadmium metabolism, Environ. Health Perspectives 28,
     (1979), pp. 131-136.

[22] M. R. RABINOWITZ, G. W. WETHERILL, AND J. D. KOPPLE, Kinetic
     analysis of lead metabolism in healthy humans, J. Clinical
     Investigations 58, (1976), pp. 270-286.

[23] E. BATSCHELET, L. BRAND, AND A. STEINER, On the kinetics of
     lead in the human body, J. Math. Biol. 8, (1979), pp. 15-23.

[24] S. R. BERNARD, Dosimetric data and metabolic model for lead,
     Health Physics 32, (1977), pp. 44-46.

[25] C. N. CAWLEY, W. G. CALE, AND N. T. CHEHROUDI, Simulating metabolic response of a young adult male to changing levels of atmospheric lead, Proc. Summer Computer Simulation Conference, (1979), Houston Texas.

[26] J. B. HURSH, Retention of 210-Pb in beagle dogs, Health Physics 25, (1973), pp. 29-35.

[27] A. H. MARCUS, The body burden of lead, Environ. Res. 19, (1979), pp. 79-90.

[28] J. H. MARSHALL ET AL., Alkaline earth metabolism in adult man, Health Physics 24, (1972), pp. 124-221.

[29] A. H. MARCUS, Alkaline earth metabolism: The ICRP model reformulated as a semi-Markov model, Health Physics 38, (1980), pp. 825-832.

[30] G. E. HARRISON, Whole body retention of the alkaline earths in adult man, Health Physics 40, (1981), pp. 95-99.

[31] A. H. MARCUS AND A. BECKER, Power laws in compartmental analysis, Part II, Math. Biosci. 34, (1977), pp. 27-45.

[32] J. NEYMAN AND P. S. PURI, A structural model of radiation effects in living cells, Proc. Natl. Acad. Sci. 73, (1976), pp. 3360-3363.

[33] J. NEYMAN AND E. L. SCOTT, Statistical aspects of the problem of carcinogenesis, Proc. Sixth Berkeley Symp. Math. Stat. and Prob., Vol. IV, (1967), pp. 707-720, University of California, Berkeley Press, Berkeley, CA.

[34] P. J. GEHRING AND G. E. BLAU, Mechanisms of carcinogenesis: Dose response, J. Environ. Pathol. Toxicol. 1, (1977), pp. 163-179.

[35] P. J. GEHRING, P. G. WATANABE, AND C. N. PARK, Resolution of dose-response toxicity data for chemicals requiring metabolic activation, Toxicol. Appld. Pharmacol. 44, (1978), pp. 581-591.

[36] M. W. ANDERSON, D. G. HOEL, AND N. L. KAPLAN, A general scheme for the incorporation of pharmacokinetics in low-dose risk estimation for chemical carcinogenesis: Example-Vinyl chloride. Toxicol. Appld. Pharmacol. 55, (1980), pp. 154-161.

[37] A. L. HODGDON, A. H. MARCUS, P. ARENAZ, J. L. ROSICHAN, T. P. BOGYO, AND R. A. NILAN, The ontogeny of the barley plant as related to mutation expression and detection of pollen mutations, Environ. Health Perspectives 37, (1981), pp. 5-7.

[38] J. G. WAGNER, Do you need a pharmacokinetic model and if so, which one?, J. Pharmacokin. Biopharm. 3, (1975), pp. 457-478.

RISK ASSESSMENTS,
ENVIRONMENTAL MEASUREMENTS

Some Principles
of Collective Decision-Making:
Risk-Benefit Analysis
in Health and Environmental Issues

J. C. Bailar III*

Abstract. The essential elements for making decisions are data, values (individual and/or collective), rules, and machinery. "Data" include all of the information considered in coming to a decision. "Values," including some kind of scaling, relate to individual preferences, even when they are used for collective decisions. "Rules" provide a framework for the integration of data with values; examples include utilitarianism, solipsism, and "you divide, I choose." "Machinery" needed to implement the rules may range from the simple aggregation of individual acts (e.g., the shift from animal to mechanical transport) to highly structured processes (e.g., OSHA'S recent proposal to categorize and regulate carcinogens by risk classes).

In the process of decision-making, we must operate with what we think we know at the time we make the decision. Thus the data may be incomplete, misunderstood, or simply wrong. The data may be derived from scientific investigation, from personal experience, from introspection, or even from divine revelation.

The next essential element is values, including some kind of ranking or scaling of the possible outcomes of various decisions. Values are defined by, and in terms of, individuals. What are sometimes called collective or social values are either the sum of individually held values or a set of rules, mechanisms, or procedures to make collective decisions. While social values in this sense are nearly indispensible in the formulation of collective decisions, it would be a serious error to assume that they have any moral force or validity of their own, and in complex matters it is virtually certain that any possible set of social values will be in sharp conflict with the personal values of some members of that society.

*U.S. Environmental Protection Agency, and Harvard School of Public Health

Supported in part by a grant from the Alfred P. Sloan Foundation.

147

There are many possible sets of rules for selecting one decision rather than another, whether the decision is individual or collective. Some have been reduced to a few expressive words:

The greatest good for the greatest number.
Women and children first.
Look out for Number One.
Play it safe.
You break, I take.
One person, one vote.
Big brother knows best.

Different rules will quite commonly lead to different decisions, even when values are the same.

Decision machinery, like decisions themselves, may be individual or collective, and the latter may range from the simple aggregation of individual acts to highly structured mechanisms. An example of the former - collective decision by individual acts - was the switch from animal to mechanical transport, despite the costs and risks of millions of self-propelled internal combustion engines. The other extreme, a highly structured mechanism for a set of collective decisons, is exemplified by the recent scheme of OSHA to categorize potential carcinogens by risk classes based on the nature of the experimental data, volume of use, probability of exposure, and other stystematically considered features of the substance.

1. Introduction. This paper surveys some aspects of Risk-Benefit Analysis (RBA) as it may be applied to decisions that involve human welfare, health and survival. The survey is not intended to be complete, nor is there much that an expert would regard as new. The review is rather intended to be an introduction to the basic concepts of RBA, problems in its application, and ways around some of those problems. Along the way I will raise some of the larger issues of the ways we cope with hazard and the ways we resolve controversy. I will generally assume that risk analysis (the task of assessing what would happen if certain exposures occur) has been completed, but that we must still determine the likelihood that exposure will occur under various sets of conditions, and that we must then make some policy decisions in light of that information.

From one point of view, RBA is simply a means of organizing information and making decisions. As such, it must compete with other principles for making decisions such as cost effectiveness (attaining maximum return for a fixed, rather than variable, expenditure of resources), lowest attainable risk, or simply muddling through.

What is RBA? It is a direct extension of cost-benefit analysis, or CBA. A standard textbook (1) on CBA begins with the sentence:

"The general question that a cost-benefit analysis sets out to answer is whether a number of investment prospects, A, B, C, etc. should be undertaken and, if investment funds are limited, which one, two, or more among these specific projects that would otherwise qualify for admission, should be selected."

CBA is based on the fundamental principle that one can assess both the probability and, on a single scale, the value (positive or negative) of all effects that might flow from one or another of the actions analyzed. In classical CBA, the single scale of valuation is a monetary scale. While CBA may be very complex in practice, its basic premises are simple.

It is a long way from this definition of classical CBA to such extensions as an analysis of the effects of motorcycle helmet laws (2), the biologic principles of energy conservation by honey bees (3), or the impact of automobile emmission control in Los Angeles on health in neighboring communities (4). Such extensions are commonly grouped together as RBA.

Some of the conceptual extensions in RBA are:

° Values may be expressed in units other than monetary ones (e.g., "utilities").

° New problems of interpersonal scaling arise.

° There are questions of equity (distribution of good and bad effects).

° Consent of affected persons becomes an issue.

° Mechanisms for making and implementing decisions differ.

There will be two underlying themes to my remarks. First is the notion that because of these extensions RBA is a tool of analysis, not a rule for decison-making. Second is the notion that RBA applied to medical and environmental issues is not fundamentally a matter of medicine, statistics, science, or even economics. RBA uses statistical and scientific data and concepts, but they are embedded in a complex matrix of politics, philosophy, ethics, individual and collective values, good sense, and even religion. Unfortunately, in the real world, real problems afflict real people and demand real responses now; responses that may be constrained by each of the items I have mentioned, responses that must often be based on grossly inadequate data, and responses that may be vigorously opposed by one or another powerful segment of society.

Many of these issues have been examined in one or more of five recent books that reflect the views of, respectively, an economist (5), a government regulator (6), a risk assessor (7), a physical scientist (8), and a committee (9). I recommend all five books for serious readers, but I have felt especially enriched by reading Lowrance's monograph (8). It is the account by a perceptive and well-informed observer of his own struggles to come to grips with some of the difficult aspects of risky societal decisions.

2. Elements For A Decision Process. There are four essential elements for making decisions: data, values, rules, and machinery. I use these terms as follows. "Data" include all of the information considered in coming to a decision. "Values", including some kind of scaling, are defined by and in terms of individuals, even when they are used for collective decisions. "Rules" provide a framework for the integration of data with values; one example is utilitarianism. "Machinery" needed to implement the rules may range from the simple aggregation of individual acts to highly structured processes. Each of these elements needs some discussion.

In the process of decision-making, we must operate with what we think we know at the time we make the decision. Thus, data may be incomplete, misunderstood, or simply wrong. They may be derived from scientific investigation, from personal experience, from introspection, or even from divine revelation. The important thing is what we think we know, however we may come to know it. The most relevant data in decision-making are likely to relate some of the possible decisions to their consequences, including assessment of the relative likelihoods that one set of consequences will occur rather than another. Data may be quantitative only in the roughest sense and they may omit outcomes that are common but trivial, serious but rare, not (yet) recognized as consequences, or hard to evaluate.

The quality, extent, and relevance of data are often the most important single issue in discussions on the control of risks. The consequence of the recent decision by EPA (10) to curtail most uses of the herbicide 2,4,5-T provides a good example of the conflicts that arise when limited and inadequate data suggest but do not prove a large risk. The EPA decision was triggered by one limited and very small study (in Alsea, Oregon) of a high degree of relevance to humans (frequency of miscarriages), though there was already substantial information from laboratory studies showing a risk of teratogenesis and carcinogenesis. An estimated four million people would have been exposed had spraying of the compound been allowed to continue as usual. The Dow Chemical Company challenged the suspension (11) on the grounds that "the bulk of scientific data gathered to date over 3 decades of use demonstrate that there has never been a single documented incident of human injury resulting from normal agricultural use of these products." There are now widespread efforts to expand the base of data on the risks of 2,4,5-T as various challenges and counter-challenges make their way through regulatory and legal channels.

The next essential elements are values and rules including some kind of ranking or scaling of "value" of the possible outcomes of various decisions. My use of the word "values" specifically excludes any moral connotation. I am convinced that values must be defined by, and in terms of, individuals, although persons with other orientations (e.g., Marxists) might disagree. It may be helpful to recall the distinction between values and ethics; that is, between what is (the present state of our preferences) and what ought to be (moral principles in some higher system), or between that which is preferred and that which is preferable (12).

Consideration of values in the present context inevitably leads to consideration of ethics in another way, because of the effects of the latter in shaping our values (and the ways we express them). While values are individual, ethics are generally collective.

While there are many ways to view a system of ethics, it is perhaps best for the purpose here to define ethics as a set of rules for translating values into actions; special importance is attached to the rules (the ethics) we use when values collide.

There are many possible sets of rules for selecting one decision rather than another, whether the decision is individual or collective. Some have been reduced to a few expressive words:

> The greatest good for the greatest number.
> Women and children first.
> Look out for Number One.
> Don't make anyone worse off (Pareto) principle of
>   economics).
> Play it safe.
> You divide, I choose.
> One person, one vote.
> Big brother knows best.
> Primum non nocere.

The last means "Above all, do no harm" - often claimed to be the best guide in problems of medical practice, although few of us would want our own physicians to follow this principle too closely. "Above all, do some good" might be an improvement (14).

The force of such pungent maxims may be great, although each is ambiguous. (Does "Play it safe" tell us to aggregate individual utilities, as per Arrow's social welfare criterion, or to aggregate over uncertainty? Does "Primum non nocere" refer to outcomes across persons or across states of nature? Different rules will quite commonly lead to different decisions, even when values are the same. Thus, a decision rule that emphasizes avoidance of clear and immediate bad outcomes (miscarriage), no matter how rare those outcomes may be, might lead to a ban on 2,4,5-T regardless of the level of benefits to others, while a decision rule that considers more diffuse bad outcomes (reduced grain production) or a rule that acts on the sum of all individual costs and benefits ("the greatest good for the greatest number") might not.

What are sometimes called collective or social values are either
the sum of individually held values or a set of rules, mechanisms, or
procedures to make collective decisions (which are in fact an
expression of ethics, not values). While social values in this
latter sense are nearly indispensible in the formulation of
collective decisions, it would be a serious error to assume that they
have any moral force or validity of their own, and in complex matters
it is virtually certain that any possible set of social values will
be in sharp conflict with the personal values of some members of that
society.

The proposition that science is value-free is at least arguable.
For example, Adams (13) has argued that value concepts are an
essential part of the science of ecology, not just a means for
assessing whether ecology is really helping us to obtain our goals.

Again, it seems that what matters in decision-making is what the
members of a society, or the persons making decisions on behalf of
the society, think are the appropriate ways to assess, integrate, and
use our personal values and ethics, though these may be incomplete,
inconsistent, poorly understood, poorly communicated, or in striking
conflict with other values held at the time. Thus, EPA's action in
the 2,4,5-T matter was something we can like or dislike (a value
judgment), or something right or wrong (an ethical judgment), only as
the action is seen in some context of values and ethics. To some
pregnant women in Oregon it seemed right; to some farmers facing
serious crop losses it seemed wrong; pediatricians, stockholders of
Dow, and others might also have strong and conflicting opinions,
while much of the public might be indifferent because it does not
feel that its (individual) values have been touched.

Decision machinery, like decisions themselves, may be individual
or collective, and the latter may range from the simple aggregation
of individual acts to highly structured mechanisms. An example of
the former - collective decision by individual acts - was the switch
from animal to mechanical transport, despite the costs and risks of
millions of self-propelled internal combustion engines. The other
extreme, a highly structured mechanism for a set of collective
decisions, is exemplified by the recent scheme of OSHA to categorize
potential carcinogens into risk classes based on the nature of the
experimental data, volume of use, probability of exposure, and other
systematically considered features of the substance (14).

Many objections to the use of RBA have been raised. The following
list is based on a list originally developed by Pope (15); I present
these points as reflecting the opinions of some thoughtful observers
although I do not agree that each of them is necessarily a serious
weakness:

1. RBA requires values (utilities) for noneconomic factors that
    have values that are inherently indeterminate.

2. RBA requires estimates of the probabilities of uncertain consequences, but reasonably accurate estimates are rarely available.

3. Results of RBA may be manipulated by one side or another when there is an imbalance among sides in access to information or in supporting resources.

4. There are serious inequities in the common practice of devaluing future outcomes that will affect us or our contemporaries.

5. We do not have the knowledge, even less the right, to assign values to outcomes (good or bad) that will affect future generations.

6. It is immoral to put a price tag on the life, health, or welfare of other persons.

7. RBA itself may involve substantial costs and benefits (e.g., delay).

8. RBA is used as a surrogate for, or even to disguise, arguments over deeper questions of power and ideology.

While I largely agree with Pope about each of the abuses he has noted, and have myself embellished some and added others, I believe that those abuses can be contained without abandoning other useful aspects of RBA. I suspect that Pope's strictures, or similar points, would apply to any other broad approach to decision-making. There is the further point that I have been able to find remarkably little firm data for thoughtful analysis to support any of these contentions, though they seem inherently reasonable.

Pope concluded (15):
"RBA is not an objective tool. It does not produce values for the various risks and benefits which are genuinely comparable. It cannot tell us whether or not a given toxic substance generates more in the way of benefits than it imposes in risks. And it has built into it systematic biases in favor of those who benefit and against those who incur the risk from toxic materials."

The reason Pope and I differ is that his condemnation applies principally to RBA as a decision tool, whereas I believe it is properly seen, and can be usefully employed, as an analytic tool.

I cannot in fact accept any of these objections in isolation from consideration of alternatives to RBA, and I have not yet seen any balanced analysis that objectively compares RBA with other analytic (or decision-making) strategies.

Despite many recognized problems, appropriate use of RBA can provide useful increases in our understanding of complex problems. Some of its uses are to:

°   direct attention to gaps in knowledge

°   indicate priorities for research, and stimulate the accumulation of needed data and analysis

°   contribute to public understanding of relevant issues and problems

°   provide an initial screen of both problems and solutions for the guidance of decision-makers.

The Committee on the Biological Effects of Radiation (9) has provided some discussion of these points.

Although RBA is a valuable analytic tool for use in the decision-making process, it has been misused, and this misuse is often cited by critics as a deficiency of RBA. RBA has been misused in two ways: it has been carried out with a value scale - money - that has not been used so as to express preferences accurately, and there has been no agreement on (often no consideration of) the decision strategy. Specifically, a Bayes strategy should not be used unless it has been explicitly justified. RBA can accommodate a Minimax or other strategy just as well, as the choice of strategy is a matter of politics and philosphy, not of science or logic. The decision strategy is not dictated by RBA; it is one of the variable inputs, although it has generally been chosen to maximize the values of the choosers. The critics of RBA should not claim that the instrument is faulty. RBA is simply a tool to organize, reveal and perhaps explain the data and the preference relations that must underlie any decision. If we do not like the results, we should criticize the expressed preferences (or the users), not the tool.

Likewise, the value-scaling problem is not a flaw in RBA. The flaw, if there is one, is rather in the ambiguity and obfuscation with which society approaches problems that mix various benefits and costs, such as economic status and human life. It does no good to say that life is priceless - that it must be valued above everything else. That is nonsense, because our society simply does not have the resources to insure each of us an absolute maximum in life span, and we would quite possibly not want to live in a society that did. We do, indeed, find maximum protection of human life to be less than imperative. RBA forces us to recognize that fact.

3. CONCLUSIONS. It is evident that there are far more questions about risk control and decision-making than there are answers, and it is virtually certain that we will have to contend with these matters more and more in the future. We as statisticians should start coming to grips with them now.

One last comment. I have said some things that are sharply critical of RBA, and other things that are sharply critical of the critics. There is virtue on both sides, and I hope that this will be recognized in further discussion.

REFERENCES

(1) E. J. Mishan, Economics for Social Decision: Elements of Cost-Benefit Analysis, Praeger, New York, 1973.

(2) A. Muller, Evaluation of the costs and benefits of motorcycle helmet laws. Am. J. Public Health 70, (1980), pp. 586-592.

(3) W. M. Schaffer, et al. Competition foraging energetics and the cost of sociality in three species of bees, Ecology 60,(1979), pp. 976-987.

(4) N. deNevers, Human Health Effects and Air Pollution Control Philosophies, Lung 156,(1979), pp. 95-107.

(5) E. J. Mishan, Cost-Benefit Analysis, New Expanded Edition, Praeger, New York, 1976.

(6) R. W. Kates, Risk Assessment of Environmental Hazard, J. Wiley and Sons, Inc., New York, 1978.

(7) W. D. Rowe, An Anatomy of Risk, J. Wiley and Sons, Inc., New York, 1977.

(8) W. W. Lowrance, Of Acceptable Risk: Science and the Determination of Safety, W. Kaufman, Inc., Los Altos, CA 1976.

(9) BEIR Committee, Consideration of Health Benefit-Cost Analysis for Activities Involving Ionizing Radiation Exposure and Alternatives, National Academy of Sciences, Washington, DC, 1977.

(10) News and Comments. EPA halts most use of herbicide 2,4,5-T, Science 203, (1979), pp. 1091.

(11) The Dow Chemical Company's comments on the Administrators Emergency Suspension Orders. In re: Emergency suspension order for 2,4,5-T, and Silrex. FIFRA Docket numbers 409 and 410. 26 March 1979.

(12) D. Hume, Treatise of Human Nature (1739). L. A. Selby-Bigge, ed. Oxford University Press, Oxford, 1941.

(13) E. M. Adams, <u>Ecology and value theory</u>, Southern J. Philosophy 10,
      (1972), pp. 3-6.

(14) C. P. Stewart and A. Stolman, eds. <u>Toxicology: Mechanisms and
      Analytical Methods</u>. Academic Press, Vol. 112.

(15) C. Pope, <u>Problems in the toxic substance area</u>, In Toxic Substances:
      Decisions and Values, Part I, Technical Information Project,
      Washington, DC, 1979.

Much Ado About Next to Nothing,
Or What to do with Measurements
Below the Detection Limit

R. C. Rhodes*

Abstract. When the true value of a measurable characteristic approaches zero, the imprecision of the measurements approaches that for the noise distribution of the measurement process at a zero level. There exists a risk that a given measurement value reflects the presence of the characteristic when in fact none exists. To avoid this risk, certain "detection" limits are defined such that measurement values below the "detection" limit are given special treatment with respect to reporting and interpreting the results.

The non-reporting or reporting of such data in some arbitrary way may create some problems in data handling, summarization, and analysis. Also, biased statistical estimates of population parameters are obtained from measurements of samples.

The determination of which noise distribution to use in arriving at detection limits, the procedure to be used in generating data for the noise distribution, the particular computational procedure to use in computing the limits, and the way in which measurement values below the detection limit should be reported depend upon (1) the objective of obtaining the sample measurements, (2) previous knowledge and experience of the user in working with similar data, (3) the assumptions which the user wants to make concerning the origin of the samples, and (4) the specific risks the user desires to take.

Continued progress in science involves the capability of measuring smaller and smaller quantities, generally employing more sophisticated and costly measurement methods. Measurement data from these methods should be used to the fullest extent of the information contained therein.

1. Introduction. With many measurements the results are far removed from zero and have considerable precision compared to the magnitude of the chemical or physical quantity being measured. In such cases, for all practical considerations, the imprecision or inherent variability of the measurement method is often ignored, and the reported values are considered as the "true" values of the items or samples of the population being measured. Each item or sample of the population

---

*U.S. Environmental Protection Agency, Environmental Monitoring Systems Laboratory, Research Triangle Park, NC 27711

has some _true_ value, which would be approached if larger and larger numbers   of measurements were to be made of the same item. The variability of these replicate individual measurements of the same sample
would represent the precision (or imprecision) of the measurement
system at that particular level.

However, in other measurement situations the chemical or physical
quantity or characteristic being measured is very small, such that the
imprecision of the measurement cannot be ignored. In fact, as the true
value of the quantity being measured approaches zero, the only distribution which exists is that for the imprecision, the standard deviation
for which could be represented by s_o. Various techniques are used to
estimate s_o depending upon the scope of the measurement process for
which "repeatability" or "noise" is defined.

2. _Limit of Detection_. It is common practice to use some multiple
of s_o, defined as the detection limit, LD, to indicate the value below
which the measurement result _may_ be due solely to the imprecision of
the method. An extensive treatment has been given by Currie concerning
various definitions of limit values, which are functions of inherent
variability components of the measurement process [1].

The question which arises in practice with the measurement of items
or samples which may or may not have some actual true level of the
quantity being measured, is what to do with measurement data which are
less than the detection limit. The mere fact that a value is below
the detection limit does not _per se_ indicate that a true zero quantity
exists.

All of the above considerations are concerned with the risk of
reporting or labeling a _single_ routine measurement as a real value
when in fact the true value of the item or sample may be zero.

3. _Reporting of Data_. A number of alternative procedures are used
in the reporting of data from the analytical laboratory to the data
analyst. Several procedures for the handling of data below the LD are
commonly used, for example:

   (1) Do not report values below LD.

   (2)   Report all values below LD as zero.

   (3)   Report all values below LD as some positive quantity less
than LD, e.g., 1/2 LD.

   (4)   Report all values below LD as "below LD."

4. _Use of Data_. Problems are created for the statistical analysis
of data sets which originally contained measurement values below LD
and which have been altered or not reported.

Data Summarization. The summarization or reduction of such reported measurement data by the calculation of ranges, averages, and standard deviations will obviously give differing results, depending upon the prior data manipulations. Obviously, if one wants to estimate the measurement distribution, a procedure which is logically correct is to use the original data before it has been altered.

Summarizing the data after alteration may produce biased estimates of the distributional parameters. The extent of such biases will depend upon the relative variances of the distributions of the true values and that of the imprecision, and the location of the mean of the distribution of true values.

Other complications and unnatural conditions result when simple histograms, cumulative percentage plots, or tabulations of percentiles are prepared. Such graphical or tabular representations reflect the censored and/or disjoint distributions resulting from the altered data.

Data Analysis. Further, complications are created for the person desiring to perform statistical analysis of such data sets. The results of standard statistical tests, regression analyses, analyses of variance, multivariate analyses--in fact, most any standard statistical analyses using altered data may be distorted or biased. Moreover, unless missing values (values which have been deleted) are somehow estimated to make the data sets complete, many analyses would be impossible or very complicated. It seems unrealistic for a statistician in order to properly analyze a set of data, to resort to some estimation procedure to fill in missing values which were not missing in the first place.

Practical Problems. In addition to the above points, there are some very practical reasons why values below the LD should not be altered or eliminated prior to data analysis.

(1) The alteration or elimination is an additional operation which must be performed and which introduces chances for error. Manual review of large sets of data to identify those values below the LD to make the stipulated substitution or deletion requires additional effort and can introduce errors.

(2) How does one compare or combine different sets of data from the same measurement process but which have been obtained at different times having different LD values?

(3) As the LD is usually defined as ks_o where k is the appropriate multiple corresponding to some specified risk, how does one compare or combine different sets of data (even having the same s_o) if different k values (i.e., different risks) are used?

(4) If duplicate or replicate analyses are made on the same sample, and some of the measurements are below the LD and some above,

does one report only the values above the LD? What is the best estimate of the mean for the sample?

   5. Statistical Considerations.

        Averaging of the Noise. In some cases, it should be appropriate
to consider the effects of averaging the noise both in the development
of the detection limit and in the analysis of data. If the limit of
detection, LD, is defined as ks_o when applied to individual measurements, the LD when applied to averages of n independent measurements
should be $ks_o/\sqrt{n}$. Theoretically, the LD value can be reduced to near
zero by replicating the analyses of each sample a large number of times.
Dattner has suggested the use of a "minimum detectable mean" to define
the LD when consideration is being given to the mean of observed
measurements [2].

        Aggregates of Data. In arriving at the detection limit consi-
deration is usually given to the risks which apply to a single routine
measurement. Seldom, if ever, is a single measurement used in isolation to itself. Ultimate decisions and courses of action are usually
made on the basis of groups or aggregates of data. The meaningfulness
of a given datum should be considered in relation to the total of all
the data available, the particular objective of the data analyst, and
the assumptions the data analyst is willing to make.

   For example, if the data are to be used as a control check of a
process which is intended to be, and historically has been, controlled
at zero, it could be assumed that the true level of zero is being
attained or maintained as long as the results fall within the noise
band in the expected random pattern. Thus, if most or all the individual values fall below the LD, then it might well be concluded that
the true level for all the individual values is near zero.

   On the other hand, if experience has indicated and conditions of
sampling are such as to expect the presence of some small quantity of
the characteristic being measured, and many of the measurements are in
fact above the detection limit, then all of the results, including
those below the detection limits should be considered.

        Conservatism. It has been proposed by some that the reason for
conservatism in the internal reporting of data below the detection
limit is that (1) the accuracy and precision of results are extremely
poor and should not be considered as numerically meaningful or reproducible, and (2) the numerical results may be difficult or impossible
to confirm by a different method. Although it is true that all very
low results should be interpreted with respect to the detection limit
and the available information on accuracy and precision, these considerations do not necessarily mean that the results are not meaningful
or reproducible. The measurements must be reproducible--otherwise
there has been no basis for arriving at the detection limit in the

first place. Further, the fact that the results may be difficult or
impossible to confirm by a different method does not per se mean that
the results are not meaningful. There may well be biases or differences
in precision between methods. However, the purpose or objective of a
study may be to determine differential effects or simply to make comparisons in which case one is concerned only with the stability of the
method used for the particular study, and the internal consistency of
the data set being analyzed for a specific objective.

   If it is necessary or desirable to consider, in using or interpreting
a given set of data obtained from a given measurement system, the variation or biases between laboratories or between methods, then information
concerning such variation or biases should be obtained by or made available to the analyst of the data in addition to information on the detection limit. Such information should be used if between-laboratory or
between-method comparisons or considerations are necessary or pertinent
to the objective of the study.

   If the analyst wants to consider or interpret data in light of
between-laboratory or between-method variability it should be done
using estimates of the between-laboratory or between-method variability,
not information on the detection limit.

   6. Other Considerations. There are obvious risks of misusing
measurements in the noise band without knowledge or proper consideration
of the detection limit and other inherent variabilities of the measurement process. Different rules may be needed for the reporting of
measurements to the local data analyst and the reporting of measurements
to an unknown potential user far removed from the measurement process.

   7. Summary. It is the responsibility of the data analyst to determine how measurement values should be treated in light of knowledge of
inherent variations of the measurement process and the particular
objective in using the data. The particular treatment and interpretation of the data will also depend upon previous experience with results
from samples obtained under similar conditions and circumstances and
with the assumptions which the analyst may wish to make.

   As science continues its progress, the measurements of smaller and
smaller quantities are capable of being made and the effects of smaller
and smaller chemical and physical quantities are being estimated.
Generally, the analytical methods involved in the measurement or detection of these smaller and smaller quantities become more and more
sophisticated and costly. Consequently, the measurement data from these
methods should be used to the fullest extent of the information contained therein.

REFERENCES

[1] L. A. Currie, Limits for qualitative detection and quantitative
     determination, Analytical Chemistry. 40:3, (1968), pp. 586-593.

[2]   S. L. Dattner, <u>Defining minimum detection limits by use of the</u>
      <u>minimum detectable mean</u>, 73rd Annual Meeting, Air Pollution Control
      Association, June 1980.

                            BIBLIOGRAPHY

 1.   B. Altshuler and B. Pasternak, <u>Statistical measures of the lower</u>
      <u>limit of detection of a radioactivity counter</u>, Health Physics,
      (1963), p. 293.

 2.   American Chemical Society, <u>Guidelines for acquisition and data</u>
      <u>quality evaluation in environmental chemistry</u>, Analytical
      Chemistry, 52:14, (1980), pp. 2242–2249.

 3.   R.V. Cheeseman and A.L. Wilson, <u>Manual on analytical quality</u>
      <u>control for the water industry</u>, Water Research Centre, Technical
      Report TR 66, Medmenham, Marlow, Buckinghamshire, England, (1978).

 4.   Environmental Protection Agency, <u>Definition and procedure for the</u>
      <u>determination of the method detection limit</u>, Revision 11.1,
      Environmental Monitoring and Support Laboratory, Cincinnati, Ohio,
      January 1981.

 5.   A. Hubaux and G. Vos, <u>Decision and detection limits for linear</u>
      <u>calibration curves</u>, Analytical Chemistry, 42:8, (1970), pp. 849–
      855.

 6.   J.D. Ingle, Jr., <u>Sensitivity and limit of detection in quantita-</u>
      <u>tive spectrophotometric methods</u>, J. of Chem. Education, 61:2,
      (1974), pp. 100–105.

 7.   H. Kaiser, <u>Quantitation in elemental analysis, Part II</u>, Analytical
      Chemistry, 42-4, (1970), pp. 53A–58A.

 8.   E.J. Kushner, <u>On determining the statistical parameters for</u>
      <u>pollution concentration from a truncated data set</u>, Atmospheric
      Environment, 10, pp. 975–979.

 9.   F.J. Linning and J. Mandel, <u>Which measure of precision? The</u>
      <u>evaluation of the precision of analytical methods involving</u>
      <u>linear calibration curves</u>, Analytical Chemistry, 36:13, (1964),
      pp. 25A–32A.

10.   G.H. Morrison, <u>Trace analysis, physical methods</u>, Interscience
      Publishers, (1965), pp. 2-3.

11.   W.J. Owen and T.A. DeRouen, <u>Estimation of the mean for lognormal</u>
      <u>data containing zeroes and left-censored values, with applications</u>
      <u>to the measurement of worker exposure to air contaminants</u>,
      Biometrics 36, (1980), pp. 707–719.

HEALTH EFFECTS

Ambient Air Pollution—
Hazardous to Our Lungs?

Alice S. Whittemore*

Abstract. This paper presents a brief review of epidemiologic
evidence for the role of ambient air pollution in respiratory disease.
It is argued that existing epidemiologic data do not provide an adequate basis for setting air quality standards. This is due to inadequate control for confounding variables, and to lack of statistical
power. The subject is divided into four areas according to type of
potential respiratory damage: chronic and acute mortality, and
chronic and acute morbidity. The paper discusses difficulties,
advantages and possible improvements in design and analysis of studies
in each of these areas. Particular emphasis is given to statistical
issues in need of further work. Recommendations for future research
are outlined.

1. Introduction. The task of evaluating the respiratory hazards
of air pollution is exceptionally difficult. The three strategies for
doing so are animal experiments, controlled human studies, and epidemiological studies of populations receiving either occupational or
ambient exposures. Each has its limitations; yet each provides an in-
dispensable source of data. This paper provides an overview of statistical problems that arise in the design and analysis of epidemiological studies concerning respiratory disease and ambient levels of
certain air pollutants. These pollutants are described briefly in
Section 2. Section 3 discusses the various study designs, their major
findings, and their strengths and weaknesses. Some statistical issues
in design and analysis are presented in Section 4, followed by a con-
cluding section on recommendations for future research. A more extensive consideration of some of the topics outlined here and references
to further reading can be found in (1).

*Department of Family, Community and Preventive Medicine, Stanford
University Medical School, Stanford, CA 94305. This work was sup-
ported by grants to the SIAM Institute for Mathematics and Society
from the National Science Foundation, the Department of Energy, the
Environmental Protection Agency and the Rockefeller Foundation, by a
Research Career Development Award from the National Institute of
Environmental Health Sciences, and by grant number CA 23214-01 from
the National Cancer Institute.

2. Pollutants. The U. S. Clean Air Amendments of 1970, which are
scheduled for review by the Congress in 1981, mandate the Environmental Protection Agency to promulgate and to periodically review
national air quality standards for each of several pollutants. Those
which are now regulated and their current standards are shown in
Table 1.

TABLE 1

U.S. PRIMARY AIR QUALITY STANDARDS

Pollutant	Standard	Averaging time
Sulfur Dioxide (SO_2)	80 µg/m^3 (0.03 ppm)	Annual arithmetic mean
	365 µgm/m^3 (0.14 ppm)	Maximal 24-hour average
Total suspended	75 µg/m^3	Annual geometric mean
particulates	260 µg/m^3	Maximal 24-hour average
Photochemical oxidants	0.12 ppm	Maximal 1-hour average
Nitrogen Dioxide (NO_2)	100 µg/m^3 (0.05 ppm)	Annual arithmetic mean
Carbon Monoxide (CO)	10 mg/m^3 (9 ppm)	Maximal 8-hour average
	40 mg/m^3 (35 ppm)	Maximal 1-hour average

Concern about community exposures to carbon monoxide has focused
not on respiratory hazards but rather on cardiovascular and central
nervous system damage. Therefore this pollutant will not be
considered here.

Sulfur oxides and particulates often occur simultaneously as a result of fossil fuel combustion. Other sources for sulfur oxides are
smelters and sulfuric acid manufacturers, while particulates are also

generated by such industrial point sources as grain elevators and lumber mills. These pollutants do not form a chemically or physically specific mixture, but one which varies both temporally and spatially in chemical character, oxidation state and particular size distribution. These properties of the sulfur oxide/particulate complex make it extremely difficult to indite individual chemical components as hazards to health.

Photochemical oxidants are produced by nitrogen oxides, hydrocarbons and solar radiation in a complex reaction. Combustion of fossil fuels and motor vehicle emissions provide major sources for the reactants. Ozone is generally the principal component and the one believed to be the most irritating to the respiratory tract. Also present but not usually measured are peroxyacetyl nitrate, acrolein, peroxybenzoyl nitrates and aldehydes. Apart from NO_2, little is known about the respiratory effects of nitrogen oxides. While exposure to very high levels of NO_2 can be fatal, epidemiological studies have not shown a relationship between excess mortality and increased ambient NO_2 or oxidant levels, after adjusting for temperature. Moreover, little is known about the effects of chronic exposure to these pollutants.

3. <u>Epidemiological Studies</u>. Population-based investigations of ambient air pollution and respiratory disease can be classified into four types, depending upon whether their endpoint is respiratory mortality or respiratory morbidity, and whether they deal with the short-term or the long-term effects of pollutant exposures. Here I briefly describe these four types of studies, and summarize their findings concerning the above pollutants, as well as their chief strengths and weaknesses.

A. <u>Respiratory mortality: Long-term effects</u>. An important question in public health research is whether chronic exposure to elevated pollutant levels increases the chance of respiratory disease. Many workers have investigated this question by examining geographic differences in mortality rates due to bronchitis, emphysema, lung cancer, and other chronic respiratory disease. (See for example, 2-4.)

As indicated in Table 2, these investigations have shown a fairly consistent pattern of association between respiratory mortality and residence in areas of heavy particulate and sulfur oxide pollution. However the assignment of an etiologic role for air pollution on the basis of such data is difficult because of the design limitations described below.

STRENGTHS: (i) Aggregate mortality data are relatively accessible and inexpensive to collect.

LIMITATIONS: (i) Data are limited or lacking on important determinants of mortality such as smoking habits, socioeconomic status,

TABLE 2

RESPIRATORY HAZARDS: CONCLUSIONS OF EPIDEMIOLOGICAL STUDIES

Study	Pollutant		
	SO_2/Particulates	Oxidants	Oxides of Nitrogen
Mortality			
Long-term effects	Positive (2-4)	Unknown	Uknown
Short-term effects	Positive (5,6)	Negative (12,13)	Negative (12,13)
Morbidity			
Long-term effects	Positive (7-9)	Negative (14)	Positive (17,18)
Short-term effects	Positive (10,11)	Positive (10,15,16)	Unknown

occupation, preexisting disease, ethnic background and diagnostic
accuracy in filling out death certificates. It is quite plausible
that consistent confounding due these factors might explain the consistency of the associations found. For example, people with lower
socioeconomic status (SES) tend to smoke more cigarettes (19) and live
in more polluted areas than do those with higher status. Thus
cigarette smoking and SES probably follow an air pollution gradient
throughout most of the geographical areas studied. Further, because
heavily industrialized areas are often heavily polluted as well,
occupation among males might well be consistently correlated with residence in a dirty area. (ii) Geographical differences in pollutant
levels are usually assessed at the same time as (or even later than)
mortality occurrence. Thus one must assume that these relationships
have not changed over the lifetimes of the populations at risk of
death. (iii) There is little or no control for selective migration in
and out of polluted areas. (iv) Aggregate measures of exposure are
inadequate for evaluating nonlinear exposure-response relationships.

The first and fourth limitations are illustrated with some hypothetical data on cigarette smoking and lung cancer mortality, shown in
Table 3. In this table the populations of two fictitious census
tracts are classified by cigarette consumption. The age-adjusted lung
cancer mortality rates are assumed proportional to the square of daily
smoking rate. It can be seen that although tract B has a greater proportion of smokers and a greater per capita cigarette consumption,
tract A has the higher mortality rate. This anomaly indicates that
the use of aggregate indices may not adequately control for smoking
and other potential confounders of the pollution-mortality relationship.

B. Respiratory mortality: Short-term effects. The strongest
evidence against air pollution has been the excess mortality observed
in past "killer fog" episodes (20-22). These episodes have prompted a
number of studies on possible associations between temporal fluctuations in mortality and in sulfur oxide/particulate pollution. The
sensitivity of such studies depends on a number of factors, including
the size of the study population and the variability in pollutant
levels to which the population is exposed. Thus most of the investigations have taken place in large industrialized cities such as
London (23), New York (5), and Tokyo (6), although there have been
others in smaller cities (e.g. 24, pp. 263-309, 25, 26).

STRENGTHS: (i) Mortality and pollutant levels in a single population are compared in various time periods. Thus unlike cross-
sectional comparisons of mortality in different geographical areas, the
population under study serves as its own control. This means that
smoking habits, occupational exposures and socioeconomic status are
less likely to obscure the relationship between mortality and
pollution. (ii) There is no need to infer previous pollution exposures from contemporary aerometric data. (iii) The data are relatively inexpensive to collect.

TABLE 3

NUMBER OF RESIDENTS (THOUSANDS) BY CENSUS TRACT AND SMOKING HABIT (HYPOTHETICAL DATA)

Census Tract	Smoking Habit				% smokers	per capita cigarette consumption (packs/person/day)	age-adjusted lung cancer mortality rate*
	nonsmoker	1 pack/day	2 packs/day	Total			
A	6	1	3	10	40	0.7	.013
B	1	8	1	10	90	1.0	.012

*up to a proportionality constant, assuming the rate is proportional to the square of daily smoking rate.

   LIMITATIONS: (i) Temporal variables such as influenza epidemics,
temperature extremes, season and holidays must be carefully controlled.
(ii) Findings at one time and place are not easily generalized because
of variability in pollutant mix and in the elderly and infirm population at risk. (iii) Those who by virtue of age or preexisting disease
are at risk of death are apt to spend most of their time indoors.
Thus density of cigarette smoke, type of heating and cooking fuel, and
other determinants of indoor air quality may have more relevance to
mortality than do moderate variations in outdoor levels as measured
some distance away. (iv) Temporal studies must deal with variable and
unknown lags between stimulus (air pollution) and response (death due
to respiratory dysfunction). (v) Because of sizeable decreases in
pollution levels in the U. S. and Western Europe following Clean Air
legislation (see Figure 1), relatively weak "signals" emitted by
current milder pollutant fluctuations are likely to be swamped by
random and nonrandom variations in daily deaths.

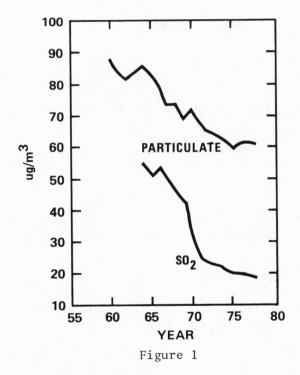

Figure 1

Average annual levels of total suspended particulates and sulfur
dioxide in U.S. during 1960-1978. Particulate levels represent annual
geometric means of daily values averaged over 95 sites during
1960-1971 and over 3000 sites during 1972-1978. Sulfur dioxide levels
represent annual arithmetic means of daily values averaged over 32
sites during 1965-1971 and over 1322 sites during 1972-1978.
Reprinted with permission from William F. Hunt, Environmental
Protection Agency, personal communication.

The last three limitations cited tend to decrease a study's ability to detect an air pollution effect, if one exists. This may explain the negative findings for oxidants and oxides of nitrogen shown in Table 2. On the other hand, these studies have persistently shown a pattern of increased mortality on days or weeks of increased sulfur oxide/particulate pollution. Although the studies have justifiably played a major role in regulating these pollutants, their data are too crude for determining the exposure-response relationships needed to set standards.

C. Respiratory morbidity: Long-term effects. Morbidity studies of respiratory damage due to chronic pollutant exposures usually fall into one of two categories: (i) cross-sectional studies of respiratory status and pollutant levels at a single time in two or more geographical units (e.g. 14, 17); (ii) cohort studies comparing temporal changes in respiratory status and in pollution for several geographic units (e.g. 7, 8).

STRENGTHS OF CROSS-SECTIONAL STUDIES: (i) the data are cheaper to collect than are data from the cohort studies.

LIMITATIONS OF CROSS-SECTIONAL STUDIES: Although there is often some attempt to control for important intervening factors, these studies suffer from many of the severe limitations affecting the chronic mortality studies. There is little data on past exposures, and little or no control for selective migration in and out of polluted areas. Note: these limitations pertain much less to cross-sectional studies of respiratory morbidity in children than to such studies in adults. The advantages of working with children are discussed further in Section 5.

STRENGTHS OF COHORT STUDIES: (i) Control for intervening variables is possible. (ii) Pollutant exposures can be measured over a period of several years. (iii) Pollutant exposures can be related to changes in respiratory status.

LIMITATIONS OF COHORT STUDIES: (i) They are time-consuming and expensive. (ii) Loss to followup (possibly due to selective migration) can be a serious problem. (iii) Pollution exposures are measured with large errors.

D. Respiratory morbidity: Short-term effects. Studies comparing temporal changes in respiratory status with concomitant pollution fluctuations are generally designed to examine one of three respiratory endpoints: (a) daily or weekly self-assessed symptom reports (panel studies) (e.g. 11, 15, 16); (b) measures of pulmonary function (e.g. 27, 28); (c) hospital or clinic visits (e.g. 29, 30).

STRENGTHS: (i) The study population can serve as its own control. Indeed, for studies of types (a) and (b) each individual can serve as his or her own control. This type of analysis eliminates interpersonal

variation. (ii) There is no need to infer previous pollutant exposures from contemporary pollution data.

LIMITATIONS: The first four problems associated with studies of
acute mortality effects—confounding by weather and season, specialized
pollution or population at risk, inaccuracy of exposure estimates, and
unknown lags—must also be addressed in acute morbidity studies. In
addition to these problems, panel studies are vulnerable to the
vagaries of self-assessed symptom reporting and, unless the subjects
are blind to the study's goals, to the possibility of reporting bias.

4. Statistical Issues. There are a number of unsettled issues in
the design and analysis of epidemiological studies of air pollution
and respiratory disease. They are classified into problems of pollution exposure assessment, and problems of respiratory disease
assessment.

A. Pollution exposure assessment.

PROBLEM: Intercorrelation among several different aerometric and
meteorologic variables that may affect respiratory status.

RESULT: Inability to indict specific pollutants.

NEEDED: Further theoretical and Monte Carlo study of the relative
merits of existing statistical techniques for dealing with multi-
collinearity. Such techniques include ridge regression, factor
analysis, and principal components analysis.

PROBLEM: Missing aerometric data. The multivariate procedures
available for the analysis of air pollution studies provide useful
techniques for the control of confounding and the evaluation of combined effects and interactions. However, application of these techniques is problematical when some of the pollution data is missing or
unreliable.

RESULT: Loss of information, decreased sensitivity.

NEEDED: Further theoretical and Monte Carlo study of the EM
algorithm (31) and other procedures for dealing with missing covariates
in multiple regression.

PROBLEM: Uncertainty in estimates of individual exposures to
pollution.

RESULT: Regression coefficients can be biased downward. Further,
errors of measurement in intervening variables can confound regression
coefficients of interest.

NEEDED: Further work on personal pollution monitors; further work
on the idea of allocating study subjects' time into specific microenvironments (home, office, motor vehicle, etc.) and of sampling pollutant concentrations in the microenvironments; standardization of
methods for differentiating particles chemically and for measuring
those of a given size distribution; research into application of
existing methods (32) for adjusting regression coefficients to account
for error in independent variables.

B.   Respiratory disease assessment.

PROBLEM: Autocorrelation in serial measurements of respiratory
status.

RESULT: Potential for bias in regression coefficients and other
measures of association.

NEEDED: Further application of time series methods to short-term
studies of temporal fluctuations in respiratory morbidity.

PROBLEM: Lack of knowledge concerning the precision with which
lung function measurements (e.g. forced expiratory volume, peak expiratory flow rate) predict the development of disabling disease.

RESULT: Research efforts may be expended on an insignificant
physiological endpoint.

NEEDED: Better methods of analyzing data from long-term studies of
decline in pulmonary function (see 33).

PROBLEM: Lack of standardization of the protocol for pulmonary
function testing.

RESULT: Incomparability of different studies.

NEEDED: A uniform approach to such questions as how many tests an
individual should receive at one sitting, whether to take the mean or
the maximum spirometry reading; how to adjust the measurement differences between instruments and between technicians (see 34).

PROBLEM: Missing response data in short-term morbidity studies.

RESULT: Study insensitivity; potential bias in measures of
association.

NEEDED: Theoretical and Monte Carlo study of missing data
algorithms applied to the special needs of these data.

Perhaps the greatest weakness of all population-based air pollution
studies is the presence of large random and nonrandom errors in measured pollutant exposures. Such uncertainties reduce the power of a

study. Other sources of insensitivity are insufficient variability in
exposures to pollutants, inadequate control for confounding factors,
insufficient sample sizes, and the chance that reactions of sensitive
subgroups will go unnoticed. Temporal studies of acute effects are
further weakened by unknown lags between exposure and effect, while
cross-sectional studies of chronic effects are muddied by migration in
and out of geographical units.

   Because of these limitations, negative results cannot automatically
be interpreted as evidence of safety. At best, such results provide
crude upper bounds for effects. At present the lack of documented
evidence on adverse effects at levels slightly above the standards
cannot be construed as evidence in favor of relaxing them. More sensitive studies are needed. What must be done to achieve them?

   5. Recommendations for Future Studies. The data base used for
setting air quality standards can be improved in three ways: (a) reduction of uncertainty in pollution exposures; (b) better study
design; and (c) better data analysis.

   A. Reduction of exposure uncertainties. Attempts should be made
to reduce pollution exposure uncertainties with more accurate, better
calibrated, standard measuring devices located close to the nose and
mouth of the population at risk. It is possible that personal pollution monitors may one day become portable and cheap enough for use on
the large scale needed for epidemiological studies. Until then the
notion of parcelling subject's time into specific microenvironments
and sampling pollutant levels in these environments should be imple-
mented in short-term morbidity studies.

   B. Improved study design. We should abandon hope of elucidating
chronic effects by studying current or former smokers. Cigarette
smoking so dominates air pollution as a respiratory hazard that such
people cannot provide information on chronic effects without precise
control of such myriad smoking modifiers as duration, pattern, amount,
depth of inhalation, and tar and nicotine content. The impracticality
of doing this suggests that future chronic effects studies be restricted to lifelong nonsmokers. Similar comments apply to strong
occupational respiratory hazards.

   For these reasons studies in children are uniquely valuable. In-
sults to the respiratory tract in childhood may be one of the important
determinants of chronic respiratory diseases in adulthood. To clarify
this, cohorts of children whose exposures are being documented and
who remain nonsmokers should be followed into adulthood for
chronic disease. Unfortunately, the necessary restriction of study to
nonsmokers precludes the investigation of possible interaction between
cigarette smoke and air pollution in the induction of respiratory
disability.

Because of the limitations discussed in Section 3, further cross-sectional studies of chronic effects in adults are not likely to be useful in determining standards. Long-term cohort studies of geographical differences in pulmonary function changes share some of these limitations and thus should be undertaken only with the greatest care. Current air quality monitoring and data storage and retrieval are sufficiently developed so that within the next few decades, national data banks on average air pollution levels by time and place of residence could be available. It may thus be feasible to conduct retrospective studies of lifetime exposures among nonsmoking, non-occupationally exposed victims of chronic lung disease as compared with exposures among suitably chosen controls. As with all chronic effects studies, the sensitivity of these retrospective studies would be compromised by large errors in exposure estimates. Further, they would be subject to at least as many potential biases as are corresponding cohort studies. Nevertheless, because the frequency of chronic lung disease is low, they would be substantially cheaper and more efficient than the cohort studies.

Short-term studies of acute nonfatal events as they vary with pollution over time, while unable to answer the important questions concerning chronic effects, have the best prognosis for sensitivity, reliability, and feasibility. It is important that existing studies of this type be duplicated using improved design, exposure assessment techniques, and analysis.

C. _Better data analysis_. Future investigators should use state-of-the-art statistical methodology for controlling intervening variables and for increasing sensitivity. The sensitivity and validity of many short-term morbidity studies can be enhanced by relating disease to exposure on an individual rather than an aggregate level, as described earlier. Finally, study plans should include more careful sample size estimates. In complex situations such estimates could be generated by Monte Carlo simulations.

REFERENCES

(1) WHITTEMORE, A. S., _Air pollution and respiratory disease_, Ann. Rev. of Public Health, (May 1981), in press.

(2) WINKELSTEIN, W., JR., KANTOR, S., DAVIS, E. M., MANERI, C. S., and MOSHER, W. E., _The relationship of air pollution and economic status to total mortality and selected respiratory system mortality in men_, Arch. Environ. Health 14 (1967), pp. 162-169.

(3) LAVE, L. B. and SESKIN, B. P., _Air pollution and human health_, Science 169 (1970), pp. 723-733.

(4) STOCKS, P., _Cancer and bronchitis mortality in relation to atmospheric deposit and smoke_, Br. Med. J. 1 (1959), pp. 74-79.

(5)   SCHIMMEL, H. and GREENBERG, L., A study of the relation of pollu-
      tion to mortality, New York City 1963-1968, J. Air Pollution
      Control Assoc. 22 (1972), pp. 607-616.

(6)   LEBOWITZ, M. D., TOYAMA, T., and MCCARROLL, J., The relationship
      between air pollution and weather as stimuli and daily mortality
      as responses in Tokyo, Japan, with comparisons with other cities,
      Environ. Res. 6 (1973), pp. 327-333.

(7)   FERRIS, B. G., JR., HIGGINS, I. T. T., HIGGINS, M. W., and
      PETERS, J. M., Chronic nonspecific respiratory disease in Berlin,
      New Hampshire, 1961 to 1967: A follow-up study, Am. Rev. Resp.
      Dis. 107 (1973), pp. 110-122.

(8)   LUNN, J. E., KNOWELDEN, J., and ROE, J. W., Patterns of respira-
      tory illness in Sheffield junior school-children: A follow-up
      study, Brit. J. Prev. Soc. Med. 24 (1970), pp. 223-228.

(9)   LAMBERT, P. M. and REID, D. D., Smoking, air pollution and
      bronchitis in Britain, Lancet 1 (1970), pp. 853-857.

(10) LAWTHER, P. J., WALLER, R. E., and HENDERSON, M., Air pollution
      and exacerbations of bronchitis, Thorax 25 (1970), pp. 525-539.

(11) WHITTEMORE, A. S. and KORN, E. L., Asthma and air pollution in
      the Los Angeles area, Am. J. Public Health 70 (1980), pp. 687-696.

(12) BIERSTEHER, K. and EVENDIJK, J. E., Ozone, temperature and
      mortality in Rotterdam in the summers of 1974 and 1975, Environ.
      Res. 12 (1976), pp. 214-221.

(13) OECHSLI, E. W. and BUECHLEY, R. W., Excess mortality associated
      with three Los Angeles September hot spells, Environ. Res. 3
      (1970), pp. 277-285.

(14) COHEN, C. A., HUDSON, A. R., CLAUSEN, J. L., and KNELSON, J. H.,
      Respiratory symptoms, spirometry, and oxidant air pollution in
      nonsmoking adults, Am. Rev. Resp. Dis. 105 (1972), pp. 251-261.

(15) SCHOETTLIN, C. E. and LANDAU, E., Air pollution and asthmatic
      attacks in the Los Angeles area, Public Health Reports 76 (1961),
      pp. 545-548.

(16) HAMMER, D. I., HASSELBLAD, V., PORTNOY, B., and WEHRLE, P. F.,
      Los Angeles student nurse study, Arch. Environ. Health 28 (1974),
      pp. 255-260.

(17) SHY, C. M., CREASON, J. P., PEARLMAN, M. E., MCCLAIN, K. E.,
      BENSON, F. B., and YOUNG, M. M., The Chattanooga school children
      study: Effects of community exposure, and results of ventilatory
      function testing, J. Air Pollu. Control Assoc. 20 (1970),
      pp. 539-545.

(18) PEARLMAN, M. E., FINKLEA, J. F., CREASON, J. P., SHY, C. M.,
      YOUNG, M. M. and HORTON, R. J. M., Nitrogen dioxide and lower
      respiratory illness, Pediatrics 47 (1971), pp. 391-398.

(19) Smoking and health: A report of the Surgeon General, DHEW Publ.
      No. (PHS) 79-50066, U. S. Dept. Health, Educ., Welfare, 1979.

(20) FIRKET, J., The cause of the symptoms found in the Meuse Valley
      during the fog of December 1930, Bull. Acad. Roy. de Med. de
      Belgique 11 (1931), pp. 683-741.

(21) SCHRENK, H. H., HEIMANN, H., CLAYTON, G. D., GAFAFER, W., and
      WEXLER, H., Air pollution in Donora, Pennsylvania: Epidemiology
      of the unusual smog episode of October 1948, Public Health
      Bull. 306, Washington, D. C., GPO, 1949.

(22) LOGAN, W. P. D., Mortality in London fog incident, Lancet 1
      (1953), pp. 336-338.

(23) GORE, A. T. and SHADDICK, W., Atmospheric pollution and mortality
      in the County of London, Br. J. Prev. Med. 12 (1968), pp. 104-113.

(24) Natl. Acad. Sci., Proc. Conf. Health Effects of Air Pollutants,
      U. S. Sen. Comm. Publ. Works, Print Ser. No. 93-15, Washington,
      D. C., GPO, 1973.

(25) KENNEDY, J., KEVANY, J., and ROONEY, M., Air pollution and ill
      health, Ir. J. Med. Sci. 144 (1975), pp. 102-118.

(26) LINDBERG, W., Air Pollution in Norway, Oslo: Smoke Damage
      Council, 1968.

(27) LAWTHER, P. J., BROOKS, A. G. F., LORD, P. W., and WALLER, R. E.,
      Day-to-day changes in ventilatory function in relation to the
      environment: I. Spirometric values, Environ. Res. 7 (1974),
      pp. 24-40.

(28) STEBBINGS, J. H., FOGLEMAN, D. G., MCCLAIN, K. E., and
      TOWNSEND, M. C., Effect of the Pittsburgh air pollution episode
      upon pulmonary function in school children, J. Air Pollut.
      Control Assoc. 26 (1976), pp. 547-553.

(29) GOLDSTEIN, I. F. and BLOCK, G., Asthma and air pollution in two
      inner city areas in New York City, J. Air Pollut. Control Assoc.
      24 (1974), pp. 665-670.

(30) DURHAM, W. H., Air pollution and student health, Arch. Environ.
      Health 28 (1974), pp. 241-254.

(31) DEMPSTER, A. P., LAIRD, N. M., and RUBIN, D. B., Maximum likeli-
      hood from incomplete data via the EM algorithm, J. Roy. Statist.
      Soc. B 39 (1977), pp. 1-22.

(32) GLESER, L. J., Estimation in a multivariate 'errors in variables'
      regression-model: Large sample results, Ann. Statist. 9 (1981),
      pp. 24-44.

(33) FLETCHER, C. M., PETO, R., TINKER, C. M., and SPEIZER, F. E.,
      The Natural History of Chronic Bronchitis and Emphysema, Oxford
      University Press, 1976.

(34) FERRIS, B. G., JR., Epidemiology standardization project, Am.
      Rev. Resp. Dis. 118 (1978), pp. 1-120.

Modeling Dose Response Relationships
for Health Effects Data

Victor Hasselblad*

Abstract. Guidelines for dose response curves to be used in environmental research are given. Six example data sets were chosen for their use or potential use in the process leading to regulatory decisions. Dose response models are given for each data set. Where more than one model gave an adequate fit, the conclusions remained the same.

1. Introduction. The Environmental Protection Agency has been making regulatory decisions for 10 years. Many of these decisions are based on documents which contain studies of adverse health effects, with consideration for an appropriate margin of safety. These studies are most useful when they provide a well defined dose response curve for an accepted adverse health effect. Unfortunately there are relatively few such studies in the literature. I have chosen six studies which either have been considered in the regulatory decision process, or at least have the potential for consideration. Before discussing them individually, I would like to discuss some guidelines for dose response curves, with the hope of generating criticisms, modifications, or just increased interest in this area.

2. General Guidelines. The field of dose response curves in general is a very broad field, with several books already written by outstanding researchers. What I would like to present are some guidelines for dose response curves in environmental research which will help them contribute to the regulatory decisions process. The guidelines are:

1. The response variable should be an accepted adverse health effect.

2. The dose variable should be a good estimate of the exposure of each individual unit in the study.

3. The model should include any important covariates in a manner consistent with the known effect of those covariates.

*Biometry Division, Health Effects Research Laboratory, Environmental Protection Agency, Research Triangle Park, NC 27711

4. The curve should model the smallest unit of response, i.e. an
    individual instead of a group.

5. The error term should be appropriate, i.e. binomial for
    dichotomous variables, poisson for counts, normal for continu-
    ous variables.

In discussing each study, the extent to which these guidelines are met
will be discussed.

   The actual curve fitting process often requires sophisticated
statistical software. Although both SAS and BMDP provided useful
routines for analysis of some data sets, the only system which reflects
the philosophy of the guidelines given earlier is the GLIM system.
This is a British system developed at the Rothamsted Experimental Station, and is part of the larger GENSTAT system. Hopefully, other
packages which are more readily available in this country will recognize the usefulness of these improvements.

   3. The Azar Lead Study. The first two studies which will be
discussed have a continuous reponse variable, and are studies of the
effects of lead on humans. The first of these, the study of Azar, et
al. [1], is one of the best examples of a dose response curve with good
individual exposure estimates. This study was conducted on 150
subjects in 5 U.S. cities. The independent variable was air lead
measured by means of personal air samplers which were run from two to
four weeks. The dependent variable was blood lead, measured at least
twice in each individual. After excluding one individual suspected of
illicit moonshine whiskey consumption, linear models were fitted to the
logs of both variables. The models fitted included ones with different
intercepts by city along with both different and common slopes. The
results are summarized in Table 1. A model using a common slope with

TABLE 1

Analysis of Variance Table of the Azar Study

Factor	D.F.	S.S.	M.S.	F	p-value
Slopes	5	.9828	.1966	2.89	.016
Common slope	1	.9412	.9412	13.84	<.001
Different slopes	4	.0416	.0104	.15	.963
Intercepts	4	8.3617	2.0904	30.74	<.001
Error	139	9.4503	.0680		
Total	148	18.7948			

different intercepts is the simplest model giving an adequate fit, and
is the model given by Azar, et al [1].

This curve is in Figure 1. along with the actual data.

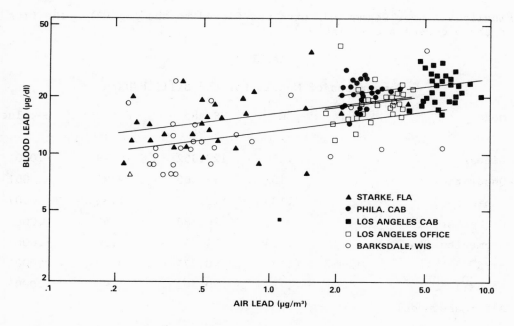

Figure 1. Fit of blood lead to air lead for the Azar study.

The study design and analysis are both excellent, and the study
was one of three which had a major impact on the national ambient air
lead standard. One problem with the analysis is that the independent
variable is assumed to be measured without error. As a result, the
estimated slope is biased low, although it is difficult to quantify
the amount. Most studies, even designed toxicological studies, have
this same problem.

4. The Billick Blood Lead and EP Data. As part of a large scale
screening program, New York City collected blood samples from
thousands of children from the core urban area. The data have been
collected since 1970, and were described by Billick, et al [2]. The
data included here are the 1976 and 1977 values of blood lead and
erythrocytic porphyrin (EP) among those children who were being
screened for the first time. Because blood lead provides a good
estimate of recent lead exposure, blood lead becomes the independent
variable in this analysis. The variable EP is an indicator of undue
lead exposure and is used along with blood lead for screening purposes.
The interesting feature of these two variables is that their relationship is clearly nonlinear (with or without logarithmic transforma-
tions).

Several different curves were fitted to the data. These included
linear, quadratic and cubic polynomials. Also fitted was a general
nonlinear dose response curve:

$$\log(EP) = (A + BX^C)\exp(-DX)$$

Finally a linear segmented curve was fitted to the log(EP). The fits of these curves are in Table 2.

TABLE 2

Comparison of Models for the Billick Data

Model	D.F.	R^2	SS above error	F-test	p-value
Linear	1	.150	122.962	10.99	<.0001
Quadratic	2	.181	32.465	2.97	<.0001
Cubic	3	.185	19.775	1.85	.0007
Hockey stick	2	.183	26.288	2.40	<.0001
Segmented line	3	.184	24.149	2.26	<.0001
$A+BX^C$	2	.178	40.271	3.68	<.0001
$(A+BX^C)e^{-DX}$	3	.185	20.302	1.90	.0004
All means model	45	.232	–	–	–

The best fits are given by the models with 3 degrees of freedom. The curves are very similar; the cubic curve is shown in Figure 2, along with the geometric mean EP value for each blood lead level. The predicted values for the three curves are in Table 3. All curves give

TABLE 3

Comparison of Predicted Values for the Billick Data

Model	Blood Lead (µg/dl)				
	10	20	30	40	50
Cubic	23.5	24.3	37.1	66.0	107.6
Segmented line	22.5	23.8	38.3	65.8	112.9
$(A+BX^C)e^{-DX}$	23.6	24.4	37.5	66.8	117.0

very similar values through 40 µg/dl, and differ only slightly at 50 µg/dl blood lead. Only 16 of the 9409 blood lead values were 50 µg/dl or larger.

Although the data give a well defined dose response curve, elevated EP is at best a questionable adverse health effect. EP data were discussed in the Air Quality Criteria Document for Lead, but had little impact on the standard itself.

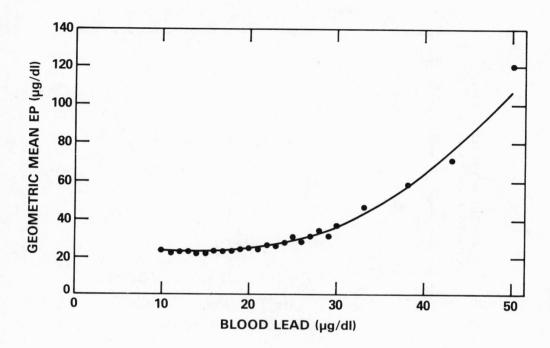

Figure 2. EP as a function of blood lead in New York children.

5. The Ott Arsenic Exposure and Mortality Study. Ott et al. [3]
studied the mortality experience of workers of a chemical company.
Expected deaths due to respiratory malignancy were fitted as a function
of age and year of death. Expected deaths in the exposed group were
calculated from the white male U.S. mortality experience. Expected
respiratory deaths were calculated from this using the fitted prediction equation. The ratio of observed to expected deaths, and the
actual numbers of deaths are shown in Figure 3.

Assuming that these counts of deaths follow a Poisson distribution
with parameter λ, the following model can be fitted:

$$\lambda_i = A(E_i + BE_i As_i^C),$$

where E_i is the expected number of deaths, As is the arsenic dose, and
A, B, and C are parameters to be estimated. This model gives a
reasonable fit as measured by a standard chi-square test. A likelihood
ratio test for A = 1, a test that the background rate for the exposed
group is the same as the control group, is non-significant. Thus the
data do not contradict the calculated expected values. Using A = 1,
the test for the effect of arsenic gives an asymptotic chi-square of
29.02 for 2 degrees of freedom, which is highly significant. Table 4
gives the various models, goodness of fits, and likelihood ratio tests
for the Ott data.

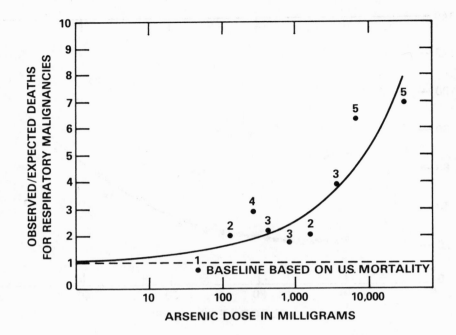

Figure 3.   Ratio of observed to expected respiratory
            malignancy deaths as a function of arsenic
            dose.

TABLE 4

Fits of Various Models for the Ott Study

Model	Log-likelihood	Chi-square	D.F.	p-value
Sample	−13.215	−	−	−
Full	−14.573	2.66	6	.850
A = 1	−14.747	2.96	7	.889
A = 1, no As	−29.256	64.68	9	<.001

Likelihood ratio test for A = 1: $X^2 = 0.35$, D.F. = 1, p = .555
Likelihood ratio test for no arsenic effect: $X^2 = 29.02$, D.F. =
   2, p < .001

   There are some problems with these analyses. First, the method of
computing the expected deaths is not standard. Secondly, the numbers
of actual deaths are small. This affects the confidence in the
predicted curve, as well as the α levels of the tests since they
require asymptotic theory. Finally, the dose estimates are probably
very crude at best. The purpose of the analysis is to show how such
data can be analyzed using the fact that the data are counts, rather
than using the more common least squares regression. The data set

itself is being considered by the Environmental Protection Agency in its assessment of the carcinogenic potential of arsenic.

6. Claxton's Mutagenic Screening Data. The Ames test, using Salmonella bacterial strains to measure increased induction of mutation has become a standard screening method for suspected carcinogenic compounds. The test consists of exposing specific mutant strains to a compound on agar plates deficient in histidine. Revertant colonies are then counted, usually with an automatic colony counter. The particular compounds in a study by Claxton and Kohan, [4] were fluorenone and various nitrofluorenones. Various doses of each compound were used on the TA98 strain of Salmonella typhimurium, with 3 replicates at each dose.

Models were fitted for each compound assuming that the counts followed a Poisson distribution where the parameter λ_i was given by

$$\lambda_i = (\beta_0 + e^{\beta_1 + \beta_2 \log x_i}) e^{-\beta_3 x_i}$$

where x_i is the dose. The term β_0 corresponds to the background rate, β_1 and β_2 describe the mutagenicity, and β_3 describes the toxicity.

All models were fitted using maximum likelihood methods. Figure 4 shows a curve fitted to data resulting from the testing of 3-nitrofluorenone. Reduced models with the β_3 term or the β_1 and β_2 terms eliminated were also fitted. The results of these fits along with goodness of fit tests and likelihood ratio tests are in Table 5.

TABLE 5

Analysis of Likelihoods for 3-nitrofluorenone

Model	D.F.	Log-likelihood	Test Against	Chi-square	p-value
(A) Sample	21	−80.958	−	−	−
(B) All means	7	−90.285	(A)	18.65	.179
(C) Full	4	−93.264	(B)	5.96	.114
(D) No toxic.	3	−113.687	(C)	40.85	<.001
(E) No mutag.	2	−1869.043	(C)	3551.56	<.001

The analysis indicates that both toxicity and mutagenicity are present, but mutagenicity has the larger chi-square. Similar analyses were made for fluorenone and three other nitrofluorenones. All compounds except fluorenone showed strong mutagenicity, and the estimated increase over background for each compound is in Table 6.

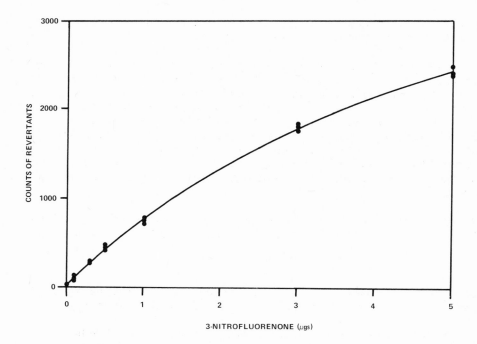

Figure 4.   Counts of revertants as a function of 3-nitrofluorenone dose

TABLE 6

Mutagenicity by Compound for Kohan's Data

Compound	Estimated Increase in Counts by Dose			
	.1	.5	1	5
Fluorenone	0.	0.	0.	0.
3-Nitrofluorenone	100.	435.	820.	3579.
2,7-Dinitrofluorenone	1055.	2763.	4184.	10963.
2,4,7-Trinitrofluorenone	1362.	3005.	4225.	9319.
2,4,5,7-Tetranitrofluorenone	358.	1374.	2453.	9420.

Although the curves appeared to fit the counts fairly well, there were certain problems with the model testing. In order for the Poisson assumption to hold, the doses and numbers of bacteria applied per plate would have to be the same for each replicate. The variances of the revertant counts for large mean count values (>100) were larger than would be expected from a Poisson distribution, indicating that the doses or numbers of bacteria were probably not that uniform. This problem may affect the tests of significance presented, but should have little effect on the curve fitting. Since all of the nitrofluorenones were so highly significant, the effect on these data is probably minimal.

These kinds of data sets will undoubtedly have an impact on decisions about toxic substances.

7. The Winkelstein Buffalo Mortality Study. Winkelstein, et al. [5] studied mortality in Buffalo and Erie County, New York, for the years 1959 through 1961. Pollution estimates were made from a network of 21 sampling stations which were operating from July 1961 to June 1963. Both total suspended particulates (TSP) and sulfur dioxide were measured. Sulfur dioxide was measured using the lead candle method, which is extremely unreliable. The original analysis by Winkelstein, et al. grouped the data into 16 groups of census tracts split by average TSP levels and socioeconomic level. The total mortality rates for white males age 50–69 are in Table 7.

TABLE 7

Average Annual Death Rates Per 1000

Socio-economic level	1(low)	TSP 2	3	4(high)
1(low)	–	36	41	52
2	24	27	30	36
3	–	24	26	33
4	20	22	27	–
5(high)	17	21	20	–

The denominators for these rates were taken from the 1960 U.S. census. This analysis showed no tests of significance, but descriptively showed increasing mortality rates with increased TSP exposure across all socioeconomic levels.

The data, as presented by Winkelstein, can be analyzed using several different models, including linear and log-linear models for contingency tables, as well as multiple probit and logit analyses. A comparison of these methods is in Table 8.

The probit and logit analyses were done using GLIM [6]. The GSK method [7] gives weighted least squares estimates, and was done using both a linear and loglinear model. The loglinear model is the same as that used by LOGLIN, which is a maximum likelihood method described by Bishop, Feinberg, and Holland [8]. The differences between these two methods are a function of the method of estimation. Note that logit analysis and loglinear models using maximum likelihood are equivalent in this case. It is clear that the conclusions do not depend on the method. There is a clear effect of socioeconomic status and TSP, with no evidence of an interaction.

TABLE 8

Comparison of Methods of Analysis for
the Winkelstein Mortality Study

Method	X^2 error D.F.	X^2 TSP D.F.	X^2 SES D.F.
Probit	4.16	72.95	155.73
Logit	4.02	73.10	155.88
GSK–Linear	5.33	67.94	145.71
GSK–Loglinear	3.89	75.69	160.64
Loglin	4.02	73.10	155.89

The Winkelstein study has been criticized by Holland et al. [9] for several reasons. Having the pollution data for a period after the mortality data is an obvious flaw. Holland et al. also state that the data "...have not been satisfactorily standardized with respect to the effects of age, social class, ethnicity, occupation, mobility of population or, in particular, smoking habits". Although data on occupation, mobility, and smoking habits are not readily available, some additional work can be done using more specific socio-economic and age information.

The data from Winkelstein's study are available by census tract. The 21 station aerometric network was interpolated to give TSP estimates for each of the 72 census tracts in Buffalo. The stations and census tracts are shown in Figure 5.

Several socioeconomic variables are available from the 1960 census, including percent unemployment, median years of schooling, median income, and percent of homes sound. Age data for both the population and the deaths were available in 5 year intervals. Using these smaller units results in 288 cells for analysis. Linear models with TSP, age group, and one of the four socioeconomic variables were fitted using multiple probit analysis. The results are in Table 9. The contribution for TSP appears somewhat smaller, and the contribution of socioeconomic status appears larger when compared with the previous analysis. In particular, percent unemployment appears to be the best socioeconomic predictor of mortality. Age, is highly significant, which is to be expected. The coefficient for TSP in the linear model in Table 8 was .00295, which is very similar to the value of .00289 for the linear model in Table 9.

There were a few of the 288 cells which contributed heavily to the significant lack of fit of the model, and these are difficult to explain without more information about the specific census tracts.

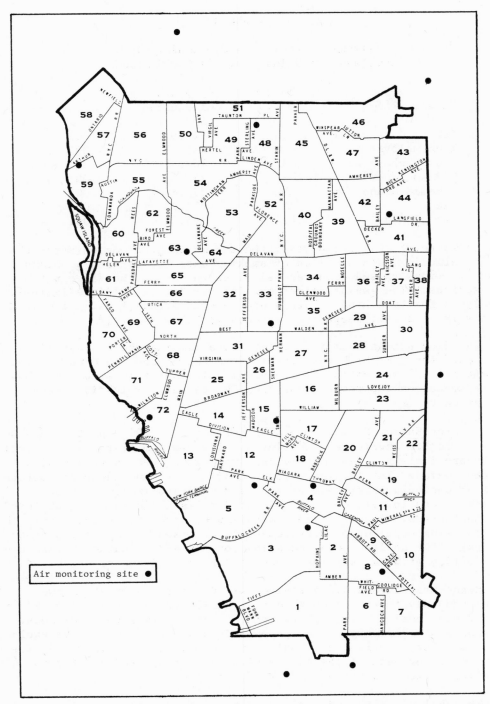

Figure 5.   Census tracts and stations used in the Winkelstein
study of mortality in Buffalo.

TABLE 9

Analysis of the Buffalo Mortality Data
by Census Tract Using Multiple Probit Analysis

Factor	D.F.	Asymptotic Chi-square	p-value
TSP	1	42.97	<.001
% Unemployment	1	261.28	<.001
Years Schooling	1	162.55	<.001
Median Income	1	240.85	<.001
% Homes Sound	1	221.87	<.001
Age	3	913.75	<.001
Fit of Model	282	395.93	<.001

In spite of this reanalysis, the two major problems of after-the-fact pollution data and lack of smoking data are serious problems. The questions raised about social class and age do not appear to be as serious. The use of either multiple probit or multiple logit analysis for this kind of study provides a method of using linear model analysis in a case where the response is binomial.

The data set had a major role in establishing the ambient air standard for TSP which was set nearly a decade ago. Because of the limitations just mentioned, it is unlikely that this study will have much impact on the revision of the TSP standard, which is currently in process.

8. The Hammer Nurse Study. Hammer, et al. [10] reported on student nurses in Los Angeles who completed daily symptom diaries for a period of approximately 3 years. Several symptoms showed increases with higher oxidant levels, including eye discomfort and chest discomfort. The oxidant exposure was measured at the Air Pollution Control District Station #1, which is within 2 miles of the schools attended by the nurses. The original analysis used group rates and fitted these to the single pollution measurement using a segmented function (hockey stick). The analyses did not allow for individual nurse differences or for day of week, seasonal changes, or annual trends.

Since many nurses did not give very complete information, we included only those nurses reporting on 75 percent of the days for the 3 year period. We also restricted the analyses to nonsmokers. A few nurses never reported any symptoms, and so they had to be excluded. Analyses were restricted to only include weekdays. Separate analyses were made for each of the two hospitals: California Lutheran and Los Angeles County General.

The analysis method described by Korn and Whittemore is especially attractive for this kind of study. For convenience, we used probit analysis, and used a model which included maximum hourly oxidant

values, day of week, season, and year. Also included were dummy
variables for each nurse, and for each nurse's previous response. A
summary of the likelihood ratio tests for the 8 nurses included from
California Lutheran Hospital is in Table 10.

TABLE 10

Analysis of Likelihoods for Hammer's Nurse Study
Eye Irritation Data from Lutheran Hospital

Factor	D.F.	Chi-square	p-value
Common slope	7	20.64	.004
Oxidant	1	156.70	<.001
Day of week	4	11.32	.023
Season	3	2.89	.409
Year	3	3.55	.315
Previous day	8	243.62	<.001
Nurse differences	7	328.44	<.001

The analysis shows large effects from individual nurse differences,
previous responses, and oxidant pollution. There was evidence
that the nurses varied in their response to oxidant pollution (common
slope). All other factors were much less important. The coefficients
for oxidant pollution for the 8 nurses were: -.013, .042, .044, .050,
.051, .054, .060, and .071. Thus, one nurse appeared to show no
effect from the pollution, whereas the other 7 reacted about the same.

Similar analyses were made for 19 nurses at Los Angeles County
General, although they were split into two groups because of size
restrictions of the program. Both groups showed a highly significant
effect from oxidant pollution. The effect of chest discomfort is less
clear, with only the California Lutheran nurses showing a marginally
significant effect from oxidant pollution. These results are
summarized in Table 11.

TABLE 11

Likelihood Ratio Tests for Hammer's Nurse Study

Effect	Lutheran Hospital X^2	Lutheran Hospital p-value	L.A. County General X^2	L.A. County General p-value
Eye irritation	156.70	<.001	43.80*	<.001
			30.62*	<.001
Chest discomfort	3.94	.047	.04	.850

*split in two groups due to program size restrictions

It is difficult to depict such analyses graphically. For
simplicity, we looked at eye discomfort for California Lutheran
nurses on days where they had no previous symptoms. The data,
pooled by oxidant level and fitted by a simple probit curve, is in
Figure 6. The strong effect of oxidant pollution on eye discomfort
is clear.

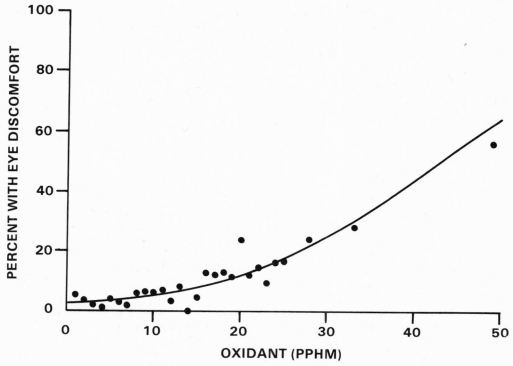

Figure 6. Percent eye discomfort of California Lutheran
Nurses as a function of oxidant level.

The report of Hammer, et al. [10] also includes the symptoms of
headache and cough, which were not reanalyzed. Although the dose
response curve for eye irritation is statistically highly significant,
it is not as important as a health end point as the symptoms of cough
or chest discomfort. The study is useful in describing the effects of
oxidant pollution on these symptoms, and was included in the Air
Quality Criteria Document for Ozone.

9. Summary. Although there are problems with each of the studies
described, it should be clear that a good model derived from a well
done study is extremely useful to the regulatory decision process.
Even though a few examples do not prove a point, I feel that the
choice of the model is relatively unimportant if it is a reasonable
one, and if it is not extrapolated beyond the body of the observed
data.

Models which describe individual responses are especially useful. These models can allow for individual differences, and often give much more information than do models which look only at overall rates. The use of an appropriate error term may also provide an estimate of goodness of fit, which is desirable in any study.

Hopefully, future studies will be designed with an appropriate model for the analysis specified before the data are collected. This not only makes the final analysis easier, it also should result in a better study from data collection to the final paper.

REFERENCES

[1] A. AZAR, R. D. SNEE, and K. HABIBI, An epidemiologic approach to community air lead exposure using personal air samplers, Environmental Quality and Safety, Supplement II: Lead, 37, (1975), pp. 12-145.

[2] I. H. BILLICK, A. S. CURRAN, and D. R. SHIER, Analysis of pediatric blood lead levels in New York for 1970-1976, Archives of Environmental Health, 31, (1979), pp. 180-190.

[3] M. G. OTT, B. B. HOLDER, and H. L. GORDON, Respiratory cancer and occupational exposure to arsenicals, Archives of Environmental Health, 29, (1974), pp. 250-255.

[4] L. CLAXTON, and M. KOHAN, Mutagenicity of nitrofluorenones in the forward and reverse Salmonella assays, to be submitted.

[5] W. WINKELSTEIN, S. KANTOR, E. W. DAVIS, C. S. MANERI, and W. E. MOSHER, The relationship of air pollution and economic status to total mortality and selected respiratory system mortality in men, 1. Suspended Particulate", Archives of Environmental Health, 14, (1967), pp. 162-171.

[6] R. J. BAKER, and J. A. NELDER, The GLIM System Release 3, Numerical Algorithms Group, Oxford, England, (1978).

[7] JAMES E. GRIZZLE, C. FRANK STARMER, and GARY G. KOCH, Analysis of categorical data by linear models, Biometrics, 25, (1969), pp. 489-504.

[8] Y. M. M. BISHOP, S. E. FIENBERG, P. W. HOLLAND, Discrete Multi-Variate Analysis: Theory and Practice, The MIT Press, Cambridge, Mass., pp. 57-122.

[9] W. W. HOLLAND, A. E. BENNETT, F. R. CAMERON, D. duV. FLOREY, S. R. LEEDER, R. S. F. SCHILLING, A. V. SWAN, and R. E. WALLER, Health Effects of Particulate Pollution: Reappraising the Evidence, Amer. J. Epidem., 110, (1979), pp. 533-659.

[10] D. I. HAMMER, V. HASSELBLAD, B. PORTNOY, and P. F. WEHRLE, Los Angeles Student Nurse Study, Daily Symptom Reporting and Photochemical Oxidants, Archives of Environmental Health, 28, (1974) pp. 255-260.

Issues in Health Risk Assessment
with Application to
Ambient Sulfur Oxides
and Particulate Matter

J. H. Ware*

Abstract. Increasingly subtle trade-offs between public health and
economic considerations sometimes create the need for risk analysis as
a basis for environmental decision making. One component of that
analysis is health risk assessment, the evaluation and synthesis of
information about the health effects of a potential hazard. This paper
considers some conceptual and methodologic issues in health risk assessment and examines the contrast between theory and the task of assessing
the health effects of ambient sulfur oxides and particulate matter.
When substantial information is available in several forms, the principle methodologic issue in risk assessment involves the approach to combining evidence. When information is sparse, as with sulfur oxides and
particulate matter, the assessor should focus on the limitations of the
evidence and the potential value of additional research.

1. Introduction. Federal agencies have an increasing need for
analytic approaches to decision making in the regulation of environmental hazards. Regulations often have substantial economic and public health significance, yet are based on inadequate information. A
case in point is the determination of air quality standards for sulfur oxides and particulate matter.

The application of decision analytic techniques to environmental
risks has been called environmental risk analysis. Risk analysis consists of several distinguishable analytic and information gathering
tasks, one of which is health risk assessment. Health risk assessment
involves the evaluation and synthesis of information about the environmental hazard under consideration. This paper considers the conceptual
and methodologic aspects of health risk assessment and illustrates the
contrast between theory and practice by reviewing some of the available
evidence on the health effects of ambient sulfur oxides and particulate
matter.

*Harvard School of Public Health, Boston, MA 02115

*This research was supported in part by grant ES01108 from the Nation-
al Institute of Environmental Health Sciences and Electric Power Research Institue Contract No. RP 1001 EARI.

2. <u>Health Risk Assessment.</u> We distinguish between:
a. estimating the probability of catastrophe such as nuclear war,
nuclear accident or dam failure; and
b. estimating the effects of low risk hazards such as auto accidents,
carcinogens or air pollutants when the responses of different individuals are approximately independent.

These two types of problems differ in a variety of ways. The psycho-
logic impact of catastrophe is quite different from the persistent and
substantial effect of auto accidents or scattered deaths with uncertain
attribution to environmental hazard. A more important distinction for
the statistician is the potential for gathering observational or experimental data in the second set of problems. We will focus on this
type of hazard. Here, the objective of risk assessment is estimation
of the <u>exposure-response</u> <u>function</u>.

For categorical responses such as disease, recorded as present or
absent, the exposure-response function gives the expected disease frequency (incidence or prevalence according to the setting) at each
level of exposure. For measured responses, such as forced vital capacity, the exposure-response function gives the expected average level of
response at each level of exposure.

Health risk assessment utilizes the available scientific evidence
to characterize the exposure-response function. Data sources may
include
          -In vitro studies
          -Animal studies
          -Occupational studies
          -Population based epidemiology.
Important information is often obtained from studies of related agents
and this evidence must be included in a quantitative assessment.

We can identify two stages in a health risk assessment:

          -<u>Evaluation</u> <u>of</u> <u>individual</u> <u>studies</u>
          -<u>Combining evidence</u>.
Both tasks involve statistical skills in combination with understanding of the biologic effects of the agent under investigation.

The evaluation of individual studies or items of evidence is a
familiar statistical scientific task. Ordinarily, one seeks to establish criteria for such an evaluation, and gather all relevant criti-
cism. Although many assessments have been restricted to the binary
choice between accepting or rejecting individual studies, a richer
set of choices might be desirable. One possibility would be to report
subjective measures of uncertainty for individual studies that reflect
the limitations of the evidence such as potential bias or weaknesses
in the study design.

The task of combining disparate evidence is equally important, but less well studied. We consider some of the issues in the next section.

3. <u>Combining Evidence</u>. The simplest problem of this type involves pooling evidence from replicates of a single type of study. Various methods have been proposed for this problem, including Fisher's technique for combining P-values and the Mantel-Haenszel method for combining evidence from several 2×2 tables (Mantel and Haenszel, 1959). When an "effect" parameter is assumed to be constant across studies, it is usually possible to define a model across several studies that allows pooled estimation of the parameter of interest. Of course, the adequacy of the model is always a concern.

A more interesting formulation assumes that the effect parameter varies randomly over studies with a mean value that represents the average effect. This <u>random</u> <u>effects</u> formulation has a natural appeal, in that it recognizes the variation in the strength of associations arising from variation in the study design. This concept leads to the fitting of mixed models to data combined from several studies. Although mixed linear models have been extensively studied for measured response (for example, Harville (1977)) comparatively little has been done for the analogous problem with categorical response.

Bayesian methods have a natural appeal for the problem of combining evidence. They are closely related to random effects models and offer the potential for linking subjective and data based information. It is likely that Bayesian ideas will be central in future work. Nevertheless, the linkage between subjective probabilities (expert judgment) and data is complex even with a Bayesian formulation, since expert opinion usually represents a composite of the available information rather than a priori.

Some recent investigations have considered the problem of combining evidence in the risk assessment setting. Crouch and Wilson (1979) considered the data from the animal carcinogenesis experiments sponsored by the National Cancer Institute and suggested that the data supported constant relative sensitivity between species over a spectrum of carcinogenic agents. This concept has subsequently been formalized by DuMouchel and Harris (1981), who combine the notion of constant interspecies relative sensitivity with a Bayesian analysis of data from exposure of several species to several agents found in diesel emissions. We discuss this work in some detail to illustrate the potential value of Bayesian methods in this setting.

DuMouchel and Harris consider the problem of combining evidence from studies of human lung cancer incidence, skin tumor initiation in mice, viral transformation in hamsters, and mutagenesis experiments carried out for several related agents. They assume that each investigation is adequately summarized by the logarithm of the slope of an estimated linear exposure-response function. If

$$Y_{kl} = \text{log of the slope of the estimated dose response function for species } k \text{ and agent } l,$$

the summary statistics form a matrix as shown in Table 1.

TABLE 1

Matrix of log slopes of dose-response functions for agent by study type.

Study type	Agent 1	2	.	.	.	L
1	Y_{11}	Y_{12}	.	.	.	Y_{1L}
2	Y_{21}	Y_{22}				Y_{2L}
.	.	.				.
.	.	.				.
.	.	.				.
K	Y_{K1}	Y_{K2}				Y_{KL}

We assume that the true log slopes, denoted θ_{kl}, have a linear representation

$$\theta_{kl} = \mu + \alpha_k + \beta_l + \delta_{kl} .$$

Then

$$\tau_{kk'} = \alpha_k - \alpha_{k'}$$

$$= \text{log relative sensitivity of different modalities } k \text{ and } k',$$

and

$$\rho_{ll'} = \beta_l - \beta_{l'}$$

$$= \text{log relative potency of different agents } l \text{ and } l'.$$

There is no need to independently establish conversion factors for relating animal or mutagenesis experiments to human exposure, since conversion factors are estimated in the data analysis.

The factor δ_{kl} represents the deviation of θ_{kl} from the additive model. If

$$\delta_{kl} \sim N(0, \sigma^2)$$

that is, has a normal distribution with mean 0 and variance σ^2, and

$$y_{kl} \sim N(\theta_{kl}, c_{kl}^2)$$

with c_{kl}^2 estimated from the data and treated as known, analysis of the resulting two stage model will produce estimates of θ_{kl} that are smoothed across strata and study type.

There is a natural link between Bayesian analysis and the study of subjective probability distributions as quantification of expert opinion. Many investigators have studied the problem of eliciting expert opinion (Wallsten and Budescu (1980), and Henrion (1981)) as well as the potential for distortion in the elicitation (Tversky and Kahneman (1974)). Although such expressions of expert judgment may eventually be an important part of health risk assessment, there is presently no accepted procedure for their explicit use.

4. Assessing Sulfur Oxides and Particulate Matter. The Environmental Protection Agency is currently engaged in assessing the health risks of ambient sulfur oxides and particulate matter. Many of the difficult issues in that assessment are characteristic of environmental risk assessment. We consider only the health effects associated with chronic, that is, long term, exposure.

The potential sources of information in that assessment are animal experiments, occupational studies and population based epidemiology. Although animal studies have been of some value in exploring mechanisms for health effects of pollutants, including reduced ciliary clearance, increased airways resistance and increased susceptibility to infection, they have not been helpful in characterizing the shape of the exposure-response function. This is in part due to our imperfect understanding of the chemistry of air pollutants and the biology of their effects. It has been established that SO_2 as a pure gas is relatively harmless except at very high doses because of high absorbency in the nose. However, studies of particulate exposure, possibly combined with SO_2, are difficult to summarize or synthesize because "particulate matter" has been defined in strikingly different ways in different laboratory investigations. Consequently, our current knowledge of the exposure-response relationships for exposure to the SO_x - PM mixture characteristic of fossil fuel combustion is based primarily on epidemiologic studies.

The general view is that occupational studies are also of limited value, both because of the special characteristics of exposure in

occupational settings and the exclusion of children, the aged, and
sensitive individuals from occupational groups. However, as more
emphasis is placed on gathering information from related settings for
risk assessment, occupational data may help to characterize the exposure-response function.

Epidemiologic Studies We first consider some of the important
limitations of epidemiologic studies of air pollution, then examine
some epidemiologic studies of sulfur oxide and particulate matter
exposure. A more detailed assessment is provided in a forthcoming
paper (Ware et al. 1981).

Epidemiologic studies of air pollution ordinarily have three significant limitations:
    a) personal exposure is inaccurately measured,
    b) respiratory disease history is self-reported, and
    c) important confounding variables are poorly controlled.

a) Measurement of personal exposure

The link between outdoor concentration at a central site and personal exposure is often weak. The linkage might be portrayed graphically as

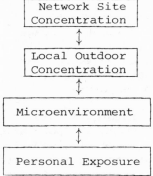

Spengler and his colleagues have been directing a systematic study
of these relationships in conjunction with the Harvard Six-Cities
Study, a large epidemiologic investigation. In a study of personal
exposure to respirable particulates in two cities (Dockery and Spengler, 1981), they found that only 48% of the variation in personal exposure among individuals was explained by outdoor levels. The impact
on epidemiologic studies of the resulting error in measuring the independent variable, exposure, is bias in the exposure-response function toward no association.

b) Measurement of respiratory disease history

Most epidemiologic studies of respiratory disease use self reports
of disease history and symptom prevalence based on standard question-
naires. Such data are subject to significant errors of reporting,
again diluting the relationship between exposure and response.

c) Control of confounding variables

Background variables will be confounding in studies of air pollution and health if:
    i)   they are casually related to the outcome under study or they are surrogates for casual variables;
    ii) they are associated with air pollution concentration.

In air pollution studies, variables like smoking, socioeconomic status, and occupational exposure are often difficult to measure accurately in epidemiologic studies. In addition, the effects of cigarette smoking on respiratory health are highly variable (Fletcher et al., 1976). Yet these variables frequently have stronger associations with respiratory health than does air pollution exposure. The result is substantial potential for bias that is difficult to control.

In an effort to reduce subjectivity in evaluating individual studies of air pollution exposure, we considered five criteria to be met by individual studies:
    a)   They were reported in the open literature
    b)   Concentrations of sulfur oxides and particulate matter were adequately measured and reported.
    c)   Major confounding factors were considered.
    d)   The exposure concentrations were relevant to current or possible future standards.
    e)   No significant errors of design, conduct or analysis were noted.
Although no study can fully achieve these criteria (particularly c) and d)) in this setting, these criteria were helpful in evaluating individual studies.

Mortality Studies One source of information about health effects of chronic exposure to air pollution is a group of mortality studies, using vital statistics and air pollution data from standard metropolitan statistical areas. The work of Lave and Seskin (1970,1977) exemplifies this approach. The major limitation of these studies is inadequate control of smoking, SES, and occupational exposure. The information used in controlling for these factors is often either derivative or nonexistent, leaving open the possibility that associations detected are attributable to these factors or other characteristics of urban living not controlled in the analysis.

For example, Lave and Seskin (1977) performed various multiple linear regressions with deaths per 10,000 persons as the response variable. In one such regression, the result was

$$M = 20 + 0.04\overline{P} + 0.7S_{MIN} + 0.001D$$

$$+ 40(NW) + 700(>65)$$

based on results from 114 SMSA's during 1971, where

$$M = \text{deaths per 10,000 population,}$$

$\overline{P}$ = average level of Total Suspended Particulates
$(\mu g/m^3)$,

S_{MIN} = minimum observed level of sulfate particulates
during the study year $(\mu g/m^3)$,

D = population density $(persons/m^2)$,

NW = percentage of the population nonwhite,

>65 = percentage of the population over 65.

This analysis shows a positive association between pollution level and mortality. However, individual regression coefficients will be unstable over studies because of the high correlation between $\overline{P}$ and S_{MIN}.

We can compare results from several studies in terms of the

Elasticity = the predicted percentage change in M associated with a 100% increase from the mean for each pollution variable while other variables are fixed at their mean levels.

Elasticities from several regressions of Lave and Seskin (1977, LS1-4), Lipfert (1978, L1-4) and Crocker (1979, C1) are given in Table 2. These regression analyses differ principally in the choice and definition of confounding variables. The striking variation in elasticities over analyses illustrates the sensitivity of the results to model selection.

Table 2

Elasticities for Air Pollutants in Nine
Regression Analyses of Mortality

Regression	Elasticity
LS1	.09
LS2	.03
LS3	.09
LS4	.12
L1	.10
L2	.09
L3	.06
L4	.04
C1	.004

The interpretation of these studies can be debated. Wilson et al. (1981) in an informative book on the health effects of fossil fuel burning, argue that the persistently reported association is not

attributable to confounding. Ware et al. (1981) and Thibodeau (1980)
emphasize the limitations of these studies.

Morgan (1978) accepted the linear approximation to the exposure-
response function implicit in this analysis and contrasted the posterior distribution for the sulfate coefficient based on data from
four studies (dashed line in Figure 1) with his subjective probability
distribution (solid line in Figure 1) which assigned probability .01
to negative values and .14 to 0, corresponding to no association.

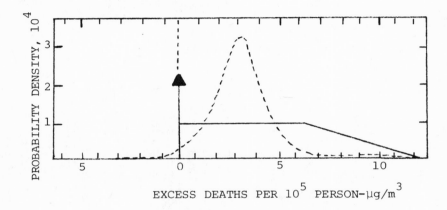

Figure 1

Posterior distribution (dashed line) and subjective probability distribution (solid line) for the slope of the exposure-response distribution linking total mortality to the concentration of sulfate particles,
as given in Morgan (1978). The subjective probability distribution
also assigns probability .01 to negative values and .14 to 0.

Morbidity Studies   Several studies, mainly of cross-sectional design, have reported associations between annual average pollution concentration and respiratory disease prevalence and/or pulmonary function. The studies cited in the assessment of Ware et al. are listed
in Table 3.

Because of differences in aerometric methods and outcome measurement, the data cannot be directly pooled across studies. Instead,
a Bayesian or random-effects approach is indicated. One approach
would treat the parameters of the exposure-response function as random effects over studies. This would allow some study-to study

TABLE 3

Summary of evidence for health of chronic
exposure to SO_2 and particulate matter. From
Ware et al (1981).

Type of Study	Reference	Effects Observed	Annual Average Pollutant Levels At Which Effects Were Noted ($\mu g/m^3$)	
			TSP	SO_2
Cross-Sectional (4 areas)	Lunn et al.	Increased frequency of respiratory symptoms; decreased lung function in five-year-olds	360	225
Cross-Sectional study across Britain	Lambert and Reid	Increased prevalence of respiratory symptoms	200	100
Cross-Sectional (2 areas)	Sawicki	More chronic bronchitis, asthmatic disease in smokers; reduced FEV%	270	125
Cross-Sectional (4 areas)	Rudnik et al.	Increased history and symptoms of respiratory illness	285	125
Longitudinal and Cross-Sectional	Ferris et al.	Higher rate of respiratory symptoms; and decreased lung function	180	55
Cross-Sectional (2 areas)	Hammer	Increased frequency of acute lower respiratory disease	135	>25

variation, but would not resolve the issue of noncomparability of exposure and outcome between studies.

First, we examine the separability of the effects of SO_2 and
particulate matter. Figure 2 shows the joint distribution of SO_2
and black smoke (BS), a measure of particulate pollution, over eight
areas studies by Lunn et al. (1967) and Rudnik (1977). This high
level of collinearity is typical, especially of European studies prior
to 1970, and greatly limits the attribution of association to individual pollutants. This collinearity arises because SO_2 and particulate matter have many common sources.

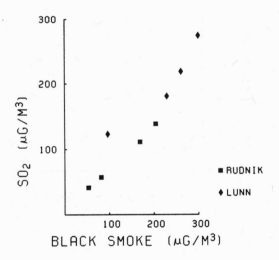

Figure 2

Plot of SO_2 and Black Smoke concentrations of four areas studied by
Lunn et al. (1967) and four sites studied by Rudnik (1977).

   A Fragment of the Health Effects Data For assessing the functional form of the exposure-response relationship, only studies with more
than two sites are helpful if we do not pool across studies. Figures
3-5 show the prevalence of persistent cough plotted against the level
of BS from the studies of Lunn et al. (1967,1970), Lambert and Reid
(1970), and Rudnik (1977). The data are consistent with a monotone
exposure-response relationship, but the paucity of information is most
notable. When we consider that the evidence consists of a handful
of studies of this sort, we realize that there is little evidence for
determining the form of the exposure-response function, and no basis
for investigating whether a threshold exists.

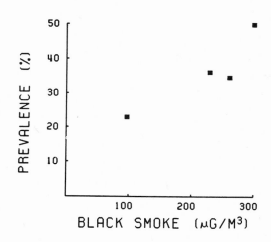

Figure 3

Prevalence of frequent cough among children in four communities studied
by Lunn et al. (1967).

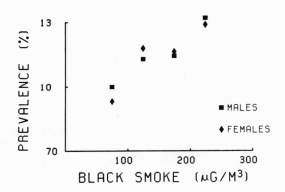

FIGURE 4

Prevalence of persistent cough and phlegm among adults by concentration of black smoke for four groups reported by Lambert and Reid
(1970).

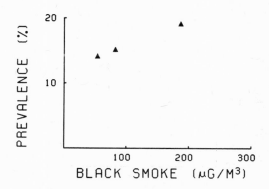

Figure 5

Prevalence of chronic cough among children by concentration of black
smoke in three areas studied by Rudnik (1977).

5. <u>Conclusions</u>. Although the determination of new SO_2 and particulate
matter air quality standards has substantial public health and economic
significance, an assessment of health risk properly begins by empha-
sizing the limitations of current evidence. While air pollution is
unlikely to be beneficial, and severe episodes have clearly produced
excess mortality and morbidity, we know very little about the exposure-response function near current ambient levels. This presents two
problems for the decision maker.
                    -How shall new standards be determined?
                    -How can the information base be improved?

Further comments are addressed to the second question.

   Animal Studies   Animal work is potentially useful for elucidating
disease mechanisms, for studying components of particulate pollution,
and for characterizing the exposure-response functions. If effects
are shown only at high concentrations, the problem of low dose extrapolation will arise in this setting as it has for carcinogens.

   Epidemiologic Studies   There is irreducible uncertainty in epidemiologic studies that arises from the potential for bias previously
described. Health effects of SO_x and PM, if they occur at present
ambient levels, may be comparable to or smaller than possible bias.
Large epidemiologic studies will help to assess that boundary. There
may also be a role for case-control studies and investigations including monitoring of personal exposure.

   Risk Assessment Methodology   The problem of combining evidence is a
challenging issue for methodologic research. Especially needed are:

        -New techniques for combining results across studies.
        -Improved methods for eliciting subjective probability
         distributions.
        -Techniques for modifying measures of uncertainty, such
         as standard errors, to reflect uncertainty not due to
         sampling variability.
        -Methods for combining subjective probabilities with ob-
         jective (data based) information.

Health risk assessment is a natural part of environmental decision
making. We are just beginning to develop the language and technology
needed in the task.

REFERENCES

(1) T.D. Crocker, W. Schulze, S. BenDavid, and A.V. Kneese. Methods
     development for assessing air pollution control benefits,
     Volume 1: Experiments in the economics of air pollution epi-
     demiology. EPA-600/5-79-001a, E.P.A., Research Triangle Park,
     NC, (1979).

(2) E. Crouch, and R. Wilson. Interspecies comparison of carcino-
     genic potency. J. Tox. and Env. Hlth. 5: pp. 1095-1118, (1978).

(3) D.W. Dockery and J.D. Spengler. Personal exposure to respirable
     particulates and sulfates. J. Air Pollution Control, Assoc.
     31: pp. 153-159, (1981).

(4) W. DuMouchel, and J. Harris. Bayes and empirical Bayes methods
     for combining cancer experiments in man and other species. Tech-
     nical Report No. 24, (1981), Mass. Inst. of Tech.

(5)   B.G. Ferris, Jr., and D.O. Anderson, The prevalence of chronic respiratory disease in a New Hampshire town. Am. Rev. Resp. Dis. 86: pp. 165-185, (1962).

(6)   B.G. Ferris, Jr., I.T.T. Higgins, M.W. Higgins, and J.M. Peters, Chronic nonspecific respiratory disease in Berlin, New Hampshire, 1961-1967. A follow-up study. Amer. Rev. Resp. Dis. 107: pp. 110-22, (1973).

(7)   B.G. Ferris, Jr., H. Chen, S. Puleo, and R.L.H. Murphy, Chronic nonspecific respiratory disease in Berlin, New Hampshire, 1967-1973. A further follow-up study. Am. Rev. Resp. Dis. 113: pp. 475-485, (1976).

(8)   C.M. Fletcher, R. Peto, C. Tinker, and F.E. Speizer, The Natural History of Chronic Bronchitis and Emphyzema. Oxford University Press, Oxford, (1976).

(9)   D.I. Hammer, Frequency of lower respiratory disease in two southeastern communities, 1968-1971. Sc. D. dissertation, Harvard University, (1976).

(10) D.A. Harville, Maximum likelihood approaches to variance component estimation and to related problems. J. Am. Statist. Assoc. 72: pp. 320-340, (1977).

(11) M. Henrion, Assessing probabilities: A review. Dept. of Engineering and Public Policy, Carnegie-Mellon University, (1981).

(12) P.M. Lambert, and D.D. Reid, Smoking air pollution and bronchitis in Britain. Lancet 1: pp. 853-857, (1970).

(13) L.B. Lave, and E. Seskin, Air pollution and human health. Science 69: pp. 723-33, (1970).

(14) L.B. Lave, and E. Seskin, Air Pollution and Human Health. Johns Hopkins University Press, Baltimore, (1977).

(15) F.W. Lipfert, The association of human mortality with air pollution. Union Graduate School Thesis, Cincinnati, Ohio, (1978).

(16) J.E. Lunn, J. Knowelden, and A.J. Handyside, Patterns of respiratory illness in Sheffield infant school children. Br. J. Prev. and Soc. Med. 21: pp. 7-16, (1967).

(17) J.E. Lunn, J. Knowelden, and J.W. Roe, Patterns of respiratory illness in Sheffield junior school children. A follow-up study. Br. J. Prev. and Soc. Med. 24: pp. 223-228, (1970).

(18) N. Mantel, and W. Haenszel, Statistical aspects of the analysis of data from retrospective studies of disease. J. Nat. Cancer Inst. 22: pp. 719-748.

(19) M.G. Morgan, S.C. Morris, A.K. Meir, and D.L. Shenk. A probabilistic methodology for estimating air pollution effects from coal-fired power plants. Energy Systems and Policy 2: pp. 287-310, (1978).

(20)   Report of the Committee on Risk and Decision Making, National
       Academy of Sciences, (1981).

(21)   J. Rudnik, Epidemiological study on long-term effects on health
       of air pollution. Research Report 7a Nat. Research Inst. for
       Mother and child. Warsaw, (1977).

(22)   L.A. Thibodeau, R.B. Reed, and Y.M.M. Bishop, Air pollution and
       human health: A review and reanalysis. To appear in Env. Hlth.
       Persp.

(23)   A. Tversky, and D. Kahneman, Judgment under uncertainty: Heuris-
       tics and biases. Science 185: pp. 1124-31, (1974).

(24)   T. Wallsten and D. Budescu, Encoding subjective probabilities:
       A psychological and psychometric review. U.S. Environmental
       Protection Agency, (1980).

(25)   J.H. Ware, L.A. Thibodeau, F.E. Speizer, S.D. Colone, and B.G.
       Ferris, Jr., Assessment of the health effects of atmospheric
       sulfur oxides and particulate matter: Evidence from observation-
       al studies. To appear in Env. Hlth. Persp.

(26)   R. Wilson, and J.J. Harrington, Alternate Approaches to Setting
       Ambient Air Quality Standards in The Business Roundtable Air
       Quality Project, Volume 1, (1980).

(27)   R. Wilson, S.D. Colome, J.D. Spengler, and D.G. Wilson, Health
       effects of Fossil Fuel Burning. Ballinger, Cambridge, MA.,
       (1980).

OZONE DATA

Statistical Analysis
of Stratospheric Ozone Data
for Trend Detection

G. Reinsel, G. C. Tiao and R. Lewis*

Abstract. Time series modelling of monthly Dobson ground-based total ozone data is considered for the detection of trend in ozone due to the possible effects of the release of chlorofluoromethanes (CFMs). Based on ozone data from a global network of 36 ground-based Dobson recording stations over the period 1958-1979, our findings show little evidence of any trend in global ozone occurring in the 1970's. Using a random effects model for the individual station trend estimates, the global change in total ozone during 1970-1979 has been estimated as (.79 ± 1.30)%. These results differ considerably from the theoretical CFM chemical model predictions of (-1.6 ± 1.1)% change [5].

Total ozone data from the Nimbus-4 BUV satellite experiment for the period April, 1970 to May, 1977 is analyzed to: (1) provide a better appreciation and understanding of the global distribution and behavior of total ozone, with emphasis on assessing any possible trend in ozone, and (2) compare with ground-based Dobson total ozone data for possible instrument calibration and drift errors. Linear regression models containing annual, semi-annual, biennial and linear trend components are estimated for monthly time series of zonal averages of satellite data and the nature of the variation in these components with latitude is presented. An analysis of daily BUV satellite-Dobson ground ozone data is performed which shows a definite downward drift in the satellite data estimated at about -1.5 m atm-cm per year relative to a Dobson network of 36 stations.

1. Introduction. Recently, scientists have focused considerable attention on the effect of human activities on the stratospheric ozone equilibrium. Theoretical chemical models have been used to estimate that the release of various chemical compounds, such as halocarbons, to the environment have and will continue to result in excessive depletion of the stratospheric ozone layer (see [1]-[6]). Of particular importance is the effect of the release of chlorofluoromethanes (CFMs), which are widely used in aerosol products, air conditioners, refrigerators, and urethane foam manufacturing. Statistical analysis

*Department of Statistics, University of Wisconsin-Madison, Madison, WI 53706. This research is partially supported by Chemical Manufacturers' Association under Contract No. FC-78-250R and Contract No. FC 80-304.

of available stratospheric ozone measurements is important to determine
whether any changes in the ozone data consistent with the ozone depletion theory can be detected.

   In a recent paper [7], time series modelling of monthly averages of
the total column amount of atmospheric ozone (total ozone) at a network
of 36 ground-based Dobson recording stations is considered for the
detection of trend in total ozone due to the possible effects of the
release of CFMs. In Section 2 of this paper we review and update the
analysis in [7], which covers the period 1958-1978, to include recently
available total ozone data for 1979. In addition to the ground-based
Dobson ozone measurements mentioned above, an extensive set of total
ozone data from the Nimbus-4 Backscattered Ultraviolet (BUV) satellite
experiment for the period April, 1970 to May, 1977 is also available.
The first two years of the Nimbus-4 satellite data have previously been
analyzed in [8] and [9], while the entire seven years of satellite data
is analyzed in [10]. In Section 3 of this paper we summarize some of
the results of the analysis in [10].

   2. Time Series Modelling of Ground Station Ozone Data. Total
stratospheric ozone measurements using Dobson spectrophotometers and
other instruments are currently being recorded on a regular daily basis
at over 60 ground locations throughout the world. Most of the recording
stations began monitoring total ozone in the late 1950's or early
1960's. These ozone recording stations are not uniformly distributed
about the globe, but tend to be most heavily concentrated in the North
Temperate zone, especially North America and Europe. The location of
36 longer running recording stations used in our statistical analysis
are indicated in Figure 1.

   Total ozone data has been previously analyzed by a number of authors,
e.g., see [11], [12], [13], and [14], with particular interest in
quantifying long term trends. The statistical procedure commonly used
in these studies is linear regression analysis (i.e., fitting a
straight line) applied to adjusted total ozone values (e.g., deviations
from monthly means, monthly deviations from the overall mean or running
averages of these deviations for individual stations, and for averages
of stations grouped according to geographical regions, hemispheres and
the globe). However, problems arise in the interpretation of results
from these linear regression models since these models fail to take
account of the positive autocorrelation which is present in the ozone
data. Hence we consider time series analysis which accounts for autocorrelation in a quantitative trend assessment of ozone data.

   2.a. Statistical Time Series Models. Let us denote the time series
of monthly means of total ozone over time t at a particular location
by $y(t)$, t=1,2,...,T. We consider statistical models for such series
for the detection of a trend in the ozone measurements at each individual location. One prominent characteristic of the ozone data is a
strong seasonal pattern over time. In addition, the CFM chemical
theory in [5] predicts a depletion in ozone which is closely

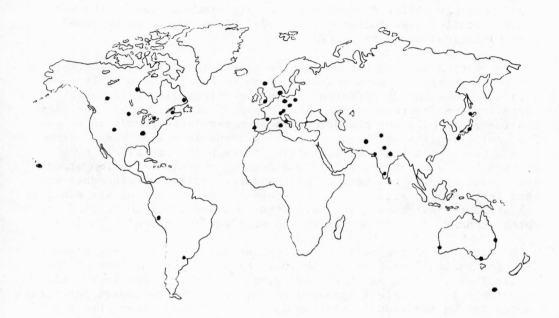

Figure 1.   Geographical Distribution of 36 Dobson Stations

approximated by a linear trend starting in 1970. Based on these considerations of the ozone data, the basic components of a time series
model for monthly ozone data will consist of an overall mean level μ,
a component s(t) which accounts for the seasonal variation over months,
a component $\omega x(t)$ which accounts for a possible trend or depletion in
ozone over time, and an unexplained error or "noise" component N(t)
which may be autocorrelated over time and hence may account for the
short-term correlation in ozone from month to month. Thus an appropriate model for the time series y(t) is

(1) $$y(t) = \mu + s(t) + \omega x(t) + N(t),$$

where the seasonal component s(t) is adequately represented as a
linear combination of sinusoidal curves of fundamental period 12
months and its harmonics (e.g., 6 months), and $\omega x(t)$ represents a
linear trend beginning in 1970, that is, x(t) = 0 for $t \leq T_o$ and
$x(t) = (t-T_o)/12$ for $t > T_o$ where T_o denotes December, 1969, and
represents the annual rate of change in ozone since 1970 at a particular location. To account for the autocorrelation over time in the
noise N(t), it is modelled as an autoregressive process

$$N(t) = \phi_1 N(t-1) + \ldots + \phi_p N(t-p) + a(t) ,$$

where a(t) is a process of independent random variables with mean
0 and possibly different variances for different months of the year.
A more detailed description of the model given above can be found in
the statistical appendix in [7].

Time series models of the above form, and in particular the rate of
change parameter ω, were estimated from the available monthly ozone
data at a total of 36 different ground locations listed in Table 1,
including the "representative global sample" of 9 stations previously
considered in [15] for the detection of man-related trends in ozone.
The series lengths of the data at the various locations ranged from
11 to 22 years of monthly data, running through 1979 at almost every
station. To account for possibly different monthly variation at each
individual station a weighted least squares estimation procedure was
used in the calculation of the estimate $\hat{\omega}$ of ω and of its statistical standard deviation. The estimates $\hat{\omega}$'s and their associated estimated standard deviations for the 36 stations are given in Table 1.

A histogram of the estimates of the annual rate of change since
1970 for these 36 stations is shown in Figure 2 (on the left of the
vertical axis). The estimates are given in % change per year. Since
from Table 1 the typical standard deviation of the estimated percentage
change for an individual location is about .151% per year, the spread
of the estimates in Figure 2 indicates that there are real differences
in the trends in ozone data at different locations. However, the estimates do seem to form a cluster about zero which suggests the absence
of an overall global trend during the period 1970-1979. In Figure 2,
the estimates are also plotted against the latitude of the station's
location. Different symbols are used to indicate the general geographic
location of the station corresponding to each estimate. The results
show that either on a global basis or on a regional basis there is no
strong evidence of an up trend or a down trend in the ozone data.

2.b. Sources of Variation in Estimating a Global Ozone Trend.
There are a number of factors which need to be taken into account in
using the data from the Dobson station network to provide an estimate
of the actual global trend in ozone. Dobson measuring instruments
are not generally calibrated with periodic regularity. Thus the instruments are subject to long term calibration and drift errors which can
affect the estimate of ozone trend. In addition, differences in long
term pressure patterns and variation in observing conditions exist between different geographic regions which may affect the estimated
trend within a region. Indeed, the spread of the histogram in
Figure 2, when compared with the standard deviation of .151% for the
trend estimate at an individual station, shows that there is more than
one source of variation among the estimates.

In an attempt to partially account for these sources of variation
in the estimated trends due to instrument and other local sources of
errors, and geographic variation, we proceed as follows. Suppose we
consider the estimated trend at an individual station within a given

Table 1

Trend Estimates from Time Series Models for Period 1958 - 1979

Station	Location	Data Period	Trend $\hat{\omega}$ (m atm-cm per year)	Estimated St.Dev.of $\hat{\omega}$ (m atm-cm per year)
Churchill, Canada	58N,94W	1/65-12/79	-.887	.421
Edmonton, Canada	53N,114W	4/58-12/79	.351	.401
Goose, Canada	53N,60W	1/62-12/79	1.160	.429
Caribou, USA	47N,68W	1/63-12/79	-.939	.349
Bismarck, USA	46N,100W	1/63-12/79	-.846	.292
Toronto, Canada	43N,79W	1/60-12/79	.449	.353
Boulder, USA	40N,105W	1/64-12/79	-.900	.239
Nashville, USA	36N,86W	3/63-12/79	.095	.350
Aarhus, Denmark	56N,10E	1/58-12/79	-.295	.864
Lerwick, UK	60N,1W	1/69-12/79	1.071	.584
Bracknell, UK	51N,0W	1/69-12/79	-.066	.353
Potsdam, G.D.R.	52N,13E	1/64-12/79	.199	.784
Belsk, Poland	52N,20E	4/63-12/79	2.749	.419
Hradec Kralove, Czech.	50N,16E	8/61-12/79	1.836	.419
Hohenpeissenberg, F.R.G.	47N,11E	1/68-12/79	-.768	.335
Arosa, Switz.	46N,9E	1/58-12/79	-.222	.281
Mont Louis, France	42N,0E	3/62-12/79	1.966	.417
Vigna Di Valle, Italy	42N,12E	1/58-12/79	.666	.337
Cagliari/Elmas, Italy	39N,9E	1/58-12/79	-.379	.920
Lisbon, Portugal	38N,9W	10/67-12/79	.853	.354
Srinagar, India	34N,74E	2/64-12/79	.312	.384
Quetta, Pakistan	30N,67E	8/69-12/79	.898	.430
New Delhi, India	28N,77E	1/63-12/79	.980	.399
Varanasi, India	25N,83E	1/64-12/79	.614	.758
Mount Abu, India	24N,72E	11/69-12/79	1.775	.547
Kodaikanal, India	10N,77E	1/61-12/79	-.255	.875
Sapporo, Japan	43N,141E	2/58-12/79	-.239	.383
Tateno, Japan	36N,140E	1/58-12/79	.083	.284
Kagoshima, Japan	31N,130E	1/62-12/79	.693	.393
Brisbane, Australia	27S,153E	1/58-12/79	-.133	.483
Perth, Australia	32S,116E	3/69-12/79	1.640	.416
Aspendale, Australia	38S.145E	1/58-12/79	-.171	.412
MacQuarie Island, Australia	54S,159E	4/63-9/79	.108	.510
Huancayo, Peru	12S,75W	3/64-12/79	.263	.425
Buenos Aires, Argentina	34S,58W	10/65-12/79	1.532	.505
Mauna Loa, Hawaii	19N,155W	1/64-12/79	-1.319	.324

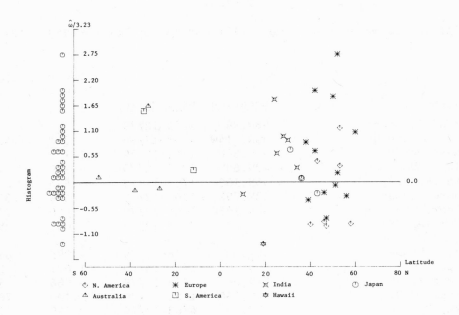

Figure 2.   Trend Estimates vs. Latitude
(m atm-cm per year/3.23)

region as consisting of the sum of the following independent components, the true global trend ω, a component due to geographic variation which is constant within a region but may differ from region to region with a variance σ_G^2, a component due to instrument error and other local sources of variation which is constant within a station but differs from station to station with a variance of σ_I^2, and a component which represents the statistical error in estimating trend within a particular station with a variance of σ_E^2. Applying standard variance component techniques (see the statistical appendix in [7]) the variances of these three components, statistical, individual station, and geographical, can then be estimated from the estimated variances of the trend estimates for individual stations, the variation of trend estimates between stations within each region, and the variation of regional estimates of trend between the different regions.

Now an assumption that is commonly made in the standard variance components model would imply in this situation that the statistical error in the trend estimate at any particular station is independent of the statistical error in the trend estimate at any other station. However, there is evidence to suggest that these errors at neighboring stations may be correlated. In fact, we have found that the

correlations between trend estimates at selected pairs of stations
within each region range from .2 to .7. To simplify the calculations,
as a rough approximation we suppose that the statistical errors in the
individual trend estimates have a common correlation of .5 between any
two stations within a given region, and are independent between
regions.

The estimate of a true global trend in ozone, obtained by appropriately weighting the individual station trend estimates, contain
error due to all three sources of variation, not just the statistical
estimation error within each station. When the geographical, individual, and statistical sources of error are taken into account, the
estimate of an actual global trend is .256 m atm-cm per year with an
estimated standard deviation of .210 m atm-cm, corresponding to an
interval estimate for total ozone change over 1970-1979 equal to
(.792 $\pm$ 1.300)%.

It is of interest to compare the preceding results obtained from
ground station data with the range of (-1.6 $\pm$ 1.1)% depletion predicted by the CFM chemical models [5] to have occurred during the
period 1970-1979. The estimated interval (.792 $\pm$ 1.300)% and the predicted range are quite different. The ground station data fail to
show statistically significant evidence of a trend in ozone during the
1970's. While the data do not completely contradict the theoretical
predictions in [5], they do provide evidence to suggest that the
theoretical predictions of the rate of depletion given in [5] may be
too large, or that possible ozone depletion due to the release of
CFMs is perhaps being offset by changes due to natural or other man-
related activities. In this regard, a recent paper [16], considers a
range of chemical model assumptions involving reaction rate coefficients, transport, trends in trace species (such as CH_4 and N_2O), and
the simultaneous effects of CFM release, increases in CO_2, and subsonic
aircraft emissions. A "most probable" trend in total ozone is predicted
there which is much more consistent with the estimated interval (.79
$\pm$ 1.30)% than is the predicted range in [5].

One important remark should be made concerning the above results.
It has been assumed implicitly that the global ozone trend estimate
that we have obtained is not seriously biased by the unbalanced
location of the 36 ground stations about the globe. Thus we assume
the results from the network of 36 stations are representative of
global conditions and are not geographically biased with respect to
the global trend behavior of ozone. In [10], an analysis is performed utilizing ozone observations from the Nimbus-4 BUV satellite
experiment, which has yielded an extensive data set for the period
1970-1977, and ozone observations from the 36 ground-based Dobson
recording stations. This analysis based on satellite and ground-based
ozone data provides information on the uncertainties in the ground data
due to instrument drift and calibration problems, and on geographic
spatial variations in ozone behavior. In particular, an analysis in

[10] indicates that, for purposes of trend detection, the 36 ground
station locations seem to provide a representative sample of the entire globe during the period of the 1970's. While the satellite ozone
data offers extensive global coverage, detection of trend in ozone
cannot be based on satellite data alone due to the shortness of the
time span over which it has been recorded.

   2.c. Temperature as an Exogenous Factor. We note that the statistical analysis presented above is only designed to obtain an estimate
of the actual global trend in ozone since 1970 regardless of the
source of this trend. Long term natural trends in ozone may exist
which could influence the estimate of global trend. Unfortunately,
the Dobson ozone data do not extend over a sufficiently long period of
time to detect such natural long term trend variations. Thus the
present analysis is not designed to distinguish between possible long
term natural trends and recent trends in ozone due to human activities.
Preliminary research has begun to help resolve this problem by investigating the relation between stratospheric ozone and other meteorological variables, such as stratospheric temperatures, whose long
term variational patterns are better known than those of ozone. The
inclusion and analysis of such meteorological data may aid in quantifying and reducing the uncertainty concerning the natural trend variations in ozone.

   We have investigated the correlation between (seasonally adjusted)
total ozone and (seasonally adjusted) measurements of stratospheric
temperature at various pressure levels taken near the Dobson ground
stations. A typical pattern of correlations (especially for locations
in the temperate zones) is characterized by a maximum negative correlation between ozone and temperature occurring in the middle troposphere,
usually at 500 mb($\approx$ 5 km), and a maximum positive correlation
occurring in the stratosphere at 100 mb($\approx$ 16 km). Thus we consider
the use of monthly temperature data at these two pressure levels as
exogenous variables in the time series models for ozone to help
account for natural variation in ozone. Specifically, time series
models of the form

(2) $y(t) = \mu + s(t) + \gamma_1 z_1(t) + \gamma_2 z_2(t) + \omega x(t) + N(t),$

where $z_1(t)$ and $z_2(t)$ are the monthly averages of temperatures at
the two selected pressure levels and the other terms are similar to
those appearing in equation (1), were estimated for the 36 ground
stations.

   The main effect of the inclusion of the temperature variables in
the time series models was to substantially reduce the variance of
the residual process $a(t)$ by an average of about 40%. Hence the
temperature variables were quite useful in "explaining" the behavior
of ozone. The strength of the ozone-temperature relation is highly
dependent on latitude, however, with only weak association between

ozone and temperature in the tropics and subtropics. However, the
inclusion of the temperature variables has little effect overall on
the trend estimates $\hat{\omega}$. This is illustrated in Figure 3 which plots
the differences between trend estimates from the time series models
with and without the temperature variables at the 36 stations. As
suggested by the rather tight concentration about zero of these
differences, the inclusion of the temperature variables in the time
series models yields no substantial changes in the conclusions concerning global trend in ozone obtained from the previous models.
Indeed, the average difference between the trend estimates from the
time series models with and without temperature variables (trend in
model without temperature minus trend in model with temperature) is
only .012% per year. One additional feature of Figure 3 that may be
noted is the distinctive grouping of the differences for stations in
North America and Europe. The inclusion of the temperature variables
tended to decrease the trend estimate $\hat{\omega}$ over European stations
while the opposite is true for stations in North America.

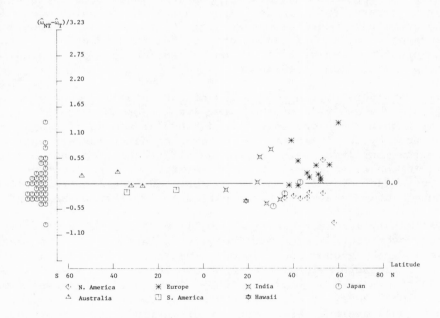

Figure 3. Difference in Trend Estimates vs. Latitude
(Trend in Model without Temperatures − Trend
in Model with Temperatures)

3. Analysis of Ozone Data from the Nimbus-4 BUV Satellite
Experiment. The Nimbus-4 Backscattered Ultraviolet (BUV) satellite
experiment has resulted in an extensive set of total ozone data for
the seven year period April, 1970 to May, 1977. This satellite data
set offers nearly a complete global coverage of total ozone measurements, with the exception of extreme polar regions (approximately 81°
-90° north and south latitudes). For this reason the Nimbus-4 BUV

data is important in the study of the global behavior of total ozone, with particular interest in any possible trends in total ozone.

The Nimbus-4 BUV satellite experiment measured total ozone at about 30 second intervals during the sunlit portion of the satellite's orbit, with measurements at any particular location usually occurring at about noon local time. Although the satellite operated nearly continuously during its first two and one-half years, its operation during the remaining years was much less consistent. In fact, the data recorded during the first two and one-half years of operation comprises approximately two thirds of the entire seven year data set.

In this paper we summarize some results of the analysis of the Nimbus-4 BUV satellite data given in [10]. In [10] we analyze the Nimbus-4 BUV satellite data in order to (1) provide a better appreciation and understanding of the global behavior of total ozone, with emphasis on assessing any possible trend in ozone, (2) compare with ground based Dobson ozone data for possible instrument calibration and drift errors, and (3) determine the extent to which ozone data at the previously mentioned network of 36 ground station locations is representative of global ozone behavior for the detection of trend. In the present paper we restrict our attention to a discussion of the first two topics mentioned above.

3.a. Analysis of Zonal Averages of BUV Satellite Ozone Data. To facilitate the analysis of the extensive set of BUV satellite data, we partitioned the globe into 540 rectangular blocks of dimension 6° in latitude by 20° in longitude. The ozone data was then aggregated by forming monthly averages of the satellite data for each block. Blocks in the range 78°-90° N and S latitude were not considered because of a lack of data. This then resulted in 468 monthly time series of ozone block averages over the period April, 1970 to May, 1977.

Preliminary inspection of the satellite data shows that variation in ozone over time depends more heavily on latitude than on longitude. To simplify the global analysis of ozone, the monthly block averages were averaged across longitude to obtain 26 zonal time series, each representing a band of 6° in latitude. To provide a general impression of the global behavior of total ozone over time, a contour plot of the monthly zonal averages as a function of latitude and time is presented in Figure 4. Some main features are rather apparent from this figure. The mean level and amplitude of annual variation depend in a rather systematic way on latitude, with the northern and southern hemispheres being complementary by seasons, and there is some evidence of a biennial variation, which is more prominent in the equatorial and south temperate zones.

As an indication of the global trend movement of total ozone, Figure 5 shows the time series of monthly global averages of ozone obtained from the 26 zonal time series as an average weighted by the surface areas. This figure indicates a definite downward trend in the

global ozone satellite data over the seven year period 1970–1976.
However, this downward trend may be due in large part to a downward
drift in the satellite instrument, as suggested by the satellite-
ground data comparisons presented later.

We now propose a simple model to describe the general behavior of
ozone. Let $y_t(\theta)$ denote the monthly average of total ozone for
month t over the latitude zone θ. Then we consider the linear regression model

(3) $y_t(\theta) = \mu(\theta) + s(t,\theta) + b(t,\theta) + \omega(\theta)\,t/12 + N_t(\theta),$

where $\mu(\theta)$ is the constant (or level) term.

$$s(t,\theta) = \alpha_1(\theta)\,\sin(\tfrac{2\pi t}{12}) + \beta_1(\theta)\,\cos(\tfrac{2\pi t}{12}) + \alpha_2(\theta)\,\sin(\tfrac{4\pi t}{12})$$

$$+ \beta_2(\theta)\,\cos(\tfrac{4\pi t}{12})$$

represents components associated with annual and semi-annual variation,

$$b(t,\theta) = \alpha_3(\theta)\,\sin(\tfrac{2\pi t}{24}) + \beta_3(\theta)\,\cos(\tfrac{2\pi t}{24})$$

represents a component associated with biennial variation, $\omega(\theta)\,t/12$

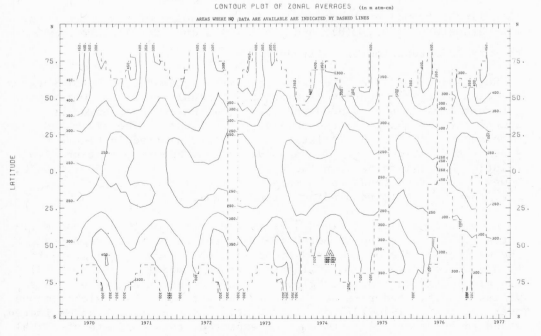

Figure 4. Contour Plot of Zonal Averages

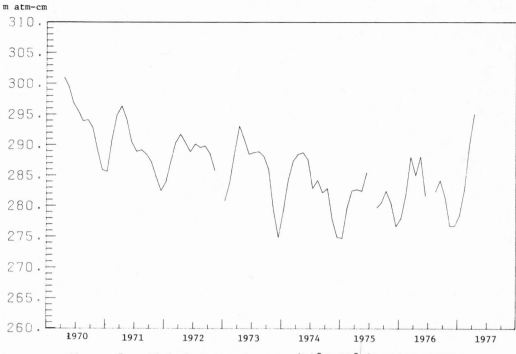

Figure 5.   Global Ozone Series (78°N–78°S), 1970–1977

is a linear trend component, and $N_t(\theta)$ is a noise or error component.
The parameters $\mu(\theta)$, $\omega(\theta)$, and the $\alpha_i(\theta)$'s and $\beta_i(\theta)$'s are assumed
to vary as a function of latitude θ.

Regression models of the above form were estimated by least squares
for each of the 26 monthly time series of zonal averages. Our main
interest lies in the trend parameter $\omega(\theta)$, which represents the
annual rate of change in the satellite ozone data. The estimated rates
of change $\hat{\omega}(\theta)$ for the 26 latitude zones are plotted in Figure 6
against the latitude θ. It can be seen from Figure 6 that no simple
relationship exists between the trend in satellite data and latitude,
however the trend tends to be more negative in the south temperate
zone than in the corresponding northern zone.

A weighted average (weighted by surface area) of these trend estimates yields the value of –1.80 m atm-cm per year, which represents
the estimated rate of downward trend in global ozone satellite data.
As a corroborative check, a linear regression model of the form (3)
was also estimated for the "global" ozone series of Figure 5. This
yields an estimated rate of change in the satellite data global ozone
over the period 1970–1977 of –1.83 m atm-cm per year with an estimated
standard error of .14 m atm-cm. As expected, this estimate of global
trend is in close agreement with the weighted average of zonal trends.

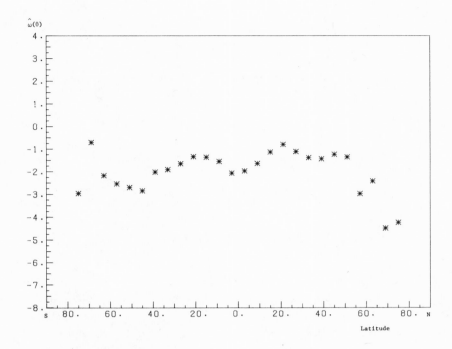

Figure 6.   Regression Analysis Using Zonal Averages
Trend Estimates vs. Latitude

Apart from the trend parameter, it may also be of interest to consider the level parameter $\mu(\theta)$ and the annual seasonal and biennial
amplitudes $R_1(\theta)$ and $R_3(\theta)$, where $R_i(\theta) = (\alpha_i(\theta)^2 + \beta_i(\theta)^2)^{1/2}$.   The
estimated levels $\hat{\mu}(\theta)$ and estimated amplitudes $\hat{R}_1(\theta)$ and $\hat{R}_3(\theta)$

of the annual seasonal and biennial components are plotted in Figures
7, 8a, and 8b, respectively. (Also plotted at the top of Figures 8a
and 8b are the percent of variance contributed by each of the components, annual and biennial, to the overall variance of the seasonal
deterministic component $s(t,\theta) + b(t,\theta)$ in (3), that is,
$\hat{R}_i(\theta)^2 / (\hat{R}_1(\theta)^2 + \hat{R}_2(\theta)^2 + \hat{R}_3(\theta)^2)$, for $i = 1$ and 3.)   The dependence
of these parameter estimates on the latitude is clearly seen.   In
particular note the lack of symmetry, at higher latitudes, between
the Northern and Southern hemispheres in the amplitude of the annual
component, and also note the prominence of the biennial amplitude in
the tropics.

   3.b.   Comparison of BUV Satellite and Dobson Ground Data.   In this
section we consider the comparison of Nimbus-4 BUV satellite data
with Dobson ground data at the network of 36 ground stations considered
in Section 2 to determine any possible calibration and drift
errors between the two types of measurements.   This comparison consists

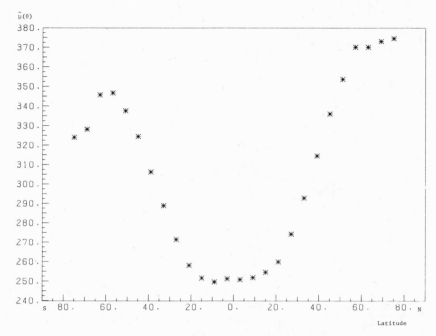

Figure 7.   Regression Analysis using Zonal Averages
            Constant (or Level) vs. Latitude

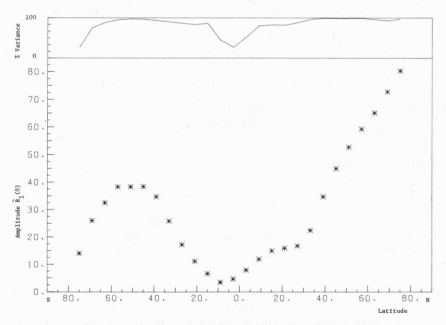

Figure 8a.   Regression Analysis using Zonal Averages
             Amplitude and Percent Variance of Annual
             Seasonal Component vs. Latitude

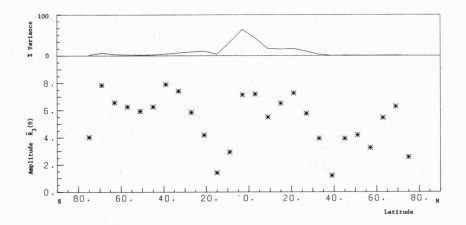

Figure 8b.   Regression Analysis using Zonal Averages
Amplitude and Percent Variance of Biennial
Component vs. Latitude

of pairing each of the 36 Dobson station's daily average ozone measurements with the daily averages of all satellite measurements recorded
on the same day within a 400 kilometer square centered at the ground
station's location.   Pairing observations in this manner over the
entire period April, 1970 to May, 1977, a total of 100 to 300 pairs of
daily observations were obtained for each of the 36 stations.   For each
station the paired differences (satellite-ground) were computed.
Although the overall behavior of the satellite and ground data are
similar, the paired differences indicate that a systematic bias as
well as a drift may exist between these two types of measurements at
individual stations.

In order to detect any possible systematic bias and drift between
satellite and individual ground station measurements over time, simple
linear regression models were estimated using the daily paired differences at each station.   To describe this, we first consider the following simple models for daily ground observations GRD_t and satellite

observations $SAT_t(\theta)$ near a particular ground station:

(4) $$GRD_t = \mu_1 + s_1(t) + \omega_1 \, t/365 + N_{1t},$$
$$SAT_t(\theta) = \mu_2(\theta) + s_2(t,\theta) + \omega_2 \, t/365 + N_{2t}(\theta) \; ,$$

where θ is the latitude of the satellite measurement and ranges over the small interval $\theta_o \pm 2°$ of length $4°$ centered at θ_o, the latitude of the corresponding ground station, μ_1 and $\mu_2(\theta)$ are "constant" terms, and $s_1(t)$ and $s_2(t,\theta)$ are components representing annual variation. Now over the small range of θ values we assume that, approximately, $\mu_2(\theta)$ and $s_2(t,\theta)$ are linear functions of θ of the form,

$$\mu_2(\theta) = \mu_2 + \mu_2^*(\theta-\theta_o),$$

$$s_2(t,\theta) = (\alpha_2+\alpha_2^*(\theta-\theta_o)) \sin(\frac{2\pi t}{365}) + (\beta_2+\beta_2^*(\theta-\theta_o)) \cos(\frac{2\pi t}{365}),$$

and

$$s_1(t) = \alpha_1 \sin(\frac{2\pi t}{365}) + \beta_1 \cos(\frac{2\pi t}{365}).$$

Then the model for the daily differences is

$$SAT_t(\theta) - GRD_t = \alpha + \mu_2^*(\theta-\theta_o) + \delta \, t/365$$

$$(5) \qquad\qquad + ((\alpha_2-\alpha_1) + \alpha_2^*(\theta-\theta_o)) \sin(\frac{2\pi t}{365})$$

$$+ ((\beta_2-\beta_1) + \beta_2^*(\theta-\theta_o)) \cos(\frac{2\pi t}{365}) + (N_{2t}(\theta) - N_{1t}),$$

where $\alpha = (\mu_2-\mu_1)$ represents the "constant" or "mean" bias, $\delta = \omega_2-\omega_1$ represents the measurement "drift" between satellite and ground measurements at the particular ground station location, and the co-efficients $(\alpha_2-\alpha_1)$ and $(\beta_2-\beta_1)$ measure any "seasonal bias". The additional terms which involve $(\theta-\theta_o)$ account for the variable latitude position of the satellite measurement relative to the fixed latitude θ_o of the ground measurement.

Using the linear regression model (5) for the data of daily differences at the 36 ground stations, we obtained an estimated aver-age "constant" bias of -9.88 m atm-cm and an estimated average drift of -1.54 m atm-cm per year from the 36 ground stations. The individual estimated bias and drift results for the 36 stations are given in Table 2 and plotted against latitude in Figures 9 and 10, respectively. Now, the average of the estimated standard deviations (for individual stations) of the drift estimates is approximately .6 m atm-cm per year. However, the drift estimates vary considerably from station to station with a standard deviation of 1.45 m atm-cm, indicating that there do exist significant differences in the drift characteristics over the different stations. Taking into account this "between station" variation in drifts, an estimate of the standard deviation of the average drift obtained from the 36 stations is

$1.45/\sqrt{36}$ = .24 m atm-cm, Thus, a 95% confidence interval for the
overall drift between daily satellite and Dobson ground station observations is (-1.54 $\pm$ .48) m atm-cm per year.

One interpretation of the estimated drift of -1.54 m atm-cm per year
between satellite and ground measurements is as follows. If, as seems
reasonable, see e.g. [6], pp. 322-323, we assume the overall drift in
ground Dobson station ozone measurements is zero over the seven year
period 1970-1976, then -1.54 m atm-cm per year is an estimate of the
downward drift experienced by the satellite measurements over the
period of the satellite's operation. The exact causes of any downward drift in the BUV satellite data are not known and this problem
is deserving of further investigation. One possible reason for an
uncorrected instrument calibration drift in the BUV satellite measurements is the degradation of the diffuser plate for solar flux measurements which caused a serious problem in maintaining long-term instrument calibration. Under the above assumption the estimate of a downward trend in the global ozone satellite data series of -1.83 m atm-cm
per year, obtained in the previous section, can be attributed for the
most part to a downward drift in the satellite measurements over the
period of the satellite's operation.

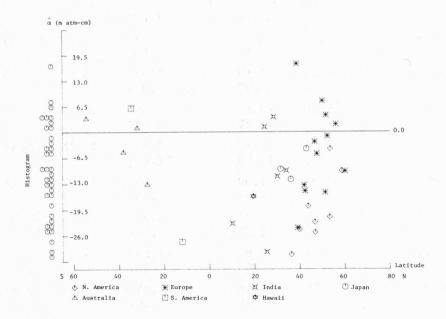

Figure 9. Daily Satellite - Daily Ground Regression Analysis
Constant Bias vs. Latitude

Table 2

Daily Satellite - Daily Ground Regression Results
at 36 Dobson Stations

Station	Latitude	Constant Bias $\hat{\alpha}$ (m atm-cm)	Drift $\hat{\delta}$ (m atm-cm per year)	Residual St.Dev. $\hat{\sigma}$	Number of Obs. (Days)
Churchill	58.8N	-9.71 (2.11)	-2.47 (.63)	20.53	281
Edmonton	53.6N	-4.18 (1.93)	-1.99 (.54)	18.03	253
Goose	53.3N	-21.31 (2.10)	-.66 (.66)	21.16	300
Caribou	46.9N	-25.10 (2.93)	-.97 (.89)	19.79	174
Bismarck	46.8N	-22.54 (1.86)	.80 (.51)	15.29	233
Toronto	43.8N	-18.52 (3.57)	-2.74 (1.05)	21.33	110
Boulder	40.0N	-24.39 (2.26)	.07 (.60)	14.60	142
Nashville	36.3N	-30.73 (2.02)	.61 (.53)	13.47	177
Aarhus	56.2N	1.99 (2.72)	-1.31 (.99)	25.51	275
Lerwick	60.2N	-9.80 (2.78)	-1.69 (.94)	22.53	235
Bracknell	51.4N	-15.12 (2.95)	-1.57 (.85)	20.18	180
Potsdam	52.4N	-1.00 (1.62)	-1.96 (.53)	15.80	262
Belsk	51.8N	4.29 (1.72)	-4.81 (.54)	15.61	247
Hradec Kralove	50.2N	7.89 (1.53)	-2.59 (.48)	14.21	272
Hohenpeissenberg	47.8N	-5.41 (1.61)	-1.23 (.50)	11.11	152
Arosa	46.8N	2.39 (1.35)	-1.00 (.42)	10.46	194
Mont Louis	42.5N	-14.76 (1.75)	-2.73 (.49)	12.76	194

Station	Latitude	Constant Bias $\hat{\alpha}$ (m atm-cm)	Drift $\hat{\delta}$ (m atm-cm per year)	Residual St.Dev. $\hat{\sigma}$	Number of Obs. (Days)
Vigna DiValle	42.1N	-13.32 (1.39)	-.96 (.44)	12.12	259
Cagliari/Elmas	39.1N	-23.97 (2.00)	1.65 (.63)	16.67	237
Lisbon	38.8N	17.38 (2.02)	-2.07 (.70)	13.21	134
Srinagar	34.1N	-9.65 (1.36)	-1.41 (.42)	9.43	142
Quetta	30.2N	-11.09 (1.61)	-1.39 (.46)	10.67	130
New Delhi	28.6N	3.83 (1.51)	-4.69 (.44)	11.37	186
Varanasi	25.5N	-30.07 (.93)	.85 (.28)	7.15	208
Mount Abu	24.6N	1.34 (.82)	-1.67 (.25)	5.89	136
Kodaikanal	10.2N	-22.88 (1.20)	.67 (.51)	5.95	83
Sapporo	43.1N	-4.16 (2.71)	-2.96 (.75)	16.14	113
Tateno	36.1N	-11.84 (2.59)	-1.09 (.70)	15.71	117
Kagoshima	31.6N	-9.28 (2.12)	-2.06 (.56)	12.21	96
Brisbane	27.5S	-13.12 (1.62)	-1.85 (.50)	9.54	108
Perth	31.9S	1.02 (2.38)	-4.29 (.65)	12.31	113
Aspendale	38.0S	-5.03 (1.56)	-2.55 (.50)	10.04	148
MacQuarie Island	54.5S	3.41 (1.85)	-2.11 (.65)	15.61	198
Huancayo	12.1S	-27.47 (.95)	-1.25 (.28)	6.68	166
Buenos Aires	34.6S	6.11 (1.54)	-1.95 (.49)	6.92	78
Mauna Loa	19.5N	-16.07 (1.37)	-.05 (.44)	8.63	128

234   G. Reinsel, G. C. Tiao and R. Lewis

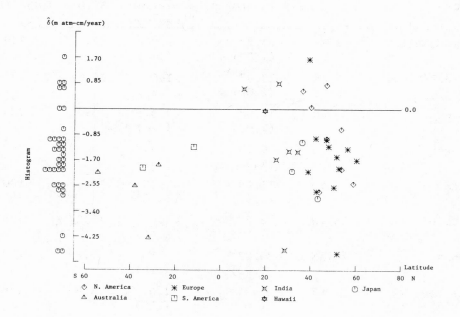

Figure 10. Daily Satellite – Daily Ground Regression Analysis
Drift vs. Latitude

REFERENCES

[1] R.J. CICERONE, R.S. STOLARSKI and S. WALTERS, Stratospheric
     ozone destruction by man-made chlorofluoromethanes, Science 185,
     (1974), pp. 1165-1167.

[2] M. J. MOLINA and F. S. ROWLAND, Stratospheric sink for
     chlorofluoromethanes: chlorine atom catalyzed destruction of
     ozone, Nature 249, (1974), pp. 810-812.

[3] National Academy of Sciences (NAS) Report, Halocarbons: effects
     on stratospheric ozone, National Academy of Sciences,
     Washington, D.C., 1976.

[4] NASA Report, Chlorofluoromethane Assessment Workshop Report,
     Goddard Space Flight Center, Greenbelt, Md., 1977.

[5] National Academy of Sciences (NAS) Report, Stratospheric ozone
     depletion by halocarbons: chemistry and transport, National
     Academy of Sciences, Washington, D.C., 1979.

[6] NASA Report, The stratosphere: present and future, NASA
     Reference Publication 1049, ed. R. D. Hudson and E. I. Reed,
     Goddard Space Flight Center, Greenbelt, Md., 1979.

[7] G. REINSEL, G. C. TIAO, M. N. WANG, R. LEWIS and D. NYCHKA, Statistical analysis of stratospheric ozone data for the detection of trends, to appear in Atmos. Environ. 15, (1981).

[8] E. HILSENRATH, D. F. HEATH and B. M. SCHLESINGER, Seasonal and interannual variations in total ozone revealed by the Nimbus 4 Backscattered Ultraviolet experiment, J. Geophys. Res. 84, (1979), pp. 6969-6979.

[9] A. J. KRUEGER, B. GUENTHER, A. J. FLEIG, D. F. HEATH, E. HILSENRATH, R. MCPETERS and C. PRABHAKARA, Satellite ozone measurements, Phil. Trans. R. Soc. Lond. A 296, (1980), pp. 191-204.

[10] G. REINSEL, G. C. TIAO and R. LEWIS, A statistical analysis of total ozone data from the Nimbus-4 BUV satellite experiment, Technical Report No. 641, Department of Statistics, University of Wisconsin-Madison, (1981).

[11] J. K. ANGELL and J. KORSHOVER, Quasi-biennial and long-term fluctuations in total ozone, Mon. Weather Rev. 101, (1973), pp. 426-443.

[12] J. K. ANGELL and J. KORSHOVER, Global analysis of recent total ozone fluctuations, Mon. Weather Rev. 104, (1976), pp. 63-75.

[13] J. LONDON and J. KELLEY, Global trends in total atmospheric ozone, Science 184, (1974), pp. 987-989.

[14] W. D. KOMHYR, E. W. BARRETT, G. SLOCUM and H. K. WEICKMANN, Atmospheric total ozone increase during the 1960's, Nature 232, (1971), pp. 390-391.

[15] W. J. HILL, P. N. SHELDON and J. J. TIEDE, Analyzing worldwide total ozone for trends, Geophys. Res. Lett. 4, (1977), pp. 21-24.

[16] J. E. PENNER, Trend prediction for O_3: an analysis of model uncertainty with comparison to detection thresholds, Lawrence Livermore National Laboratory Report UCRL-85419, submitted to Atmos. Environ., (1981).

TOXIC SUBSTANCES,
TOXICOLOGICAL TESTING

Monitoring for Toxic Substances
in Our Environment: An Overview
of Objectives and Methodology

Joseph S. Carra* and Stephen Williams**

Abstract. An evaluation of five EPA monitoring networks focused
on the uses, design and operations of each network with the following
objectives in mind: (1) improve the designs and operations so that
the monitoring data would be valid and of known quality; and
(2) determine whether we should and could integrate a wider range of
toxics monitoring into predominately pesticides networks. Our
philosophy and approach, findings and improvements are presented.
The need for and use of sample survey techniques and the
misconceptions about them are emphasized.

1. Background. The Office of Pesticides and Toxic
Substances (OPTS) currently operates five chemical monitoring
networks: the National Human Monitoring Program; the National Surface
Water Monitoring Program; the National Soils Monitoring Program; the
National Estuarine Monitoring Program; and the Suburban Air
Monitoring Program.

The networks, along with special purpose studies, monitor for
selected pesticides and other toxic chemicals. They are operated in
the Exposure Evaluation Division (EED) of OPTS to fulfill the human
and environmental monitoring mandates of both the Federal
Insecticide, Fungicide, and Rodenticide Act (FIFRA), as amended, and
the Toxic Substances Control Act (TSCA). The networks were initiated
in the mid-sixties in response to recommendations of the President's
Science Advisory Committee. In 1970 they were transferred to the EED
of OPTS in order to organizationally centralize the chemical
responsibilities for FIFRA and TSCA.

The Human Monitoring Program consists of an adipose tissue survey
and the Health and Nutrition Examination Survey (HANES). In the
former, annual national estimates of the accumulation of
organochlorene pesticides and PCB's in human adipose tissue are
obtained. The tissue, as well as associated demographic and medical
data have been collected by pathologists and medical examiners from
post-mortems and surgeries for the last 11 years. In the HANES,

*EPA (TS-798), 401 M Street, S.W., Wash., D.C.   20460
**RTI, Research Triangle Park, N.C.   27709

blood and urine specimens are obtained from a national sample of the
general population and analyzed for pesticide compounds and metals.
Additional demographic, nutritional and medical data are collected in
this survey by the National Center for Health Statistics.

From the National Surface Water Networks estimates of ambient
levels of toxic substances are obtained from 150 Geological Survey
stations across the country. The Soils Monitoring Program consists
of two national surveys, one for rural agricultural soils and one for
urban soils. The Estuarine Network is not currently operational, but
data from 180 stations in 15 coastal states have been obtained over a
seven year period. Shellfish was used in this survey as a biological
indicator of estuarine pesticide pollution. The Air Network consists
of several years worth of pesticide data from purposively selected
sites across the country.

    2. Historical Uses of Network Data. Data produced by the
networks have been used for the following: (1) to support regulatory
actions and policy decisions; (2) to detect differences between
specific demographic, age, sex, and racial groups; (3) to provide
baseline data for the proper interpretation of residue levels of
specific groups; (4) to estimate residue levels for specific
populations and identify trends; (5) to identify chemical problems or
"hot spots"; and (6) to provide a vehicle for conducting special
studies for pesticides or for other toxic substances.

    Specifically, historical data from the networks have been used to
support the DDT decision; in the aldrin/dieldrin hearings; in the
2,4,5-T/Silvex hearings; in the regulatory hearings on aldicarb; and
to establish baseline levels for pentachlorophenol (PCP),
polychlorinated biphenyls (PCB's), and many other chemicals.

    Trend assessments have also been made using data from the adipose
tissue network. These assessments show that the national estimate of
the geometric means of DDT, beta-BHC, dieldrin and oxychlordane show
statistically significant decreases over time. For alpha-BHC and
PCB's the statistic analyzed was percent of the population with
detectable levels; for this statistic, alpha-BHC shows an increasing
trend and PCB's a decreasing trend, which are both statistically
significant. It should be noted that weighted regression analysis
was used in these assessments; we shall return to this point later.

    3. Approach to Evaluation of the Networks. The existing
pesticides networks have been the subject of a comprehensive review
involving consideration of the following factors: (1) statistical
designs and their suitability to the identified regulatory needs and
uses of the resulting data; (2) quality assurance, i.e., producing
data of known quality; and (3) ADP systems supporting each network
including: (a) sample tracking system; (b) quality assurance tracking
system; (c) report generation and data analysis software.

In addition, the possibilities of integrating other toxics monitoring into the pesticides networks have been pursued. Since the networks originally were designed to monitor chlorinated hydrocarbon pesticides, they will require significant improvements to expand their capability to reliably monitor other toxic chemicals.

The goals are to produce estimates of the concentrations of toxic chemicals in various media and to measure and control the total error in each of those estimates. Since the operating components produce different types of errors, the quality assurance components must employ corresponding statistical and operational techniques to measure and control the errors, as shown below.

Types of Error	QA Control Mechanism
Sampling Error	Survey Design Based on a Probability Framework
Incomplete Sample Collection Coverage	QC Protocols, etc.
Measurement Error	Lab QC Procedures and Samples (e.g. splits, spikes, etc.)
Data Processing Error	Edit Checks, etc.
Statistical Analysis Error	Conducting Statistical Analyses Appropriate to the Design

We refer to the approach of controlling all sources of error as a total quality assurance approach to distinguish it from the prevalent view in EPA and elsewhere that quality assurance or QA refers to the control of laboratory measurements only.

Another often neglected area is the need to include in any quality assurance system provisions and guidance for the steps that should be taken when "out-of-control" situations arise so that specific sources of error are identified and corrective actions taken.

4. Statistical Survey Design Considerations. We compared the current survey design to the objectives for each of the networks in order to determine to what extent the current designs have accomplished their objectives. In general, the networks have accomplished their original objectives. However, we identified several ways in which to improve the data produced by the monitoring networks.

Probability Sampling and the Quality of Data: A monitoring
network cannot produce data of truly known quality unless it has
a complete probability sampling. Otherwise, the magnitude of
the sampling error cannot be computed.

Efficiency of Survey Design Minimizing the Overall Cost of a
Monitoring Program: We are using techniques from the field of
statistical survey design to minimize the overall cost of our
monitoring programs. These techniques: (1) enable the program
manager to obtain monitoring data of specified accuracy and of
known quality at the least possible cost; (2) can be applied to
any existing monitoring program, and will work for new programs
as well, if certain costs and variances can be estimated.

When we applied these techniques to the National Human
Monitoring Program, we succeeded in developing a new design
which achieves the same data quality for less than the current
cost. This was accomplished by increasing the number of samples
collected from each hospital.

Multimedia Monitoring: Presently, the networks are independent
systems; that is, common sites exist only by chance. However,
matched specimens have been taken on a limited basis for crops,
pond water, and sediment in a subsample of agricultural soil
sites, and for both water and sediment at surface water sites.

Although use of matched observation sites for the various
networks undoubtedly has both advantages and disadvantages, the
disadvantages seem to be less compelling. One disadvantage is
that less geographical coverage is obtained if many or all of
the monitoring sites are in the same general location for
several of the networks. Another disadvantage is that optimum
location of sites for the one medium will not necessarily be
optimum for others. On the other hand, the following advantages
are possible: (1) more can be learned of transport and fate of
chemicals so that proper precautions might be taken before the
substance or its toxic metabolites reach the final links of the
food chain; (2) if two or more of the media are highly
correlated without time lag or if one medium proves consistently
more informative than others for a particular substance, some of
the resources can be shifted to other substances or other media;
(3) cost savings may result if more information is obtained at
each site, thus reducing the number of sites needed.

Domain Estimation: The monitoring networks have as primary
objectives monitoring toxic substances for the entire U.S.
Often, particular interest is focused on some subpopulation or
subset or the entire U.S. Such a subpopulation is referred to
as a domain. Domains can consist of a stratum or a group of
strata that are built into the design or they can consist of
subpopulations that are defined independently of the design. In

either of these situations, valid domain estimates and variances
can be obtained. It follows that if valid estimates can be
obtained for arbitrarily defined domains, then valid tests can
be obtained for differences between such domains.

5. Misconceptions about Probability Sampling. As statisticians
consulting with non-statisticians in the design of monitoring systems
we became painfully aware of certain misconceptions that laymen have
about probability sampling that can seriously jeopardize
communications if not pointed out and explained at the start. Four
of the most prevalent misconceptions are given below.

(1)   "Probability sampling consists of simple random sampling
      only". This misconception causes many experts on the
      transport and fate of substances to reject "random
      sampling" as a basis for environmental monitoring. What
      goes unrecognized is that probability sampling can in fact
      utilize such expert information.

(2)   "Judgmental or haphazard sampling allows one to draw valid
      statistical inferences", or "haphazard sampling is a valid
      form of random sampling".

(3)   "Merely requesting that a statistician 'design a national
      survey' completely defines a survey design and no further
      specifications are needed."

(4)   "If you have a good survey for the whole nation, then the
      data from one of the states must constitute just as good a
      survey for the state". This is an intuitively appealing
      idea of many laymen.

6. New Survey Designs for the Networks. We have evaluated our
monitoring networks based upon the design considerations explained
above and have developed new statistical survey designs where they
were warranted. The following summarizes our results to date.

National Human Monitoring Network: We have developed a new
survey design so that the network is based on a complete
probability framework rather than the present partial one. The
new design also utilizes the cost minimization techniques
mentioned above.

National Surface Water Monitoring Program: The present design
is a non-probability sampling of the U.S. Geological Survey's
(USGS) NASQAN stations. Two design options are being
considered. Both would be complete probability frameworks for
the water network. The second option would cost less, but also
would be more limited in terms of coverage.

National Soils Monitoring Network: After extensive
investigation, we found that the National Soils Monitoring
Network already has a complete probability framework. We will,
however, use the cost minimization techniques to reduce the cost
of this network. We also plan to update the base for this
network, which is the 1967 Conservation Needs Inventory.

National Air Monitoring Network: This network operates on a
very small scale at present. Several possible modifications
using probability sampling are being considered.

National Estuarine Monitoring Network: This network is not
operational at present. Design options are being developed, but
have not yet been completed.

7. ADP Systems. In order for monitoring data to be of value,
the users must have easy access to the data. Therefore, the ADP
systems supporting each monitoring network are being improved and the
accessibility of the data from these networks has already been
expanded in several ways such as by processing backlogs of
unprocessed data, correcting data errors, simplifying procedures for
producing computer reports and for submitting report requests
directly to the computer, and creating SAS data files, including
sampling weights, to permit comprehensive statistical analysis. More
details on these items are discussed below.

Elimination of Backlog of Data: We have eliminated the backlog
of unprocessed data by entering some 12,000 records and
correcting over 5,400 data errors. Moreover, we have developed
systems to keep the data current by entering new data as it is
received by EPA, manually coding it, editing the data using the
computer, and resolving and correcting any errors in the data.

Verification of Masterfile Records: We compared source
documents to the masterfile records to assess the data
processing error. With the exception of one item, the medical
diagnostic code for patients in our National Human Monitoring
Program, the error rate was not significant.

Simplified Procedures for Producing Computer Reports: We have
simplified the procedures for producing computer reports from
the historical data files. With approximately 30 minutes of
instruction, personnel can be taught how to submit their report
requests directly to the computer from terminals in their
offices.

Statistical Analysis System (SAS): We have placed the
historical data into the commercial software package called the
"Statistical Analysis System" (SAS). SAS allows EPA personnel
to perform sophisticated statistical analyses on the data.

Sampling Weights and Computer Programs: Sampling weights have been added to our human data and appropriate computer programs obtained so that the proper statistical analyses using weighted data can be performed. The sampling weights are dictated by the specific survey design that is used.

Multimedia Toxics Information System (MTIS): The historical data from the National Human Monitoring Program have been placed into MTIS, which is also called TOXET.

It is important to have automated management control systems which track samples from sample collection through chemical analysis and data processing. EED has already developed two such systems and these systems should be expanded to reduce the amount of manual data processing occurring in the monitoring networks and also to achieve better control of both the work flow and the data quality. These systems are described in more detail below.

The Adipose Sample Tracking System (ADITRACK): This system tracks the adipose tissue specimens, as well as the data flow, from sample collection through chemical analysis and data processing. ADITRACK requires no additional data entry since data inputs to the computer are generated from the NHMP data processing system. ADITRACK also produces management reports to control work flow and data quality.

The Soil and Water Sample Tracking System (TACTRACK): All of our soil and water samples are chemically analyzed at the Toxicant Analysis Center (TAC), which is our laboratory located in Bay St. Louis, Mississippi. In addition, the TAC is the central receiving point for many samples which are then sent to other labs for chemical analysis. TACTRACK was developed for the TAC in order to provide better management control of the work in progress and to handle recordkeeping chores. We plan to expand TACTRACK to include quality control functions when the TAC's new QC program is operational. The system uses sophisticated real-time automation techniques to facilitate data entry and prevent data errors.

8. Proper Statistical Analysis of Historical Data. Proper statistical analysis must take into account the survey design of the monitoring network. For example, in previous reports, the average concentrations and trends over time were presented for several chemicals monitored in human tissue including DDT, B-BHC, dieldrin, heptachlor epoxide, hexachlorobenzene, and oxychlordane. These results were based on unweighted data. However, weighted analysis, based on the survey design, is required to properly estimate the average concentrations. It was found that the weighted averages are lower than the unweighted by about 20% for all the chemicals except B-BHC. Thus, had we stopped with the initial analysis and not

performed the proper weighted analysis, we would have overestimated
the correct values by more than 20%.

9. Special Applications of the Networks. The networks are a
valuable nucleus for special studies. By using an existing
framework, we can achieve lower costs and shorter response times. We
have taken a number of steps to increase the utilization of the
mechanisms and the personnel who operate the networks and to expand
our capability to conduct special studies in a cost-effective
manner. Essentially, our ability to monitor toxic chemicals other
than pesticides or to conduct special studies is not currently
limited in terms of survey design, field operations, or data
processing.   The limiting factor is the lack of cost-effective
chemical analytical methodologies for monitoring some of the
chemicals of interest with respect to TSCA. Some special
applications of the networks are listed below.

> Monitoring Toxic Chemical Other Than Pesticides: PCB's are
> monitored by the National Human Monitoring Program (NHMP).
> PCB's and metals are monitored by the National Soils Monitoring
> Program.

> Monitoring PCB's: PCB's are monitored by the NHMP. A special
> study was performed to examine the issue of whether or not there
> is a significant difference in residue levels of PCB's between
> racial groups. There appears to be a difference; non-whites
> have higher probability of having levels of PCB's above 3ppm. A
> multi-residue technique used to detect and measure levels of
> pesticides in human adipose tissue is used to detect some, but
> not all, isomers of PCB.

> Monitoring Toxic Metals: Since 1970, the National Soils
> Monitoring Network has accumulated experience in analyzing urban
> soil samples for arsenic, cadimum, lead, mercury, and PCB's. An
> Urban Garden Special Study will analyze soil samples for 26
> metals and vegetable samples for cadimum, copper, lead and
> nickel.

10. Expanding the Capability of the Networks to Perform Special
Studies: Any of the networks, providing they are based on a well-
designed probability framework, can be a useful nucleus for special
studies. The main benefits of utilizing the existing framework
include lower cost and shorter response time than would be possible
if the special studies were fielded independently of any ongoing
network.

A technique sometimes referred to as replicated sampling or
interpenetrating sampling has proven useful for special studies.
Basically, rather than selecting a single random sample, several
smaller independent samples are selected. One or more of these
samples can be designated at random and used jointly to comprise the

basic network. When isolated situations arise that need more
intensive investigation, already existing samples or subsamples can
be utilized in such a localized investigation. The technique of
replicated samples has also proven useful in estimating variances in
order to describe estimation precision.

One example of a study which utilized an existing network was a
special study of mirex. In this case the adipose tissue network
began to detect levels of mirex in the south. To obtain better
information this potential "hot spot" was further investigated by
supplementing the network's sites with additional sites in the south.

Statistical Issues in Toxicology

D. G. Hoel*

Abstract. Statistical research in toxicology has greatly increased in recent years. This is due, in part, to the rapid scientific developments in toxicology and its prominence in regulatory decision making. This paper reviews some of the main areas of statistical endeavor in quantitative toxicology and suggests future statistical research directions in this important biological field.

1. Introduction. Toxicology may be described in general terms as the study of adverse biological activity of exogeneous materials through laboratory experimentation. Mathematical and statistical methods have had a long and useful history of meaningful applications in this particular field of science. With heightened awareness of the value of preventive measures in public health, there is increased activity in toxicology with a resultant interest in statistical application. For the purpose of discussion, it is convenient to divide toxicology into three broadly defined areas: pharmacology, specific organ toxicity and prediction of effects in man.

The pharmacological disposition of a compound is defined as the absorption, metabolism, storage, and excretion of the material as a function of time and dose. Mathematical models based upon the mechanistic understandings of these processes have been formulated theoretically for the most common types of processes. This model-building activity has been an especially fruitful collaboration between biologist and mathematician. In fact, the terms pharmacokinetics and toxicokinetics have been coined to describe this joint research endeavor.

Organ toxicity is what usually comes to mind when the term toxicology is mentioned. Specific systems which may be affected by a toxic substance include: reproductive, immunological, neurological, etc. Familiar types of effects include carcinogenesis, mutagenesis and teratogenesis. There are a variety of laboratory assays available for assessing specific effects of a chemical to a system. Usually, mechanisms of toxicity are not sufficiently well understood to create mathematical models with any true confidence. However, considerable statistical work has been done, primarily in the direction of hypothesis testing, for dose-response effects and in the creation and estimation

---

*National Institute of Environmental Health Sciences, Research Triangle Park, NC 27711

of measures of potency. This type of statistical work has roots in the
early days of statistical method development. For example, see the
research on estimating LD_{50}'s as described in Finney's book on Probit
Analysis [1].

The most recent development in statistical applications relating to
toxicology is in the area of risk estimation or extrapolation. Basically, this involves the quantitative estimation of toxic effects at
low exposure levels in man. The paradox is that this type of estimation
is most commonly based upon relatively high-dose laboratory studies. The
obvious disparity in dose levels leads to a virtual minefield of hazards
and vociferous objections; but from a public health standpoint, the
need for even a rudimentary effort is pressing.

The purpose of this paper is to review, with a minimum of mathematical detail, some of those areas of toxicology in which there is
considerable statistical activity. Also, suggestions are offered for
prospective research directions in statistical applications. Statistical activities in toxicology can be classified within the general
categories:

  a) hypothesis testing and decision rules,
  b) model building, including risk estimation and extrapolation,
  c) bioassay design, and
  d) operational strategies for the sequence and selection of assays
      in a toxicological analysis.

These activities are reviewed for only two types of bioassay; namely,
short term _in vitro_ assays for DNA effects, and carcinogenesis bioassays
in chronic rodent studies. These two examples are explored because of
the current focus of statistical activity on them.

    2. Short-Term Tests for Heritable Effects. In recent years, toxi-
cology has witnessed the rapid development of _in vitro_ assays for
heritable effects on DNA. These assays generally involve either bacterial or cell cultures. Examples include mammalian cell transformation
assay, unscheduled DNA repair in lymphocytes, and the Salmonella mu-
tational assay of Bruce Ames. These systems are certainly less complex
than whole animal testing and offer excellent opportunities for mechanistic modeling. Furthermore, short-term tests are of high relevance
for the public health decision-maker because of their established association with carcinogenesis.

The most prominent member of the _in vitro_ assays is Ames' Salmonella
test for point mutations. His assay involves a number of different
tester stains of Salmonella, each of which is repair-deficient and
sensitive to varying types of mutations, such as base-pair substitu-
tions, frame-shift mutations, etc. The assay may also include a rat
liver homogenate in order to provide microsomes for the possible metabolism of the administered chemical.

The Ames assay has generated considerable statistical research
activity, primarily on the issue of hypothesis testing for dose-response. The assay has two main features of statistical importance.
These are the hyper-Poisson variability of the culture plates, and the
competing toxicity of the chemical. Of these two issues, the competing
toxicity is the more interesting. Since only the number of revertants
(mutated cells) per culture plate are measured, one can readily see
cases where the dose-response curve decreases at high dose, even to a
level lower than the spontaneous background rate. One solution to this
dilemma is to run a parallel assay where the competing toxicity is
measured. This, of course, is an undesirable experimental burden.
Discounting the alternative of the parallel toxicity assay, the statistician must become involved in some kind of complex modeling approaches which may provide a reasonable method for hypothesis testing.
For a more detailed discussion of the foregoing issues see Margolin et
al. [2].

A second area of interesting statistical activity centers on assessing the validity of the association between the Ames test and the
lifetime rodent assay for carcinogenesis. It has been reported that
for several broad chemical classes, the agreements between both posi-
tives and negatives are over 80%. Meselson and Russell [3] estimated
potencies for 10 compounds, showing very good qualitative agreement
over about five orders of magnitude. This work is quite preliminary
and, I suspect, overly optimistic in the high degree of agreement.

Several critical statistical issues immediately present themselves.
The first is the selection of appropriate measures of potency for both
the carcinogenesis assay and the Ames test. For the Ames test, one
might use the derivative at the origin of the dose-response function,
or more commonly, the dose which doubles the background rate. For the
carcinogenesis data, one approach which has been used is taking the
estimated dose for which 50% of the animals would have had cancer by
two years after adjusting for competing risks as the measure of potency.
This seems to be a reasonable procedure if the dose-response relations
are linear. If they are not, which is frequently the case in carcinogenesis, then the relative potency rankings of chemicals change with
modifications in the response level definition of the potency measure.
This leads directly to the unanswered question of what potency response
level is biologically appropriate in the rodent carcinogenesis assay,
performed for the purpose of comparison with a doubling dose in an in
vitro microbial assay. A second issue arises concerning the selection
of which tester strain in the microbial assay to use for comparison
purposes. In this instance, due caution must be exercised in order that
the estimate of the quantitative relationship between potencies contains no biases due to strain or species selection.

3. Carcinogenesis Rodent Bioassay. As compared with the mutagenesis in vitro tests, the life-time rodent carcinogenesis test is
biologically much more complex. This is due, primarily, to the many
types of mechanisms involved in a variety of potentially detectable

cancer types and sites. The effects of initiators, promoters and co-
carcinogens, along with the complex metabolic pathways which an administered chemical may undergo, are all possible confounding factors. In
spite of the inherent difficulties in understanding the toxicological
mechanism involved in the bioassay, the test is considered to be the
most relevant of all nonprimate assays for predicting human carcinogenicity. In addition to both government and industry in the United
States, we find foreign organizations such as the International Agency
for Research in Cancer (IARC) also depending heavily on the results of
the cancer bioassay.

Hypothesis testing for dose-response in the cancer bioassay is an
important statistical function, especially when we consider the legal
implications of regulatory actions based upon the results of these
assays. The usual approach in hypothesis testing is to assume that the
animal with the cancer type being tested has died due to that cancer.
This in turn permits the use of the usual life-table analysis such as
Cox, Mantel log-rank tests. With multiple doses, a linear trend test
is also applied. If the tumors are incidental, and not, therefore, a
cause of death, serious biases may result from incorrect application of
a life-table approach (see Hoel and Walburg [4]). Recently, IARC has
published a statistical supplement (Peto et al. [5]) detailing the
bioassay analysis techniques, with the assumption that the pathologist
is able to classify each specific tumor as either the cause of death
or, on the other hand, incidental to the animal's death.

The National Toxicology Program, which includes the National Cancer
Institute's (NCI) bioassay program, is currently analyzing tumor data
under both assumptions. The reason for this dual analysis is that many
pathologists are unwilling to make a yes-no determination on the cause
of death. If the two analyses differ significantly, the pathologist is
compelled to resolve the issue for the specific case at hand. Some
methods have been developed for the case of the pathologist giving a
score other than 0-1 for the likelihood of the tumor being the cause of
death (see Poon and Hoel [6]). These methods can further reduce the
bias in those cases where the tumor type is readily classifiable.
Competing-risk techniques in life-table analyses have also been criticized for their assumption of disease independence. In order to correct this problem, Neyman and co-workers [7] suggest using disease
state models with Markovian transitions. Unfortunately, the model is
quite complex and not of practical use for the analysis of the relatively small rodent bioassay.

A second statistical difficulty with the standard analysis of the
cancer bioassay concerns the multiple testing of tumor sites. If, in a
typical fashion, twenty different sites are tested, we would anticipate
a fairly large false-positive rate. This particular issue has been
raised by Salsburg [8] and discussed by Fears et al.[9]. The apparent
reason for the low false-positive rate is the very low spontaneous or
control rates for many of the tumor sites which results in an individual test's size being considerably smaller than its nominal level. In

addition, there are essentially four experiments for any given tumor
site, taking into consideration both sexes of two rodent species in the
standard NCI bioassay. Some statisticians have attempted to establish
decision rules for declaring a positive carcinogenic result based on
the four experiment bioassay data. I take exception with them on this
point since a predetermined decision rule is not realistic for such a
complex process. Typically, a committee of scientists of various
specialities is required to be convened for the purpose of making a
knowledgable determination of carcinogenic activity. They must weigh
many factors, from the chemical structure of the compound, to the
actual bioassay tumor frequency results, to name a few. Various tumor
sites and types also have varying biological relevance. The utter
complexity of the scientific processes leading to carcinogenesis eliminates the relevance of simplistic decision rules.

A major issue in repeated assays concerns the concept of incorpo-
rating historical control data into the statistical analysis. This is
especially pertinent when the effect being studied is relatively rare.
The toxicologist often tends to factor this historical data into his
interpretation of the data, even though the statistical analysis ig-
nores it. This occurs in all areas of toxicology, not just carcinogenesis.

A simple approach to this problem is to assume that for each experiment the spontaneous rate p of a tumor-free animal is an unknown
observation from a beta distribution, with parameters α and β. For a
given experiment, assume x tumor-free animals are observed among n
controls, and y tumor-free animals are observed among m treated
animals. We may then assume that x, given n and p, is distributed
binomially with parameters n, p. Further y, given m and π, is
also distributed binomially with parameters m, π where $\pi = \varepsilon p$
($0 \leq \varepsilon \leq 1$). We then wish to test $\varepsilon = 1$ versus $\varepsilon < 1$, which would correspond to an increase in tumor-bearing animals in the treated group.

Now, the distribution of y given ε and x can be written as an
integral (see [10]). Under the null hypothesis of no carcinogenic
effect (i.e., $\varepsilon = 1$) it follows that y, given $\varepsilon = 1$ and x, is
distributed as beta-binomial with parameters $\alpha + x$ and $\beta + n - x$. Therefore, using the critical region $y \leq y_o$, where

$$\gamma \geq \sum_{y=0}^{y_o} \Pr[y \mid \varepsilon=1, x]$$

gives an γ level conditional test of $H_o : \varepsilon = 1$. This assumes of
course, that α and β are known without error and the prior beta model
is correct.

In order to observe the impact of this model, consider Table 1. For
this example, we have used a mean spontaneous tumor rate of 1% which

should be relevant to this approach by denoting a relatively infrequent tumor. Hepatocellular carcinoma in the Fischer 344 rat has approximately this frequency. In addition, the NCI historical data on this tumor type suggests a standard deviation of 1/2% for the prior beta (i.e., α=391, β=3.95). The table indicates an increased power for the test as compared with the usual Fisher exact test. Also of interest is the fact that an exceptionally high observed background is greatly discounted by the beta prior. Although this conditional test is exact, it does require that α and β are known. Since they will be estimated in practice, this source of error should be accounted for in the procedure. Tarone [11] has also considered using a beta prior in terms of a logistic model using asymptotic likelihood methods. Because of the pressing needs of the toxicologists, statistical work in the area of historical controls should be continued in the hope that reasonable statistical procedures will be developed.

4. <u>Risk Estimation Methods</u>. Possibly the most interesting and certainly the most controversial statistical activity in toxicology has occurred in the area of risk extrapolation in the past few years. The problem can generally be considered to consist of two components. The first involves the quantitative predictability of an effect in a rodent to a similar effect in man. The second component is the familiar low-dose estimation problem. The cancer bioassay is conducted at doses many orders of magnitude higher than one would anticipate human exposure to be. Considerable faith is required to accept the extrapolated estimates, since the mathematical models needed for this type of activity are crude approximations at best, and misleading in many cases. The most pressing need is for reasonable measures of precision which incorporate both the statistical errors in the data and more importantly, the biological model errors.

The problem of mouse to man extrapolation is scientifically quite difficult with little useful data being available. Nevertheless, there is promising evidence that rodent carcinogenesis is a rather reliable predictor of human carcinogenesis. Studies conducted by IARC suggest that for 18 chemicals, compounds, or processes, there is sufficient epidemiological evidence to establish that they are human carcinogens. With the exception of arsenic, and possibly benzene, all of these agents are also established rodent carcinogens. This empirical evidence, coupled with the biological similarities of the manner in which mammalian species react to chemicals, provides the basis for the widely accepted concept of rodent carcinogenicity being presumptive of human carcinogenicity. The lifetime rodent experiment is felt to provide the most convincing evidence of human carcinogenicity short of quality epidemiology data. Even when human data become available suggesting a new carcinogen, such as the recently reported [12] association between pancreatic cancer and coffee consumption, there is still great interest in obtaining confirmatory experimental animal results from a well controlled study.

Quantitative extrapolation is based upon considerably less convincing evidence. For carcinogenesis, Meselson [13] found six of the previously mentioned 18 agents with sufficient data for calculating potencies in both man and rodent. Using as equivalent doses the amount of material per unit body weight per day, the six compounds have species differences in potencies within approximately one order of magnitude. This is certainly encouraging, considering that potencies among various chemicals in rodent tests vary up to about seven orders of magnitude. The area of quantitative species scale-up requires rigorous efforts in development and improvement, especially as new data become available.

Statisticians have devoted a great deal of their attention to the area of dose-response models and the estimation of low-dose effects. The models used have ranged from heuristic approaches assuming a linear or probit dose-response, to quasi-mechanistic models such as the multihit and multistage. Considerable statistical theory has been generated, especially for the multihit and multistage models. Estimation methods, confidence intervals, and asymptotic distributions are all available tools. Table 2, (derived from [14]) compares point estimates for two of the more popular mechanistic models using some of the best available rodent data. One observes from the table that considerable discrepancies are common, with some being several orders of magnitude in size.

Statistical confidence intervals are usually presented along with the statistical point estimates and often only one order of magnitude difference exists between the two. Clearly, these confidence estimates are misleading, since the biological errors are not included. Furthermore, the biologically unsophisticated might not appreciate how unrefined and simplistic the mechanisms underlying the mathematical model are.

For any given chemical it should be routine that the risk estimation process carefully take into consideration all possible mechanisms which might be involved in the particular carcinogenesis process being analyzed. The understanding of the kinetics of the chemical is also obligatory. Many pitfalls lurk in this area. For example, detoxification systems may or may not be saturated, toxicity may be affecting the rate of tumor production, etc. With these and other considerations at hand, the statistician might avoid the errors brought on by biological naivete by limiting the amount of realism which he attributes to his mathematical model.

TABLE 1

Cumulative Conditional Probability of Outcome
Under H_o with 50 Treated and 50 Controls

Prior Beta Distribution with Mean .99 and S.D. 0.005

	Number of Tumors in Control Group				
	0	1	2	3	4
Number of Tumors in Treated Group Minus Number In Control Group					
0	1.000	0.412	0.150	0.052	0.018
1	0.345	0.114	0.037	0.012	0.004
2	0.081	0.025	0.008	0.002	0.001
3	0.015	0.005	0.001		
4	0.003	0.001			

Cumulative Probability of Outcome under H_o
Using Fisher's Exact Test

	Number of Tumors in Control Group				
	0	1	2	3	4
Number of Tumors in Treated Group Minus Number In Control Group					
2	0.247	0.309	0.339	0.357	0.370
3	0.121	0.181	0.218	0.243	0.262
4	0.059	0.102	0.134	0.159	0.178
5	0.028	0.056	0.080	0.100	0.117
6	0.013	0.030	0.046	0.061	0.074
7	0.006	0.015	0.026	0.036	0.045
8		0.008	0.014	0.020	0.027

TABLE 2

Estimated Virtually

Safe Dose at 10^{-6}

Substance	Gamma Multihit	Multistage	Ratio VSD for Multihit/Multistage
NTA	8.0×10^{-1}	1.9×10^{-4}	4.2×10^{3}
Aflatoxin B_1	2.8×10^{-1}	7.9×10^{-4}	3.5×10^{2}
DMN	7.7×10^{-2}	1.9×10^{-3}	4.0×10^{1}
Vinyl Chloride	3.9×10^{-10}	2.0×10^{-2}	2.0×10^{-8}
BCME	3.7×10^{-2}	4.0×10^{-4}	9.3×10^{1}
Saccharin	1.1	3.3×10^{-1}	3.3
Ethylenethiourea	$3.3 \times 10^{+1}$	4.5	7.3
Dieldrin	6.3×10^{-3}	2.2×10^{-5}	2.9×10^{2}
DDT	4.8×10^{-2}	6.4×10^{-4}	7.5×10^{1}

REFERENCES

[1] D. J. Finney, Probit Analysis, Cambridge Univ. Press, London 1971.

[2] B. M. Margolin, N. Kaplan and E. Zeiger, Statistical analysis of the Ames salmonella/microsome test, (to appear Proc. Nat. Acad. Sciences).

[3] M. Meselson and K. Russel, Comparisons of carcinogenic and mutagenic potency, Origins of Human Cancer, eds. H. H. Hiatt, J. D. Watson and J. A. Winsten, Cold Spring Harbor Laboratory, NY, 1977, pp. 1473-1481.

[4] D. G. Hoel and H. E. Walburg, Jr., Statistical analysis of survival experiments, J. of Natl. Cancer Inst. 49: 361-372, 1972.

[5] R. Peto et al., Guidelines for simple, sensitive significance tests for carcinogenic effects in long-term and short-term screening assays for carcinogens: a critical appraisal (1980) International Agency for Research on Cancer, Lyon.

[6] A. H. Poon and D. G. Hoel (1981), On estimation of survival function when cause of death is uncertain. (unpublished manuscript).

[7] B. Berlin, J. Brodsky and P. Clifford, Testing disease dependence in survival experiments with serial sacrifice, J. Amer. Stat. Assoc. 74: (1979) pp. 5-14.

[8] D. S. Salsburg, Use of statistics when examining lifetime studies in rodents to detect carcinogenicity, J. of Toxicology and Env. Health, 1977, 3: pp. 611-628.

[9] T. R. Fears, R. E. Tarone and K. C. Chu, False-positive and false-negative rates for carcinogenicity screens, Cancer Research 1977 37: pp. 1941-1945.

[10] D. G. Hoel (1981), Conditional two-sample tests with historical controls, (unpublished manuscript).

[11] R. E. Tarone (1981), The use of historical control information in testing for a trend in proportions (unpublished manuscript).

[12] B. MacMahon et al., Coffee and cancer of the pancreas, N. Engl. J. Med. 1981; 304: 630-633.

[13] National Academy of Sciences, National Research Council Report, Pest control: an assessment of present and alternative technologies, Vol. 1, Contemporary Pest Control Practices and Prospects: The Report of the Executive Committee, Washington, DC, 1975.

[14] The Scientific Committee, Food Safety Council (1978) Proposed system for food safety assessment, Food and Cosmetic Toxicology 16, Supp. 2.

INDEX OF AUTHORS